Giacomo Bonan, Katia Occhi (Eds.)
Environment and Infrastructure

Studies in Early Modern and Contemporary European History

Edited by
FBK – Istituto Storico Italo-Germanico /
Italienisch-Deutsches Historisches Institut

Volume 6

Giacomo Bonan, Katia Occhi (Eds.)

Environment and Infrastructure

Challenges, Knowledge and Innovation from the Early Modern Period to the Present

DE GRUYTER
OLDENBOURG

ISBN 978-3-11-110064-7
e-ISBN (PDF) 978-3-11-111275-6
e-ISBN (EPUB) 978-3-11-111413-2
ISSN 2629-3730

Library of Congress Control Number: 2022950041

Bibliographic information published by the Deutschen Nationalbibliothek
The Deutsche Nationalbibliothek lists this publication in the Deutsche Nationalbibliografie; detailed bibliographic data available on the Internet at http://dnb.dnb.de.

Cover image: Herri met de Bles, Landschaft mit Bergwerk, Öl/Holz (*circa* 1485/1510 to 1555); Universalmuseum Joanneum GmbH Graz, Alte Galerie, Inv.Nr.55.
Typesetting: Integra Software Services Pvt. Ltd.
Printing and binding: CPI books GmbH, Leck

www.degruyter.com

Contents

Giacomo Bonan and Katia Occhi

The Hybrid Nature of Infrastructures

Until a few decades ago, the study of infrastructures was confined to a few areas of engineering, economics, transport and urban planning. Today, however, it has become the focus of a vast multidisciplinary debate that also includes the humanities and in particular history. As often happens with such kind of keywords, while the concept gained in currency it accumulated a multiplicity of definitions, sometimes resulting in haziness. The term "infrastructure" was originally coined in the second half of the nineteenth century to describe the French railway system and it was translated into other languages over the following decades. After the end of the Second World War, it became more widely used thanks to its adoption in military terminology (particularly in NATO programs) and it subsequently became a commonly used term in many different sectors, to the point of identifying virtually any element enabling the operation of modern economies and societies[1].

Dirk van Laak, one of the historians most committed in recent years to analyzing the significance and role of infrastructures, defines them as: "the stable or immobile elements that are necessary to enable fluidity, movement, and communication. They produce a networked and circularly organized society that generates trade and change, peace and prosperity"[2]. He identified their emergence in the eighteenth century, within the first developments of state modernization.

Given the central role that infrastructures played in shaping the 'built environment', it is no surprise that this concept enjoyed growing popularity within the sphere of environmental history, also in relation to two interconnected dynamics. Within the academia, the last decades have seen a convergence between

1 A. Carse, *Keyword: Infrastructure: How a Humble French Engineering Term Shaped the Modern World*, in P. Harvey / C. Jensen / A. Morita (eds.), *Infrastructures and Social Complexity: A Companion*, London 2016, p. 2739; P. Hõgselius / A. Kaijser / E. van der Vleuten (eds.), *Europe's Infrastructure Transition: Economy, War, Nature*, Basingstoke 2016.

2 D. van Laak, *Infrastructures*, in "Docupedia-Zeitgeschichte", 20.05.2021, http://docupedia.de/zg/Laak_infrastructures_v1_en_2021, http://dx.doi.org/10.14765/zzf.dok-2215.

Note: The volume is the result of shared reflections between Giacomo Bonan and Katia Occhi. Giacomo Bonan authored pages 1–5 and Katia Occhi pages 6–11. Giacomo Bonan's research has received funding, as part of "The Water Cultures of Italy, 1500–1900" Advanced Grant, from the European Research Council (ERC) under the European Union's Horizon 2020 research and innovation program (grant agreement no. 833834).

Translation: Gavin Taylor

https://doi.org/10.1515/9783111112756-001

environmental history on the one hand and the history of technology and STS (Science and Technology Studies) on the other[3]. In more general terms, since the start of the new millennium these themes have been profoundly shaped by debate on the concept of the Anthropocene, one of the characterizing aspects of which is the progressive overlapping of ecological and social dynamics, including those related to technological factors[4]. As a consequence of these developments, infrastructures have come to be considered principally as hybrid socio-ecological systems, or according to a definition proposed by Sara Pritchard, *envirotechnical systems*, that are "historically and culturally specific configurations of intertwined 'ecological' and 'technological' systems"[5].

Among the many methodological and thematic perspectives through which environmental historians have analyzed infrastructures, it is worth mentioning at least three particularly relevant fields of research, which are closely interconnected with each other and widely discussed also in the essays that comprise the present volume. The first is urban environmental history, as is already clear in one of the texts considered seminal to this historiographic genre: William Cronon's *Nature's Metropolis*. In this work, the large infrastructures realized over the course of the nineteenth century, like railways and navigable canals, are considered the linchpins around which dynamics emerged linking the urban development of Chicago to the transformation of a hinterland that extended from the Great Lakes to the Great Plains[6]. At the same time, the studies in urban metabolism that were taking shape in those years also identified the construction and operation of large infrastructures (aqueducts and sewage networks, transport and communication systems, etc.) as elements that oriented the materials and energy flows, both within the urban context and between the city and the surrounding territory[7]. A turning point in these processes was identified, at least for Europe and North America, in the nineteenth century, when the development of modern industrial-scale infrastructures provided new opportunities for urban growth through a series of improvements in sanitation, mobility, and energy

3 Cf. M. Reuss / S.H. Cutcliffe (eds.), *The Illusory Boundary: Environment and Technology in History*, Charlottesville 2010; D. Jorgensen / F.A. Jorgensen / S.B. Pritchard, *New Natures: Joining Environmental History with Science and Technology Studies*, Pittsburgh 2013.

4 K. Hetherington (ed.), *Infrastructure, Environment, and Life in the Anthropocene*, Durham 2019.

5 S. Pritchard, *Confluence: The Nature of Technology and the Remaking of the Rhône*, Cambridge MA 2011, pp. 19–20. On this see also A. Carse, *Nature as Infrastructure: Making and Managing the Panama Canal Watershed*, in "Social Studies of Science", 42, 2012, 4, pp. 539–563.

6 W. Cronon, *Nature's Metropolis: Chicago and the Great West, 1848–1893*, New York 1991.

7 J.A. Tarr, *The Metabolism of the Industrial City: The Case of Pittsburgh*, in "Journal of Urban History", 28, 2002, 5, pp. 511–545; S. Barles, *Urban Metabolism of Paris and Its Region*, in "Journal of Industrial Ecology", 13, 2009, 6, pp. 898–912.

transport and consumption. The result of these dynamics was the emergence of the so-called "networked city"[8].

The concept of a *networked city* had been developed by environmental historians starting from that of "large technological system" proposed by the historian of technology Thomas P. Hughes, when referring to the construction of large electrical infrastructures[9]. This genealogy leads to our second field of study, in which the ecological aspects of infrastructures have been frequently studied over recent years: history of energy. This dynamic area of research developed around the concept of energy systems (or regimes), a term that does not refer simply to the sum of energy sources and the necessary converters, but instead includes the social, economic, technological, and environmental aspects associated with specific models of energy exploitation. In this perspective, the study of energy systems and their transitions becomes a way to examine, through the lens of energy, the most significant ecological, economic, and social transformations of a given historical phase[10]. For example, recent research has demonstrated how modern energy transport infrastructures (canals, oil pipelines, transmission lines, etc.) are not simply connections linking supply and demand, but through the logic of economies of scale and the dynamics of path-dependence, they first 'created' new energy demands and consequently determined particular energy consumption models[11]. These transformations also redefined relations both between social actors at local or national scale, and between areas of the globe connected by the energy infrastructures on a geopolitical scale[12].

The third and final field of study, particularly well covered by environmental historians who have analyzed infrastructures, involves the management and control of water resources. A famous – and contested – reference in this respect is the theory of "Oriental despotism" elaborated by Karl Wittfogel, postulating that the transition from sustenance agriculture based on local irrigation systems, to a model based on large scale infrastructures for irrigation and flood control in Asia

8 J. Tarr / G. Dupuy (eds.), *Technology and the Rise of the Networked City in America and Europe*, Philadelphia 1988; D. Schott, *Die Vernetzung der Stadt: Kommunale Energiepolitik, öffentlicher Nahverkehr und die 'Produktion' der modernen Stadt. Darmstadt-Mannheim-Mainz 1880–1918*, Darmstadt 1999. See now S. Haumann / M. Knoll / D. Mares (eds.), *Concepts of Urban-Environmental History*, Bielefeld 2020.

9 T.P. Hughes, *Networks of Power: Electrification in Western Society, 1880–1930*, Baltimore 1983.

10 C.F. Mathis / G. Massard-Guilbaud (eds.), *Sous le soleil: Systèmes et transitions énergétiques du Moyen Âge à nos jours*, Paris 2019; I.J. Miller et al., *Forum: The Environmental History of Energy Transitions*, in "Environmental History", 24, 2019, 3, pp. 463–533.

11 C.F. Jones, *Routes of Power: Energy and Modern America*, Cambridge 2014.

12 T. Mitchell, *Carbon Democracy: Political Power in the Age of Oil*, London 2011.

encouraged the emergence of "hydraulic societies", characterized by powerful bureaucracies and centralized, authoritarian state systems[13]. Wittfogel's thesis was adopted and adapted by one of the founders of environmental history, Donald Worster. In *Rivers of Empire*, Worster analyzed the political and social dynamics linked to the realization of large-scale irrigation infrastructures, not in relation to the development of "Oriental despotism", but instead of "Western capitalism". Worster focused on the infrastructures that transformed the arid lands of the American West into one of the richest agricultural regions on the planet. The process was fuelled with massive public support, both in terms of invested resources and technical-administrative expertise, with an equally important contribution from large scale agrarian capitalism. This created a new typology of "hydraulic society" based on an interweaving of state intervention and private interests[14].

In recent decades one of the most effective ways to integrate water, energy, and urban issues has been the study of rivers. Regarding infrastructures in particular, research has shown that water courses should not be considered only in relation to the impact of large-scale infrastructures on water flow rates or the morphology of river basins. Instead, rivers should be understood as integral parts of more articulated infrastructures, in which technical elements interact with natural ones. This is an idea that already emerged in a text considered to be a turning point in the historical study of rivers, *The Organic Machine* by Richard White[15]. The author considered the Columbia River to be a sort of organic machine, in which human and natural labor were interwoven and influenced each other, transforming the surrounding territory through irrigation, energy generation, and the development of transport systems. White's methodological approach has been adopted frequently and further elaborated in subsequent decades, like for example by Sara Pritchard in her study of the Rodano River, with the aforementioned concept of *envirotechnical systems*[16].

Water courses can thus be considered as nodes in more articulated and hybrid infrastructures that have played an essential part both in urban contexts and for

13 K.A. Wittfogel, *Oriental Despotism: A Comparative Study of Total Power*, New Haven / London 1957.

14 D. Worster, *Rivers of Empire: Water, Aridity, and the Growth of the American West*, New York 1985. On this, see now G. Parrinello / S. Neri Serneri, *Water, Power, Politics: Introduction*, in "Contemporanea", 2, 2022, pp. 171–183.

15 R. White, *The Organic Machine: The Remaking of the Columbia River*, New York 1995.

16 S. Pritchard, *Confluence*. See also G. Parrinello, *Systems of Power: A Spatial Envirotechnical Approach to Water Power and Industrialization in the Po Valley of Italy, ca. 1880–1970*, in "Technology and Culture", 59, 2018, 3, pp. 652–688.

providing energy[17]. Rivers were the preferential routes of communication between urban and surrounding areas and, at least until the end of the nineteenth century, they were used for importing raw materials and exporting value added or industrial goods. A more recent use emerged from the second half of the nineteenth century, with the creation of modern aqueducts and drainage systems[18]. Water courses also played a key role in harnessing energy within more extensive infrastructural complexes. In the early modern period this included the production of hydromechanical energy, and above all rivers' role as means of transport for the main source of energy of that period: wood. The development of hydroelectric energy represented a quantitative leap in the energy that could be extracted from water courses, while the dams, generation plants, and conducting systems changed also the rates of flow, adapting them to the most varied social and economic needs through a process that has been defined as the "industrialization of rivers"[19].

Based on the brief observations and associated examples discussed so far, it is clear that in the study of the relationship between environment and infrastructure, a turning point can be identified in the technological innovations and energy regime introduced through industrialization. This observation becomes even more telling if infrastructures are considered from a 'cultural' perspective. However, the majority of studies cited so far highlight how the material and energy flows that characterized the metabolism of preindustrial societies were already organized through complex infrastructures (or *envirotechnical systems*) based on interwoven social and natural elements[20]. This framework influenced the adoption of an extensive periodization for the present volume, making it possible to identify the undeniable changes caused by industrialization, as well as the persistence of preexisting features and dynamics.

The essays presented here are the outcome of the academic discussion that emerged from the 62nd Study Week, "Environment and Infrastructures from the Early Modern Period to the Present", organized by the Istituto Storico Italo-Germanico of the Fondazione Bruno Kessler in Trento. The first essay, in the

---

17 M. Evenden, *Beyond the Organic Machine? New Approaches in River Historiography,* in "Environmental History", 23, 2018, pp. 698–720; G. Bonan, *Riflessi sull'acqua. Ricerca storica e biografie fluviali,* in "Contemporanea", 22, 2019, 2, pp. 317–328.

18 S. Castonguay / M. Evenden (eds.), *Urban Rivers. Remaking Rivers, Cities, and Space in Europe and North America,* Pittsburgh 2012; M. Knoll / U. Lubken / D. Schott (eds.), *Rivers Lost, Rivers Regained. Rethinking City-River Relations*, Pittsburgh 2017.

19 E. Jakobsson, *Industrialization of Rivers: A Water System Approach to Hydropower Development,* in "Knowledge, Technology & Policy", 14, 2002, 4, pp. 41–56; G. Bonan, *Le acque agitate della patria: L'industrializzazione del Piave (1882–1966)*, Roma 2021.

20 See also T. Soens et al. (eds.), *Urbanizing Nature: Actors and Agency (Dis)Connecting Cities and Nature since 1500*, New York 2019.

section "Overview", provides insight into the methodological and thematic context in which the most recent historical studies on the relationship between environment and infrastructure have developed. This is the broader debate on the concept of Anthropocene that has characterized the last two decades, inducing new interactions between different disciplines within the humanities (like the previously mentioned convergence of environmental history and STS) and between the humanities and the Earth System Sciences. In *Provocations to Environmental History and History of Technology: The Anthropocene*, Helmut Trischler and Fabienne Will trace back the history of the concept that defines the recent continuous transformation produced by mankind, the *Anthropos*, on the Earth system. A process of change that in recent decades has assumed such a massive and powerful scale as to compete with some of the great natural forces. The term was introduced in 2000 in geological studies and soon spilled over into the Earth System Sciences, becoming a discussion point in the human and social sciences. There was reflection on its heuristic and analytic features, debating, among many other things, causes and responsibilities for the ecological crisis and its effects, from climate change to environmental pollution and other issues. Through analysis of the Anthropocene as a geological and cultural concept and the interest it raised as a social phenomenon, the two authors investigate the positions of scientists and anthropologists as regards technology and its impact on the transformations of the planet, examining the idea of the Technosphere or Technocene. This alternative perspective considers mankind as a technical subject and part of a new stage of evolution on the planet. It thus requires a new narrative framework and a different periodization for environmental history and the history of technology in an interdisciplinary and transdisciplinary dialogue.

The role of technology and infrastructures in increasing the consumption of natural resources, and the environmental impact of human activity are the common threads that unite the essays collected here. This also applies to the ones addressing the preindustrial era and not only those regarding more recent decades. Historical analyses reveal the strategies adopted by societies and states to transform and adapt their surrounding environment in a continuous, delicate, and difficult equilibrium of diverse interests. Various means and technologies were applied according to the period, but the environmental impact over time expanded to a global scale, to the extent of necessitating collective reflection and reconsideration.

The volume is organized into three macro sections, with the first dedicated to "Urban Metabolism and the Transformation of Hinterlands", the second to "The Multiple Scales of Envirotechnical Systems", and the third to "Hybrid Landscape: Infrastructures of Water Control".

The first section starts with an essay by Georg Stöger, *Urban Environmental Infrastructure in the Eastern Alpine Region (Sixteenth to Eighteenth Century)*, with research focused on the infrastructures required for the operation of the urban metabolism in three different cities in the eastern Alpine region: Salzburg, Linz, and Vienna, all administrative and commercial centres, and transport hubs of different sizes. He considers the resources sent into the cities, how the raw materials and manufactured goods were used or transformed there, and then the final outcomes, which included unwanted by-products like effluents, waste, and emissions. The author analyzes in detail the commercial networks that supplied the cities with firewood and cereals, the water infrastructures, and finally the socio-environmental systems for fire control and floods. A system of cooperation is identified between actors inside and outside the city to sustain the urban metabolism with infrastructures, which could differ significantly in each case and were sometimes substantially transformed over time, with smaller simpler networks existing alongside or even within larger more complex systems. These infrastructures could be permanent or temporary and normally involved areas outside of the city. There was often the coexistence of a "plurality of hinterlands", which might evolve substantially over time as a result of political decisions, crises, or economic and technological developments.

The second essay, *From* Stues *to* Çates. *Infrastructures for Timber Transport in Friuli in the Early Modern Period*, is dedicated to the history of lumber transport in Carnia, one of the most critical forestry basins supplying the extensive Venetian emporium and mainland settlements. Claudio Lorenzini reconstructs the complex stages in the production chain, with a detailed description of the constructional techniques for the dams used in timber floatation. This system was already well established in the late Middle Ages with substantial changes only occurring from the start of the second half of the nineteenth century, during the period of industrialization of the main river in the region. This involved draining and irrigating the plain, and exploiting the mountain catchment basin for hydroelectric power in the early decades of the twentieth century. The essay reveals essential aspects of the infrastructural system, including some related legal issues regarding the status of collective forest property, associated organizational issues like the recruitment of specialized workers who were often foreigners, and the supply of staple foodstuffs to the forest worksites. No less important were the environmental aspects linked to the tree felling cycle and the seasonal water availability, which served to transport the logs downstream, exploiting the capacity of rivers and mountain streams to the maximum.

This is followed by a temporal leap to postwar Germany and the case of Wismut, where the largest Soviet company operated for over forty years, a sort of "State in the state" involved in the extraction of uranium during the Cold War. The essay by Astrid Mignon Kirchhof, Yaroslav Koshelev, Florian Manthey, Anna-Katharina Pelkner, Judith Schein, and Christiane Uhlig, *Uranium Stories. Making the Wismut Narrative Visible*, deals with the infrastructural systems implemented to transform Wismut. After reunification, this component of the Soviet nuclear system, and one of the biggest environmental disasters on the planet, was converted directly into a German ecological remediation company. The intervention work enabled the reconstruction of the thermal baths in Schlema with a series of associated infrastructures, reconverting a disaster zone into one of the most successful remediation projects of the ex DDR, all within a few years of the reunification of Germany. The remediation works also included conserving the memories of witnesses with the support of the Bochum Mining Museum in collaboration with other German academic institutions. Interviews were recorded with workers and their families, and these are available today in an online archive, intended to raise awareness of the social and cultural consequences of East Germany's environmental and mining history. Uranium mining transformed the economic and social profile of the area, as emerges from the testimonies of Russian and German citizens, even if there are aspects that require further research, like, for example, the associated medical consequences and the Wismut health system.

The second section, "The Multiple Scales of Envirotechnical Systems", starts with Giacomo Parrinello, who in *Water as Infrastructure and the Scalar Mismatch* shows how pollution and climate change have such a severe impact on river flows that they challenge the technical knowledge and predictive ability of those designing infrastructures for irrigation or generating hydroelectric power.

The author describes the first attempts to forecast flow rates based on historical data applied to individual water courses, with the aim of developing new irrigation canals. The Cavour Canal is used as an example, this being the most extensive hydraulic infrastructural development of the 1840s, designed to irrigate the fields of western Piedmont with the waters of the Po River. It turned out to be a failure due to incorrectly forecasting an adequate flow rate in the river to supply the irrigation canal. As the author underlines, it is predictability that transforms water into an infrastructure and this is fundamental for the existence and operation of any water-based environmental system. This emerges again in the second case study regarding the hydroelectric stations established across the entire Po River basin in the twentieth century.

Frédéric Graber addresses the relationship between infrastructures and citizens in *The Ideal Public for Infrastructures. Towards a Long-Term History of the Environment-Infrastructure-Participation Nexus*. He investigates the importance of public participation in infrastructure projects, conducted in France through public enquiries, the so-called *enquête publique*. Participatory procedures were first implemented in the eighteenth century with the public called upon to assess projects for mining, river management, drainage, production sites that created pollution, and other more general issues. Everyone was free to express an opinion of any kind, and these were recorded in a register and then assessed by a commission based in a municipality or prefecture. The author notes that there was very little public interest or participation right from the start. However, the institution survives to the present day when it remains a necessary mechanism for authorizing infrastructural developments. In the second part of the essay, this phenomenon is considered alongside what emerged from the end of the 1960s through the 1970s, when environmental issues entered the political debate, and civil society claimed a more active role in the decision-making process for major infrastructure projects.

Simone Müller's contribution *Dirty New Natures. Infrastructures and the Global Waste Economy* shifts the observational perspective to an emerging theme in environmental history: the waste economy. The author provides an interesting reconstruction of the infrastructural development project of Puerto Castilla in Honduras, arising after a tightening of environmental rules in the United States that opened the way for the exportation of hazardous waste to Central America. The drainage and consolidation of humid zones, and the creation of artificial land for the expansion of the port, combined with road construction projects, were offered in exchange for disposal facilities for waste from the Philadelphia rubbish incinerator. Some local inhabitants interpreted it as an opportunity to relaunch the local economy, but instead it rested on a heritage of colonial exploitation of areas with unstable political regimes and weak national economies. An emblematic but hardly unusual case, and the consequence of an unequal trade system that highlights the contradictions and unbalanced nature of the global environmental protection processes between the North and South of the planet.

The theme of the third part of the volume is water infrastructures, titled "Hybrid Landscape: Infrastructures of Water Control". An essay by Matteo di Tullio, *Coping with Water. Managing a Living Infrastructure in Early Modern Lombardy between Economy, Ecology, and Conflicts,* concentrates on the Po River plain, particularly in the area between the State of Milan and the western provinces of the Republic of Venice, from the fifteenth to the eighteenth century. Countless drainage and land domestication measures in the area promoted by local communities or private individuals made it possible exploit this land effectively, enabling stable settlements to grow through a complex system of ecological, economic, and social interventions. The study reveals clearly how the water network required constant attention since human intervention had given rise to a new ecosystem that had to be constantly kept in equilibrium by the inhabitants, who were an integral part of the infrastructure itself. The example demonstrates the importance of constant cooperation between users, united in consortiums that coordinated the use of the various canals. The consortiums were also relegated to resolving disputes, which were particularly numerous in moments of climate, demographic, or economic crises threatening the efficient exploitation of these living infrastructures.

The role of local people in looking after a territory and environment is taken up again in *Slow Infrastructures, Flood Protection and Extreme Weather Events. A Historical Perspective* by Tim Soens, a study dedicated to the marine coastlines of the Netherlands and Belgium from the Middle Ages to the end of the eighteenth century. The essay details the protective structures, considering the different levels of investment that indicate small somewhat *ante litteram* accelerations, with a transition from "slow" models towards increasingly "heavy" levels of capital and technological intervention. This approach is inspired by the concepts of *slowness* and *deceleration* of the *degrowth* movement, which has emerged in response to the rapid transformations of society and the environment since the second half of the twentieth century. The author underlines how the rapid climatic changes we face today oblige reflection on the need to find innovative technological solutions to protect areas once again threatened by catastrophic flooding. It is crucial to involve the inhabitants of coastal and humid regions, increasing their awareness of risk and moving beyond the model of large-scale infrastructures imposed on them from above.

In the final essay in the section, *Decadent Infrastructure? Representations of Water in the Kingdom of Naples in the Early Nineteenth Century*, David Gentilcore examines water management in the Kingdom of Naples in the nineteenth century, starting from two complementary sources. The first is a work by Teodoro Monticelli, *Sull'economia delle acque da ristabilirsi nel Regno di Napoli*, a discreetly successful volume published in 1809 by the director of the Jesuit College of Naples. It explores political issues and landscape studies, merging proto-environmentalism with concerns for the material condition of the state. The second source volume is *Statistica Murattiana*, started in 1811 on the initiative of Gioacchino Murat, brother-in-law of Napoleon and King of Naples, with the aim of gaining a deeper understanding of the natural, physical, demographic, social, and economic dimensions of the realm. This text is considered a seminal event in the so-called Franco-Neapolitan colonialism. Drawing on these two volumes, the author offers an interesting perspective on the twelve provinces of the Kingdom, based on the results of a heterogeneous study group that included Abbot Monticelli himself. Although no sections are dedicated specifically to water resources, there are numerous references to the condition and supply of water for drinking or power use. What emerges is a water policy in the Kingdom that favored the city at the expense of the countryside and with a disparity of infrastructures in the various areas. The overall situation of the local communities nevertheless appears to have been in equilibrium, thanks to their ability to maintain self-sufficiency and ensure adequate water supplies for agriculture, textile production, and sanity purposes.

John McNeill provides the *Concluding Remarks*, which retrace many key thematic ideas considered in the essays covering different historical periods. Some insightful observations are also offered on the "environment and infrastructure" binomial and its heuristic potential for environmental history.

Acknowledgements

The two editors are greatly indebted to many people. The Director, Christoph Cornelissen, the research group, and all the staff at the Istituto Storico Italo-Germanico in Trento contributed to the realization of the 62nd Study Week, out of which this book emerged. In addition to all the essay authors, we also wish to thank Christoph Bernhardt, Elisabetta Bini, Katja Bruisch, David Edgerton, Jean Baptiste Fressoz, and Joana Gaspar de Freitas. Their participation enriched the academic discussion during the conference. We would also like to acknowledge Alessandra Rosati and the Editorial Office of the FBK, as well as Gavin Taylor for their support in the preparation of this volume. Special thanks to the Fritz Thyssen Stiftung, the Rachel Carson Center of Munich and the Fondazione Universalmuseum Joanneum of Graz for permission to use the cover illustration.

I. Overview

Helmuth Trischler and Fabienne Will

Provocations to Environmental History and History of Technology: The Anthropocene

1 The Anthropocene – the genesis of a multi-polar debate

When the atmospheric chemist Paul Crutzen and limnologist Eugene F. Stoermer first mentioned the term Anthropocene in 2000, they started a scientific debate that quickly gained momentum and is now being widely discussed[1]. The publication of their proposal in a prestigious scientific journal followed two years later, when Crutzen set out his thesis succinctly and precisely in a single-page article on the *Geology of Mankind* in "Nature": humans, he suggested, have become a powerful geological force, so much so that it is necessary to designate a new geological epoch in order to accurately describe this development. At the turn of the millennium, for Crutzen and Stoermer there was no question that the Anthropocene began with the Industrial Revolution, which brought about a fundamental mechanization of economy and society[2]. Their thesis was based on data from ice cores, which show a marked increase in concentrations of carbon dioxide and methane in the atmosphere from the Industrial Revolution onwards[3]. It was not until 1879, however, that carbon dioxide levels in the atmosphere reached 290.1 ppm, exceeding the Holocene average of 280 ppm ± 10 ppm, and subsequently remained above the Holocene norm[4].

Crutzen and Stoermer were aware that their proposed dating of the Anthropocene would not be tacitly accepted if it were actually put to the test as a new geological time unit, and they seemed to expect that it would be debated: "[W]e are aware that alternative proposals can be made (some may even want to include the entire Holocene)"[5]. They would be proved right. A meta-study from 2015 identified no

1 P.J. Crutzen / E.F. Stoermer, *The "Anthropocene"*, in "Global Change Newsletter", 41, 2000, pp. 17–18.

2 P.J. Crutzen, *Geology of Mankind*, in "Nature", 415, 2002, 6867, p. 23.

3 See data in Intergovernmental Panel on Climate Change: [J.T. Houghton et al. (eds.)], Climate Change 2001. The Scientific Basis. Contribution of Working Group I to the Third Assessment Report of the Intergovernmental Panel on Climate Change, Cambridge 2001.

4 NASA, Global Mean CO2 Mixing Ratios (ppm): Observations, https://data.giss.nasa.gov/modelforce/ghgases/Fig1A.ext.txt, last accessed May 15, 2019.

5 P.J. Crutzen / E.F. Stoermer, *The "Anthropocene"*, p. 17.

https://doi.org/10.1515/9783111112756-002

fewer than nine proposals for periodization that have been seriously discussed[6]. They range from the beginning of the Neolithic Revolution around 11,700 years ago to the Nuclear Test-Ban Treaty of 1963.

All the dating proposals show that technology has played a central role in the formation of modern societies. The extent of human impact on nature and the environment – discussed today under the term Anthropocene as both a problem and an opportunity – has only been possible because of the comprehensive mechanization of all areas of life. Debates about the dating of the age of humans therefore revolve to a large extent around the question of processes of technological change and their impact on the environment and society.

From an analytical perspective, the multipolar debate about the Anthropocene can be divided into three main strands of discussion: the debate about the Anthropocene as a geological concept, the debate about the Anthropocene as a cultural concept and the debate about the Anthropocene in media, culture and the public sphere. In practice, these debates are closely interwoven and mutually influence each other[7].

1.1 The Anthropocene as a geological concept

The institutional core of the geoscientific debate is the Anthropocene Working Group (AWG). Founded in 2009, it has been entrusted with the task of examining dating proposals for their scientific evidence and, based on its own stratigraphic investigations, putting forward a plausible periodization draft for the formal recognition of the Anthropocene as a geological time unit. In order to do this, the Working Group follows the International Stratigraphic Guide (ISG), which defines various criteria for ratifying a new time unit and including it in the geologic time scale[8].

Once a dating proposal has been submitted, it must be approved with a 60% majority in each instance by the next higher geoscientific bodies – the Subcommission on Quaternary Stratigraphy (SQS), the International Commission on Stratigraphy (ICS) and the International Union on Geosciences (IUGS) – before being added to the geologic time scale. As part of formulating this proposal, the AWG is examining key geoscientific questions about the Anthropocene: can human impact on the Earth be read as measurable signals in geological strata? Is there a marked

6 S. Lewis / M. Maslin, *Defining the Anthropocene*, in "Nature", 519, 2015, 7542, pp. 171–180.

7 H. Trischler, *The Anthropocene. A Challenge for the History of Science, Technology, and the Environment*, in "NTM", 24, 2016, 3, pp. 309–335.

8 A. Salvador, *International Stratigraphic Guide. A Guide to Stratigraphic Classification, Terminology, and Procedure*, 2nd ed., Trondheim / Boulder 1994.

difference between the Anthropocene world and the stable Holocene epoch of the past 11,700 years? And where is the lower boundary of the Anthropocene? The working group has recently put forward an interim conclusion in various publications[9]. One of these articles bears the programmatic title *The Anthropocene is Functionally and Stratigraphically Distinct from the Holocene*[10]. Despite ongoing heated discussions between the AWG and the wider geoscientific community about the periodization of the Anthropocene, a consensus has emerged within the working group that the Anthropocene started in the 1950s[11]. Plutonium-239 is to serve as the primary marker for the start of the new epoch[12]. The establishment of a Global Stratotype Section and Point (GSSP), known as a golden spike, which defines the isochronous basis of a geological time unit, is still pending. However, thanks to financial support for the working group from the Haus der Kulturen der Welt (House of World Cultures) in Berlin, the process is in its final stages[13].

However, it is by no means a foregone conclusion that these next higher geoscientific bodies will agree to the proposal that the Anthropocene should begin in the middle of the twentieth century. On the contrary, objections to it range from technical arguments such as challenging the Holocene – which was only ratified in 2008 – or the long duration of possible boundary markers such as the layer of radioactive particles in the atmosphere resulting from the use and testing of nuclear bombs, to ethical and political concerns: naming, for the first time, a period of the Earth's history not only after a single species but after our own species, would strengthen the hubris that we must overcome if we are to achieve an ecologically robust Anthropocene[14]. The acting General Secretary of the International

---

9 J. Zalasiewicz et al. (eds.), *The Anthropocene as a Geological Time Unit. A Guide to the Scientific Evidence and Current Debate*, Cambridge 2019; M.J. Head et al., *The Great Acceleration Is Real and Provides a Quantitative Basis for the Proposed Anthropocene Series/Epoch*, in "Episodes", 2021, pp. 1–18: https://www.episodes.org/journal/view.html?doi=10.18814/epiiugs/2021/021031.

10 C. Waters et al., *The Anthropocene Is Functionally and Stratigraphically Distinct from the Holocene*, in "Science", 351, 2016, 6269: https://www.science.org/doi/10.1126/science.aad2622.

11 See more F. Will, *Evidenz für das Anthropozän. Wissensbildung und Aushandlungsprozesse an der Schnittstelle von Natur-, Geistes- und Sozialwissenschaften*, Göttingen 2021.

12 J. Zalasiewicz et al., *The Working Group on the Anthropocene. Summary of Evidence and Interim Recommendations*, in "Anthropocene", 19, 2017, pp. 55–60.

13 S. Turner / C. Waters, *Newsletter of the Anthropocene Working Group*, vol. 10: Report of activities 2020, s.l. 2021; M.J. Head et al., *The Great Acceleration*; J. Zalasiewicz, Subcommission on Quaternary Stratigraphy. Annual Report 2021, s.l. 2021. The presentation on the preliminary favoured GSSPs has been taken place in May 2022 at Haus der Kulturen der Welt in Berlin.

14 P.L. Gibbard / M. Walker, *The Term 'Anthropocene' in the Context of Formal Geological Classification*, in C. Waters et al. (eds.), *A Stratigraphical Basis for the Anthropocene?*, London 2014, pp. 29–37; S. Finney / L. Edwards, *The "Anthropocene" Epoch. Scientific Decision or Political Statement?*, in "GSA Today", 26, 2016, 3, pp. 4–10.

Union on Geosciences, Stanley C. Finney, even fears his own discipline becoming politicized, since the Anthropocene debate is not about scientific questions but about "a political statement"[15]. An article recently published in the geoscientific journal "Episodes", by Philip Gibbard, acting General Secretary of the ICS, in collaboration with Finney, with individual archaeological representatives of the AWG and with other authors, is sceptical and argues that the Anthropocene should be recognized as a geological event rather than a geochronological epoch. Advocates of this position see the advantage of maintaining the functionality and reach of the concept across disciplinary boundaries and into the humanities[16].

1.2 The Anthropocene as a cultural concept

The fact that the humanities and social sciences have become involved on a broad basis in the discussion about a time period shaped by humanity can only be surprising at first glance. For the term itself suggests that nothing less than fundamental anthropological questions are being negotiated here. History and literary studies, political science and sociology, philosophy and anthropology rank high among the humanities and social science communities that discuss the Anthropocene just as intensively as it now do law and religious studies. A central significance of the Anthropocene as a cultural concept lies in the fact that it blurs established boundaries – particularly those of the nature-culture dichotomy that is characteristic of modernity[17]. Critical voices are even louder among the humanities and cultural studies than in the geosciences. While some doubt the added analytical value compared with established concepts in determining the relationship between nature and culture, as well as between the environment and society,

15 S. Finney / L. Edwards, *The "Anthropocene" Epoch*, p. 4. In an excellent replication, Paul Warde, Libby Robin, and Sverker Sörlin demonstrate that in the history of geology, key concepts and issues have often been negotiated at the intersection of politics and society: P. Warde / L. Robin / S. Sörlin, *Stratigraphy for the Renaissance: Questions of Expertise for 'the Environment' and 'the Anthropocene'*, in "The Anthropocene Review", 4, 2017, 3, pp. 246–258, here pp. 248–249.

16 P.L. Gibbard et al., *A Practical Solution: The Anthropocene Is a Geological Event, Not a Formal Epoch*, in "Episodes", 2021, pp. 1–9: https://www.episodes.org/journal/view.html?uid=2248&vmd=Full.

17 B. Latour, *Agency at the Time of the Anthropocene*, in "New Literary History", 45, 2014, 1, pp. 1–18; J. Kersten, *Das Anthropozän-Konzept. Kontrakt, Komposition, Konflikt*, Baden–Baden 2014; W. Haber / M. Held / M. Vogt (eds.), *Die Welt im Anthropozän. Erkundungen im Spannungsfeld zwischen Ökologie und Humanität*, München 2016; B. Szerszynski, *The Anthropocene Monument. On Relating Geological and Human Time*, in "European Journal of Social Theory", 4, 2017, 1, pp. 111–131; C. Deane-Drummond / S. Bergmann / M. Vogt (eds.), *Religion in the Anthropocene*, Eugene OR 2017.

others harbour an even deeper apprehension. Naming a new geoscientific epoch after humans would give rampant anthropocentrism a huge boost and human respect for the intrinsic moral value of nature would dwindle further[18]. Moreover, although only small groups of people in industrialised countries would be largely responsible for the environmental problems of the modern era, the whole of humanity is held responsible, referring to the *anthropos* as a cultural entity. Instead of stimulating urgently needed social and political change, the term would obscure the attribution of concrete responsibilities – a responsibility closely linked to capitalist interests[19]. It is no coincidence that of the numerous interpretations of the Anthropocene, the Capitalocene has been particularly prominently discussed[20].

Lest there be any doubt: the Anthropocene concept hardly needs anything more urgently than a constructive critical debate about its capacities. And this is where the history of technology – with its sharp focus on the relationship between humans and technology, and the repercussions of man-made technology on the environment and society – is bound more than any other discipline to contribute critically to the Anthropocene debate. However, the accusation of reinforcing anthropocentrism, which is usually aimed at the term alone, fundamentally misjudges its normative vanishing point. Indeed, the Anthropocene is not about reaffirming the nature-culture dichotomy that has evolved during the course of modernity but rather, it is about critically challenging the resulting anthropocentrism. It is no coincidence that the Anthropocene as a cultural concept has particularly high resonance among representatives of post-humanist approaches. The blurring of boundaries between nature and culture equips non-human actors with agency – in the open space of post-humanism, hybrid forms of existence become visible. Understood in this way, the Anthropocene ultimately opens up a modified view of humans and their presumed uniqueness on Earth. In the words of literary scholar and foremost post-humanist thinker Ursula Heise, humans become part

18 J. Manemann, *Kritik des Anthropozäns. Plädoyer für eine neue Humanökologie*, Bielefeld / Berlin 2014; T.J. LeCain, *Against the Anthropocene. A Neo-Materialist Perspective*, in "International Journal of History, Culture and Modernity", 3, 2015, 1, pp. 1–28; a vehement refutation of this criticism is provided by C. Schwägerl, *Neurogeology: The Anthropocene's Inspirational Power*, in H. Trischler (ed.), *Anthropocene. Envisioning the Future of the Age of Humans*, München 2013 (RCC Perspectives, 3), pp. 29–37.

19 A. Malm / A. Hornborg, *The Geology of Mankind? A Critique of the Anthropocene Narrative*, in "The Anthropocene Review", 1, 2014, 1, pp. 62–69, here pp. 62–64.

20 J. Moore, *Anthropocene or Capitalocene? Nature, History, and the Crisis of Capitalism*, Oakland 2016; D. Haraway, *Anthropocene, Capitalocene, Plantationocene, Chthulucene: Making Kin*, in "Environmental Humanities", 6, 2015, 1, pp. 159–165; C. Bonneuil / J.-B. Fressoz, *The Shock of the Anthropocene. The Earth, History, and Us*, London / New York 2016; for an overview see F. Will, *Evidenz für das Anthropozän*, p. 208.

of "networks of distributed agents" that include animals and plants as well as chemical substances and technological objects[21]. Understanding the Anthropocene from a post-humanist perspective means becoming aware that humans are inescapably embedded in this network at all times and in everything they do.

The *Ecomodernist Manifesto*, published in 2015, shows how close the link is between the belief in technology's power to solve environmental issues and tangible economic interests. Besides AWG member Erle C. Ellis and many others, the authors of this theodicy of technology include Michael Schellenberger and Ted Nordhaus, founder of the Breakthrough Institute, a US think tank with close links to the oil and nuclear power industries. They have published highly controversial books in which they predict the end of the environmental movement, oppose climate negotiations and advocate the continued use of nuclear energy to protect and stabilize the climate[22]. Their attempt to re-calculate the cumulative costs of nuclear energy over time is particularly controversial. In doing so, the Breakthrough Institute falls back on theories that have long been disproved by economic reality, such as that "there is no inherent cost escalation trend with nuclear power" and that the costs of a nuclear reactor "rise before they fall," thus offering political decision makers a justification for building new reactors[23]. Advocates of the *Ecomodernist Manifesto* are guided by the hope that "knowledge and technology, applied with wisdom, might allow for a good, or even great, Anthropocene". A *good Anthropocene* requires "that humans use their growing social, economic, and technological powers to make life better for people, stabilize the climate, and protect the natural world"[24]. Historians are all too familiar with such professions of faith in the 'technofix'. The recourse to the secularized notion that natural science and technology having the power of salvation is, as Ulrich Wengenroth among others has emphasized, one of the guiding

21 U. Heise, *Post-Humanism: Reimagining the Human*, in N. Möllers / C. Schwägerl / H. Trischler (eds.), *Welcome to the Anthropocene. The Earth in Our Hands*, München 2015, pp. 38–42, here p. 40. Similarly, anthropologist Anna Lowenhaupt Tsing, who combines her story of the matsutake mushroom as an Anthropocene web of relationships with a lucid critique of capitalism: A. Lowenhaupt Tsing, *The Mushroom at the End of the World. On the Possibility of Life in Capitalist Ruins*, Princeton / Oxford 2015.

22 T. Nordhaus / M. Shellenberger, *Break Through. From the Death of Environmentalism to the Politics of Possibility*, New York 2007; M. Shellenberger / T. Nordhaus, *The Death of Environmentalism. Global Warming-Politics in a Post-Environmental World*, in "Geopolitics, History, and International Relations", 1, 2009, 1, pp. 121–163.

23 J. Lovering / A. Yip / T. Nordhaus, *Historical Construction Costs of Global Nuclear Power Reactors*, in "Energy Policy", 91, 2016, pp. 371–382, here p. 371.

24 J. Asafu-Adjaye et al., *Ecomodernist Manifesto*, 2015, https://static1.squarespace.com/static/5515d9f9e4b04d5c3198b7bb/t/552d37bbe4b07a7dd69fcdbb/1429026747046/An+Ecomodernist+Manifesto.pdf, last accessed September 13, 2017, p. 6.

ideas of modernity[25]. For Thomas Hänseroth, technology's promise of progress is nothing less than the sign of the epoch of "technocratic high modernism" that began with the onset of the second Industrial Revolution around 1880 and ended with the significant turning point around 1970[26]. For James C. Scott, the technofix of "high modernism" is by no means over and indeed the debate about the *good Anthropocene* demonstrates how deeply anchored is the belief in the healing power of scientific and technological creativity within the cultural establishment in modern societies, and that it recurs in a cyclical pattern[27].

Critics are concerned that such extensive trust in the ability of technology to overcome the negative consequences of human activity on the Earth and, as it were, to heal nature, would pave the way for the questionable concepts of geoengineering[28]. Both human geographer Jamie Lorimer and economist Jeremy Baskin fear that the twofold exceptionality of the Anthropocene concept – that humanity has brought planet Earth to an unprecedented state – in combination with the relevance of expert knowledge on the one hand and technological intervention on the other, which is evidenced in terms of possible solutions, could serve to legitimize the use of planetary management strategies such as geoengineering. For Baskin, this poses the risk of offloading political challenges to technology[29]. One could point to the fact that a few years ago, none other than the 'father' of the Anthropocene himself, Paul Crutzen, in despair about ongoing climate change, suggested pumping 1.5 million tonnes of sulphur dioxide particles into the atmosphere to

---

25 U. Wengenroth, *Technik der Moderne – Ein Vorschlag zu ihrem Verständnis*. Version 1.0, 2015, https://www.fggt.edu.tum.de/fileadmin/tueds01/www/Wengenroth-offen/TdM-gesamt-1.0.pdf, pp. 32, 132, 237 and others, last accessed June 5, 2019.

26 T. Hänseroth, *Technischer Fortschritt als Heilsversprechen und seine selbstlosen Bürgen: Zur Konstituierung einer Pathosformel der technokratischen Hochmoderne*, in H. Vorländer (ed.), *Transzendenz und die Konstitution von Ordnungen*, Berlin 2013, pp. 267–288; see also U. Fraunholz / S. Wölfel (eds.), *Ingenieure in der technokratischen Hochmoderne. Thomas Hänseroth zum 60. Geburtstag*, Münster 2012.

27 J.C. Scott, *Seeing Like a State. How Certain Schemes to Improve the Human Condition Have Failed*, New Haven 1998.

28 Among others B. Latour, *Love Your Monsters: Why We Must Care for Our Technologies as We Do Our Children*, in "Breakthrough Journal", 2, 2011, pp. 21–28; B. Latour, *Agency*; C. Hamilton, *The Theodicy of the "Good Anthropocene"*, in "Environmental Humanities", 7, 2016, 1, pp. 233–238; M. Hourdequin, *Ethics, Adaptation, and the Anthropocene*, in "Ethics, Policy & Environment", 24, 2021, 1, pp. 60–74.

29 J. Baskin, *Paradigm Dressed as Epoch: The Ideology of the Anthropocene*, in "Environmental Values", 24, 2015, 1, pp. 9–29; J. Lorimer, *The Anthropo-Scene. A Guide for the Perplexed*, in "Social Studies of Science", 4, 2017, 1, pp. 117–142.

reflect sunlight and thus stop global warming[30]. He was heavily criticized for this[31]. As a result of such discussions about technical interventions, whose long-term consequences on the climate and the Earth are completely unknown, the idea of the Anthropocene has acquired a bitter taste for many people.

1.3 The Anthropocene as a social phenomenon

The public debate about the Anthropocene is hardly less polyphonic. Along with the daily newspapers and mass media, museums and cultural centers as well as the arts, aesthetics and cultural theory are entering the debate – and doing so worldwide, as shown by a recent meta-study[32]. The appropriation of the Anthropocene concept is therefore not limited to theoretical discussions, but is being put into practice in a wide range of formats and thus recognised as an opportunity to bring about change. The "Anthropozän-Projekt" (Anthropocene Project), initiated in Berlin in 2013 by the Haus der Kulturen der Welt, attracted a great deal of worldwide attention, triggered many comparable projects and, not least, resulted in collaborations with the geosciences. The same is true of the special exhibition "Welcome to the Anthropocene. The Earth in Our Hands", on display from 2014 to 2016 at the Deutsches Museum, which many institutions around the world took as an example in order to bring the Anthropocene debate to public attention. For instance, the Carnegie Museum for Natural History in Pittsburgh opened an exhibition in 2017 entitled "We are Nature: Living in the Anthropocene", with Nicole Heller as the world's first Curator of Anthropocene Studies there. As mentioned, it is not only in the field of exhibitions that the subject is stimulating conceptual rethinking. The same is true for the performing arts. Here, too, the preoccupation with the Anthropocene concept is changing cultural productions. The dramaturge Theresa J. May, for example, states a change in the theatre that manifests itself in the creation of a new category: ecodramaturgy[33]. In the experimental-imaginative

---

30 P.J. Crutzen, *Albedo Enhancement by Stratospheric Sulfur Injections. A Contribution to Resolve a Policy Dilemma?*, in "Climatic Change", 77, 2006, 3/4, pp. 211–220.
31 Regarding this debate see M.G. Lawrence / P.J. Crutzen, *Was Breaking the Taboo on Research on Climate Engineering via Albedo Modification a Moral Hazard, or a Moral Imperative?*, in "Earth's Future", 5, 2017, 2, pp. 136–143; R.J. Cicerone, *Geoengineering. Encouraging Research and Overseeing Implementation*, in "Climatic Change", 77, 2006, 3/4, pp. 221–226; M.G. Lawrence, *The Geoengineering Dilemma. To Speak or not to Speak*, in "Climatic Change" 77, 2006, 3/4, pp. 245–248.
32 L. Sklair (ed.), *The Anthropocene in Global Media. Neutralizing the Risk*, Abingdon / New York 2021.
33 W. Arons / T.J. May, *Introduction*, in W. Arons / T.J. May (eds.), *Readings in Performance and Ecology*, Basingstoke 2015, pp. 1–10.

world of theatrical representation, it is possible to move a-chronologically across time and space, and at the same time to create a synergy between the planetary deep-time and the historical and human time. The Staatstheater in Nürnberg recently took up this challenge and staged a play with the title *Anfang und Ende des Anthropozäns* (Beginning and End of the Anthropocene)[34].

It is certainly too early to identify universal trends in the public discourse about the Anthropocene. Nevertheless, it is striking that, firstly, the media – and not only science-related journals but also the daily newspapers and mass media – have been picking up the scientific debate very early and reporting on new findings very promptly. Secondly, the way the topic is represented in the media is, on the one hand, closely intertwined with the debate around climate change and, on the other hand, goes way beyond this and interestingly also reflects complex epistemological questions such as the scientific evidence for a new geological epoch named after humans. It is hardly surprising, thirdly, that the public debate about the Anthropocene is highly normative, emphasizing the problems associated with human impact on the Earth and guided by the question of what needs to change – politically, economically, scientifically and technologically, as well as socially – in order to solve environmental problems or reduce their negative consequences. Fourthly and finally, it is striking that artists – with their heightened awareness of cultural-social change – became involved very early and widely in the Anthropocene debate and recognized it as an opportunity to initiate change.

In discursive practice, the multipolar debate is intertwined, interwoven and interrelated in many ways. On the one hand, it is conducted within a disciplinary context, with a range of scientific communities examining the heuristic and analytical quality of the concept against the background of their respective disciplinary framework. However, on the other hand it bursts disciplinary boundaries and develops in interdisciplinary and transdisciplinary ways.

2 The Technosphere and Technocene – new perspectives on technology

The debate about the role of technology in the age of humans has widened and deepened in recent years. The concept of the technosphere, introduced into the Anthropocene debate by Peter Haff, plays a key role here. The geophysicist, who

34 P. Löhle, *Anfang und Ende des Anthropozäns*, Staatstheater Nürnberg.

is also a member of the Anthropocene Working Group, describes the increasingly complex system of technology as the technosphere[35].

As with the Anthropocene itself, the technosphere is not an entirely new idea. It builds on earlier debates about technology from the time when, in the context of the environmental movement that began to form in the 1960s, the planetary "Limits to Growth" – the title of the Club of Rome's famous 1972 report on the future of the world economy – raised significant doubts about the technology-fixated thinking on progress that had prevailed in the postwar era. With the technosphere, research on the environment and Earth systems highlighted human intervention in global material cycles and the exchange of energy and matter. Consistently thought to its end, this results in the thesis that technology forms a discrete sphere, like the atmosphere, hydrosphere, lithosphere, cryosphere and biosphere as spaces of nature.

Haff assumes that the processes of global change subsumed under the Anthropocene concept lead to understanding the *anthropos* as a technological subject. Ingenious technical creativity has enabled humans to intervene deeply in the global metabolism.

From a system-critical perspective, Haff describes the technosphere as a newly emerged Earth system that is made up of "the world's large-scale energy and resource extraction systems, power generation and transmission systems, communication, transportation, financial and other networks, governments and bureaucracies, cities, factories, farms and myriad other 'built' systems, [. . .] all the parts of these systems, including computers, windows, tractors, office memos and humans", and he also includes intermediate social institutions such as churches and NGOs into the sphere of technology[36].

Yet Haff does not assume that the technosphere is a system made and controlled by humans. The functioning of modern society, he argues, is the product of a system that operates beyond individual and collective control and imposes its own demands on human behavior. Technology is not the consequence of human action, but the reverse is true: humans are part of the dynamic Earth system of the technosphere, which they indeed cannot control but in whose service they act. In this perspective, the technosphere, as an autonomous, dynamic and global system, represents a new stage in the evolution of the Earth.

For the Anthropocene Working Group, Haff's focus on the technosphere as a primarily physical space provides "an alternative prism" through which Anthropocene

35 P.K. Haff, *Humans and Technology in the Anthropocene. Six Rules*, in "The Anthropocene Review", 1, 2014, 2, pp. 126–136; and by the same author, *Being Human in the Anthropocene*, in "The Anthropocene Review", 4, 2017, 2, pp. 103–109.
36 P.K. Haff, *Humans and Technology*, p. 127.

phenomena can be considered[37]. The AWG has consequently embarked on quantifying the dimensions of the technosphere. Its mass, interpreted as the entire material output of any human endeavours, is estimated at around 30 trillion tonnes; this corresponds to around 50 kg per square meter of Earth. The quantity of technical objects which are suitable as potential trace fossils is estimated to be 130 million fossil types. Thus, the rapidly increasing diversity of technofossils already exceeds the richness of the dramatically shrinking biological diversity[38].

Reservations about Haff's concept are being voiced from several directions. Whilst from a geoscientific viewpoint there is criticism that direct interactions between the technosphere and other systems and factors – such as the macrosocial level – are not being considered[39], cultural scientists criticize the inherent degradation of humanity resulting from Haff's attribution of relative autonomy to the technosphere[40]. Interestingly, those who fear that the Anthropocene concept could fuel the already-rampant anthropocentrism are accusing Haff for losing sight of humans, with his theory of an autonomous technosphere.

For historical and anthropological research on technology, Haff's concept represents nothing less than a double provocation. The first provocation concerns the assumption of an autonomous technosphere. It calls into question the consensus that technology is constituted by society and, in turn, shapes culture. Technological systems do not act autonomously, but are designed by humans. How technology is linked to other social sub-systems such as politics and economy, how science and technology interact as systems of knowledge and material objects, how the production and use of technology are intertwined – these and similar questions are the subject of intense debate and considerable controversy.

However, the principle that technology is a social construction remains largely stable within cultural studies. It is not even being shaken by neo-materialistic approaches that do not see humans and culture as masters of their material environment, but rather as products of it[41]. Alongside these opposing reactions there are

---

37 J. Zalasiewicz et al., *Scale and Diversity of the Physical Technosphere. A Geological Perspective*, in "The Anthropocene Review, 4, 2017, 1, pp. 9–22, here p. 18.

38 *Ibid.*; J. Zalasiewicz et al., *Technofossil Stratigraphy*, in J. Zalasiewicz et al. (eds.), *The Anthropocene as a Geological Time Unit*, pp. 144–147.

39 J. Donges et al., *The Technosphere in Earth System Analysis. A Coevolutionary Perspective*, in "The Anthropocene Review", 4, 2017, 1, pp. 23–33.

40 See among others T.J. LeCain, *Against the Anthropocene*; J. Lorimer, *The Anthropo-scene*; P.N. Edwards, *Knowledge Infrastructures for the Anthropocene*, in "The Anthropocene Review", 4, 2017, 1, pp. 34–43; B. Szerszynski, *Viewing the Technosphere in an Interplanetary Light*, in "The Anthropocene Review", 4, 2017, 2, pp. 92–102.

41 T.J. LeCain, *Against the Anthropocene*.

also scholars who see Haff's systemic approach as productive and who are developing it further within their own fields[42]. While the sociologist Bronislaw Szerszynski, for example, adopts an interplanetary perspective in his reflections on exo-technospheres, Jeremy Davies believes that this broadening of perspective goes hand in hand with the key task of analyzing the limitations of "power relations between geophysical actors, both human and non-human" in their interrelationship[43].

The second provocation concerns the concept of technology. Haff's technosphere concept originates from a predominantly material conception of technology, and thus masks large parts of a socio-technical understood 'technosphere', as the history and anthropology of technology would conceptualize it.

Far closer to the history of technology than Haff's idea is a proposal by anthropologist and human ecologist Alf Hornborg. He also starts from the enormous social imprinting power of technology and thinks of it in a temporal perspective. Consequently, he argues for referring to the 'Technocene' rather than the Anthropocene[44]. Thereby, he adds his voice to the variety of proposals that seek to make the Anthropocene a productive source for historical-cultural research and to translate it in alternative terms, such as the 'Capitalocene'[45]. The starting point of his investigation is to question the usefulness of thinking in Cartesian categories of nature and culture, rather than stressing the added value that would result from a shift towards post-Cartesian thinking[46]. He concludes that technology, which is seemingly operating objectively, depends on the subjectively and socially constructed economy. In line with the Anthropocene thesis of the centrality of anthropogenic impact on Earth, and following the history of technology and science and technology studies, he focuses on the social and economic dimensions of technology and the critique of Eurocentric narrowness.

According to Hornborg, humanity as a collective entity has never appeared as a historical agent – not even during industrialization. Since the Anthropocene

42 B. Szerszynski, *Viewing the Technosphere*; K. Klingan / C. Rosol (eds.), *Technosphäre*, Berlin 2019; J. Gärdebo / A. Marzecova / S.G. Knowles, *The Orbital Technosphere. The Provision of Meaning and Matter by Satellites*, in "The Anthropocene Review", 4, 2017, 1, pp. 44–52.

43 J. Davies, *The Birth of the Anthropocene*, Oakland 2016, p. 62.

44 A. Hornborg, *Does the Anthropocene Really Imply the End of Culture/Nature and Subject/Object Distinctions?*, in "International Colloquium The Thousand Names of Gaia: From the Anthropocene to the Age of the Earth", September 15–19, 2014. Rio de Janeiro 2014, pp. 1–16; A. Hornborg, *The Political Ecology of the Technocene: Uncovering Ecologically Unequal Exchange in the World-System*, in C. Hamilton / C. Bonneuil / F. Gemenne (eds.), *The Anthropocene and the Global Environmental Crisis. Rethinking Modernity in a New Epoch*, London 2015, pp. 57–69.

45 For an overview see F. Will, *Evidenz für das Anthropozän*, pp. 206–209.

46 A. Hornborg, *Fetishistic Causation*. The 2017 Stirling Lecture, in "HAU: Journal of Ethnographic Theory", 7, 2017, 3, pp. 89–103.

concept misleadingly lends itself to understanding humanity as precisely this undifferentiated, collective entity, he favours the term 'Technocene' to designate the new geological epoch: "To suggest alternative designations such as the 'Capitalocene' or 'Technocene' is to evoke the very real logic of a blind socioecological system, not the subjective choice of the ruling class"[47].

The discussion about the conceptual proposals of the technosphere and the Technocene demonstrates, firstly, that debates about the Anthropocene are inseparable from basic techno-anthropological questions, such as mankind's place on Earth, human self-images, the relationship between humans and technology, people as technological subjects and their actor status in relation to non-human actors and actants. Secondly, it always raises ethical questions, such as those of responsibility, equality and also inequality. Normative perspectives on the relationship between humans, technology and the environment, which are usually negotiated rather implicitly in works on the history of technology, are at the center of debates about the Anthropocene in general and the technosphere and Technocene in particular.

3 New narratives for environmental history and history of technology from the Anthropocene perspective

Unsurprisingly, the Anthropocene is being intensely discussed among historians, particularly in the history of the environment and technology. As experts in the periodization of human history, historians – like stratigraphers – are directly affected by the Anthropocene thesis, because debates about the beginning of the Anthropocene ultimately tackle central questions of the history of technology. Engaging in the discussion about the Anthropocene as a cultural concept means nothing less than taking on the challenge of critically examining established narratives and temporalities.

Numerous leading international historians have accepted this conceptual challenge and are re-telling their stories in the light of the Anthropocene. Dipesh Chakrabarty, a prominent thinker in subaltern and postcolonial studies, is calling for nothing less than a "climate change" in history as well, as a consequence of man-made climate change. He, too, considers the separation between nature and culture

47 A. Hornborg / A. Malm, *Yes, It Is All about Fetishism. A Response to Daniel Cunha*, in "The Anthropocene Review", 3, 2016, 3, pp. 205–207, here p. 206.

that is characteristic of modernity, to be outdated and instead argues that human history and natural history are no longer independent but interwoven into an integral geohistory. In the Anthropocene, cultural, economic, social and political systems co-evolve with natural orders, requiring shifting perspectives and novel narratives. Chakrabarty considers the classical historical understanding to be outdated, because history as a discipline "exists on the assumption that our past, present, and future are connected by a certain continuity of human experience. We normally envisage the future with the help of the same faculty that allows us to picture the past. [. . .] Thus, our usual historical practices for visualizing times, past and future, times inaccessible to us personally – the exercise of historical understanding – are thrown into a deep contradiction and confusion"[48].

A multi-disciplinary analysis of Chakrabarty's theses, published in 2016, demonstrates that they are a particularly powerful and effective appeal for new narratives on the relationship between humans and the environment and that they are vitally important for cultural interpretations of the Anthropocene[49]. A recent book project between Jan Zalasiewicz – longstanding chair of the AWG and now acting chair of the SQS – the biologist Mark Williams and historian Julia Adeney Thomas points to the historiographical potential of cross-disciplinary cooperation[50].

Based on his participation in the Anthropocene Working Group, John R. McNeill– with Peter Engelke as co-author – draws on his experience as a member of the AWG to narrate the global history since the Second World War as a history of the unfolding of the Anthropocene, which resulted from the Great Acceleration[51]. As an environmental historian interested in the circulation of resources, he particularly refers to the use of nuclear energy, carbon dioxide and sulphur dioxide emissions, fresh water use and irrigation, fertilizer use, and the release of toxic chemicals to name just a few indicators of environmental change since the Great Acceleration. For the geologists in need of a clear-cut 'golden spike', he suggests examining the bones and teeth of mammals born in the 1940s and 1950s, which for the first time in history

48 D. Chakrabarty, *The Climate of History: Four Theses*, in "Critical Inquiry", 35, 2009, 2, pp. 197–222, here pp. 198–199; see also by the same author, *The Climate of History in a Planetary Age*, Chicago 2021.

49 R. Emmett / T. Lekan (eds.), *Whose Anthropocene? Revisiting Dipesh Chakrabarty's "Four Theses"*, München 2016 (RCC Perspectives, 2); similar to this J. Davies, *The Birth of the Anthropocene*, pp. 48–62.

50 J.A. Thomas / M. Williams / J. Zalasiewicz, *The Anthropocene. A Multidisciplinary Approach*, Cambridge / Medford 2020.

51 J. McNeill / P. Engelke, *Into the Anthropocene: People and Their Planet*, in A. Iriye (eds.), *Global Interdependence. The World After 1945*, Cambridge 2014, pp. 365–533; J. McNeill / P. Engelke, *The Great Acceleration. An Environmental History of the Anthropocene since 1945*, Cambridge / London 2014.

include a chemical signature that resulted from nuclear weapons tests. The 1963 Test Ban Treaty then weakened this radioactive imprint again. Some of these bones and teeth may become part of a sedimentary layer that distinguishes the mid-twentieth century from all that went before and all that came after.

Global historian Paul Dukes, on the other hand, chooses a different temporality. He frames his world since the end of the Seven Years' War as a story of the "Anthropocene era from 1763". Dukes goes away from the meaning of the Anthropocene in a strict geological sense and takes the liberty of using the term as analytical tool to narrate global history over the last 250 years, starting with the invention of the steam engine by James Watt (1764). In the Anthropocene, humans have inscribed themselves into the Earth thanks to their scientific and technological creativity. Dukes understands his narrative as a pan-disciplinary response to the ongoing crisis showing that "after aeons of the development of planet Earth, we have created the mess in no more than two centuries"[52]. To him, the Anthropocene concept offers a unique tool for linking geological time with historical time, while simultaneously focusing on "major advances in the natural sciences and their applications"[53]. Confined to the comparatively recent past, the Anthropocene concept particularly suits his ambition to narrate environmental change resulting from mankind's scientific creativity and technical ingenuity since the start of industrialization. The historian of technology and the environment Daniel R. Headrick has recently shown in a comprehensive compendium on human-nature interaction that mankind has always had a transformative effect on its surrounding environment. He tells a long and global story of the Anthropocene from the emergence of homo erectus to the present day, impressively pointing to the variety of those processes and developments that have brought about the geological Anthropocene. Despite the consensus within the geosciences to let the Anthropocene begin in the mid-twentieth century, Headrick's perspective, with its focus on causal connections as opposed to the effect-centeredness of stratigraphy, is thoroughly insightful[54].

A particularly instructive example for the analytical and narrative potential that can emanate from the Anthropocene hypothesis is the brilliant study by historian of technology and the environment Gregory T. Cushman on the career of guano, the phosphate-rich natural fertilizer derived from the excrement of Peruvian boobies.

---

52 P. Dukes, *Big History, Deep History and the Anthropocene*, in "History Today", 63, 2013, 11, pp. 4–5, here p. 5.

53 P. Dukes, *Minutes to Midnight. History and the Anthropocene Era from 1763*, London 2011, pp. 4–5.

54 D.R. Headrick, *Humans versus Nature. A Global Environmental History*, Oxford 2020 (in German: *Macht euch die Erde untertan. Die Umweltgeschichte des Anthropozäns*, Darmstadt 2021).

Cushman examines the dramatic, global historical consequences of the exploitation of the guano reserves on islands near the Pacific coast of Peru starting in the 1840s. If history is written from the perspective of this resource, that so profoundly altered the world, there is much to support dating the beginning of the Anthropocene at around the mid-nineteenth century. In Cushman's words: "Nitrogen compounds have turned the Andean legend of El Dorado into reality, down to the nitrogen-based cyanide now used to leash gold from its ore". And he extends the line of historical continuity of such materials far into the future. "Our waste nitrogen phosphate is likely to leave a mark that will last until our planet died in the red blazing fire of our aging sun"[55].

It is no coincidence that studies which focus on the rapidly growing consumption of natural resources such as fossil fuels or minerals in the course of industrialization are particularly clearly inspired by the Anthropocene thesis. Resources were – and are – the lubricant of industrialized societies in the era of capitalism. Their growing use can be measured quantitatively and assessed qualitatively, as can their environmental impact. Cushmann has analyzed the use of important raw materials such as phosphorous between 1830 and 1913 and, based on the rate of resource consumption that he identified, proposes "that industrial civilization's unprecedented exploitation of the lithosphere in the decades leading up to 1913 as part of the Second Industrial Revolution should become our primary marker for the onset of the Anthropocene"[56]. It is not the second acceleration in the 1950s but this first acceleration that marks the actual distinctive turning point on the way to the Anthropocene, which he therefore also refers to by alternative terms such as "Plantationocene" or "Eurocene"[57].

Environmental history and history of technology have recently made considerable efforts to reflect critically on the narrative of progress that is deeply embedded in the history of industrialization. In particular, the numerous works that argue around the intersection of the history of technology, science and the environment, have contributed to a differentiated picture of the transformation of environment and society, resulting from industrialization[58]. From a post-industrial

55 G.T. Cushman, *Guano and the Opening of the Pacific World. A Global Ecological History*, Cambridge 2013, p. 346.

56 G.T. Cushman, *Phosphorus and the Opening of the Anthropocene*, https://technosphere-magazine.hkw.de/p/1-The-Phosphorus-Apparatus-czfdPRXcpUj4nxj8aQQ1GZ, last accessed February 17, 2022.

57 R. Emmett / D.E. Nye (eds.), *The Environmental Humanities. A Critical Introduction*, Cambridge / London 2017, p. 98. They instructively illuminate the potential of the Anthropocene for the booming Environmental Humanities (pp. 93–116).

58 Exemplary of this is F. Uekötter, *Im Strudel. Eine Umweltgeschichte der modernen Welt*, Frankfurt a.M. 2020; J. Radkau, *Technik in Deutschland. Vom 18. Jahrhundert bis heute*, Frankfurt a.M.

perspective, this raises, among other things, the challenge of culturally dealing with the outdated industrial heritage, the so-called culturalized industrial landscape or industrial nature, as it is found in Germany, for example, in the Ruhr region, in Saarland and in the Lausitz region of Saxony. Inspired by the debate about the Anthropocene as a cultural concept, a research group at the Deutsches Bergbau-Museum recently proposed replacing the rather de-functionalized term 'industrial nature' with 'Anthropocene landscape'. Creating an Anthropocene narrative of this kind would enable "a conceptual integration of post-industrial landscape elements that form part of culturalist industrial landscapes", would act as a corrective to the de-historicization of industrial sites that is often found in industrial heritage practices, highlighting the far-reaching effects of industrial landscape use[59].

It is not only historical sciences that come up against the limits of their discipline when trying to approach the subject adequately. The geosciences are also challenged with leaving behind their classical approach and integrating a perspective from other disciplines to their methodology[60]. The question of the 'golden spike' for the Anthropocene forces stratigraphers to imagine how geological strata will look like in a distant future and which future fossils will last, to provide a record of the beginning of the Anthropocene epoch. A particular difficulty here turns out to be that the "idea of the Anthropocene fossilizes an idea of responsibility in the stratigraphy from which it is hard to return"[61].

To recognize the potential of the Anthropocene to open up new perspectives by juxtaposing vastly different time scales, it is not necessary to look ahead to the end of the Earth in several billion years or backwards to the Big Bang nearly 14 billion years ago that began everything, as proponents of "Big History" advocate[62]. The Anthropocene concept makes it possible to connect geological time and

---

2008; D. Blackbourn, *The Conquest of Nature. Water, Landscape, and the Making of Modern Germany*, London 2006.

59 J. Golombek / T. Meyer, *Das (post-)industrielle Erbe des Anthropozän – Überlegungen zu einer Weitung des Blickfelds*, in "Der Anschnitt", 68, 2016, 6, pp. 198–215, here p. 210. For the discussions about landscape in the Anthropocene from a post-human point of view see for example A.L. Tsing / A.S. Mathews / N. Bubandt, *Patchy Anthropocene: Landscape Structure, Multispecies History, and the Retooling of Anthropology*. An Introduction to Supplement 20, in "Current Anthropology", 60, 2019, S20, pp. 186–197.

60 F. Will, *Evidenz für das Anthropozän*.

61 P. Warde / L. Robin / S. Sörlin, *Stratigraphy for the Renaissance*, p. 250.

62 Programmatical here: D. Christian, *Maps of Time. An Introduction to Big History*, Berkeley 2011; Big History Project OER Project, https://www.oerproject.com/Big-History, last accessed June 29, 2021; P. Dukes, *Big History, Deep History*.

historical time in new narratives that are based on new temporalities[63]. Earth history and human history no longer run independently of one another, but instead combine to form an integrated geo-history. Humankind shapes the Earth and, in turn, is shaped by geological signatures on which humans, again, have had a hand in creating. This twofold interaction, accompanied by the blurring of boundaries between nature and culture, becomes the sign of the Anthropocene, which interweaves different timescales. The Anthropocene connects the long history of human alteration of the Earth starting during the Neolithic Revolution with the present of the 'long now' and the resulting responsibility for the future. Pointing out that geology emerged from the humanities, anthropologist Bronislaw Szerszynski formulates a paradox. The strict separation and seeming incompatibility of historical and geological time, he argues, just represents another mental construct, that also goes hand in hand with the categorical separation of nature and culture in the modern era[64]. This certainly does not diminish the challenge and achievement of the Anthropocene in re-uniting these two temporal dimensions. However, the feasibility of bringing them back together is becoming more tangible. Instead of narrating historical change on a horizontal plane, it is necessary both to develop non-linear narratives and to locate history on a vertical plane – the project 'Integrated History and Future of People on Earth' (IHOPE) shows how this can look in practice[65].

An environmental historian puts the need of synchronizing the different temporal dimensions as follows: "[W]hat I think synchronizers do [. . .] through the Anthropocene, they're going to link between the geological time scale, and the agency of humanity in the world, and then also linking the individual human life into the temporalities of the planetary, and the temporalities of the environment, and the temporalities that are ultimately geological. [. . .] A new logic comes into time"[66].

The project launched by the Californian utopian Steward Brand and his Long Now Foundation, to build a "Clock of the Long Now", which will keep time for 10,000 years or more without the need for human maintenance, impressively points to the feasibility of a new connection between passages of time, and to the dialectical constellation that humans must take responsibility for the consequences of their actions, which will continue into the unimaginably distant future,

63 H. Trischler, *The Anthropocene.*

64 B. Szerszynski, *The Anthropocene Monument*, p. 116.

65 International Geosphere-Biosphere Program, "Developing an Integrated History and Future of People on Earth (IHOPE): Research Plan". IGBP Report No. 59, Stockholm 2010.

66 The quote is from an interview that took place on March 26, 2018 in Munich between Fabienne Will and an environmental historian involved in the Anthropocene debate.

without knowing how they can adequately fullfill this responsibility[67]. This dialectic is also evident, for example, in the German Standortauswahlgesetz (German Repository Site Selection Act, or StandAG) to select a long-term repository site for radioactive waste. The law requires that such a storage site must ensure safety for one million years. This desperate effort borders on hubris, reminding us that highly radioactive waste is a substance that we cannot control, but rather, as legal scholar Jens Kersten puts it, "will control us humans – as long as we still exist in the next million years"[68].

The problems of nuclear waste management stress that the temporalities of the Anthropocene stretch far beyond any human experiences, comprehension and imagination. Clive Hamilton, Christophe Bonneuil and François Gemenne surmise that as "we appear to have taken control over nature and have become the principal force of its transformation, we also appear ill equipped, and perhaps unable, to govern a world under the influence of these changes"[69]. This striking paradox of the Anthropocene asks us to reassess the instruments of global, or more accurately, Earth governance.

4 The provocation of the Anthropocene – responses from history of technology and the environment

Despite the momentum of the current debate about the age of humans, it will take many years, if not decades, for the Anthropocene concept to unfold its full provocative potential to stimulate new research questions, both in the natural sciences and in the humanities and social sciences. However, the Anthropocene has already become an area of remarkable collaboration across the broad academic spectrum. This means that much has already been gained, because there is hardly anything society needs more urgently than a dialogue that reaches across traditional boundaries and addresses human responsibility for the Earth in the past, present and future.

---

67 The Long Now Foundation, "The 10,000 Year Clock", http://longnow.org/clock/, last accessed June 12, 2019.

68 J. Kersten, *Eine Million Jahre?*, in J. Kersten (ed.), *Inwastement – Abfall in Umwelt und Gesellschaft*, Bielefeld 2016, pp. 269–288, here p. 285.

69 C. Hamilton / C. Bonneuil / F. Gemenne, *Thinking the Anthropocene*, in C. Hamilton / C. Bonneuil / F. Gemenne (eds.), *The Anthropocene and the Global Environmental Crisis*, pp. 1–13, here p. 10.

The history of technology and the environment offers a 'natural' opportunity to take on the role of an interdisciplinary and transdisciplinary hinge in this dialogue, to cast a critical light on established narratives, and to tell new stories on the basis of the new questions and new temporalities that result from the collision of historical and geological timescales. This is particularly true for an anthropologically orientated history of technology, because in the Anthropocene debate and the resulting discussion on the role of technology, the *anthropos* is negotiated as a cultural, technological and geological subject.

In practice, human action in these different actor modes is difficult to separate from each other. However, the *anthropos* as a technological subject acts as a hinge in two respects: firstly, it appears as a link between man as a cultural subject and man as a geological subject. As the discourse about the periodization of the Anthropocene shows, it was only the advent of technology that turned humans from cultural to geological subjects. Secondly, it connects the geological (vertical) and historical (horizontal) dimensions of time, insofar as it plays a central role in both temporalities.

To conclude, we want to highlight five fields of reaction to the provocation of the Anthropocene and related challenges for the history of technology and the environment:

Firstly, as Dolly Jørgensen has recently pointed out, historians of technology and the environment are producing innovative results in fields in which they closely cooperate. Yet, in order to fully utilize the epistemological potential of their field, Jørgensen has called on historians of technology to broaden their understanding of what constitutes technology. Aligning with Actor-Network-Theory and neo-materialist approaches, Jørgensen's definition of technology encompasses not only material artefacts but also animals and plants. By the same token, she understands technology as an integral part of the ecosystem[70]. The Anthropocene debate calls for a new conceptual and methodological step further and for seeking cooperation with the geosciences, in the spirit of the much-vaunted great interdisciplinarity[71].

Secondly, the connection between human and geological histories confronts historians of technology and the environment with the challenge of decoupling from outdated linear timescales to a greater extent than ever before. Instead of narrating historical change along a horizontal plane, historians have both to

70 D. Jørgensen, *Not by Human Hands. Five Technological Tenets for Environmental History in the Anthropocene*, in "Environment and History", 20, 2014, 4, pp. 479–489.

71 R. Costanza / L.J. Graumlich / W. Steffen (eds.), *Sustainability or Collapse? An Integrated History and Future of People on Earth*, Cambridge / London 2007; L. Robin / W. Steffen, *History for the Anthropocene*, in "History Compass", 5, 2007, 5, pp. 1694–1719.

develop non-linear narratives – which many have already convincingly demonstrated – and to locate history on a vertical axis. Whilst stratigraphers read the Earth's history vertically, by looking at geological strata in order to identify phases of planetary-scale disruption as well as periods of normal change, historians have to conceptualize stratigraphic models of historical temporality[72].

Thirdly, the Anthropocene debate extends history not only in temporal dimensions but also in spatial ones. Global history has indicated ways of overcoming narrow nationalism and Eurocentrism to analyze transnational entanglements that focus in particular on the circulation of technological artefacts and scientific knowledge. While global history operates at the *Flughöhe der Adler* (the altitude of an eagle), the Anthropocene concept charges us with the task of going further to take a planetary perspective on our history[73].

It is one of the basic methodological and theoretical assumptions that every historiography is inevitably framed by the present day; and thus, current historical research is also Anthropocene history. Fourthly, however, Anthropocene narratives are not only shaped by present-day concerns, but also by concerns about our future. They connect the long history of our present with implicit and explicit normative assumptions about our future, in particular with respect to the role of technology in solving problems that we have identified in our present and projected into the future. Exposing these normative dimensions of the Anthropocene debate in a multidimensional way, as expressed in concepts of the technosphere and the Technocene, opens up perspectives that are both exciting and highly promising.

Fifthly, the provocation of the Anthropocene also manifests itself as a struggle for historical interpretive power. Stratigraphers complain vividly that the humanities and social sciences are depriving themselves of the *arcanum* of their field of research: the periodization of the history of the Earth. Their discipline risks to lose its epistemic strength and even to become a playground for political interests[74]. Conversely, the humanities are also taking a stance: human history is the subject of cultural studies and whatever stratigraphers ultimately decide regarding the formal recognition and periodization of the Anthropocene is of little relevance to the humanities, and certainly not binding. On the contrary, one of the primary tasks of history in approaching the Anthropocene is to develop alternative interpretations

72 D. Armitage / J. Guldi, *The History Manifesto*, London 2014.

73 J. Osterhammel, *Die Flughöhe der Adler. Historische Essays zur globalen Gegenwart*, München 2017; B. Szerszynski, *Viewing the Technosphere*.

74 P.L. Gibbard / M. Walker, *The Term 'Anthropocene'*; S. Finney / L. Edwards, *The "Anthropocene" Epoch*.

of the role of the *anthropos* as a subject of history, and to fill the concept with more practical meaning through its localization[75].

Becoming mired in sterile professional political debate, however, takes a great deal of energy and ultimately helps no one. Instead, the potential of interdisciplinary cooperation and transdisciplinary dialogue should be emphasized. The history of technology and the environment can be grateful to the Anthropocene debate for these epistemological provocations.

75 C. Hamilton / C. Bonneuil / C. Gemenne (eds.), *The Anthropocene and the Global Environmental Crisis*; C. Bonneuil / J.-B. Fressoz, *The Shock of the Anthropocene*.

II. Urban Metabolism and the Transformation of Hinterlands

Georg Stöger

Urban Environmental Infrastructure in the Eastern Alpine Region

(Sixteenth to Eighteenth Century)

1 Introduction

Urban environmental history usually deals with infrastructure from the nineteenth century onwards. This is not surprising, since there was a boom in urban network and infrastructure creation during this period[1]. Nevertheless, an increasing number of studies are researching infrastructure from the perspective of urban metabolism and urban hinterlands in the early modern period[2]. Metabolism can be understood, according to the rather broad but apt definition provided by Sabine Barles and Martin Knoll, as "the material and energy flows necessary to sustain human life and human activities"[3]. Metabolism therefore comprises the resources that are brought into the city, the use or transformation of these materials and products in the city, and finally the output, which includes products, but also (as unwanted by-products) effluents, waste, or emissions.

To date most studies have tended to focus on a specific part of the urban metabolism, but the present essay will combine different strands of urban material flows and urban infrastructure, and query the motives and techniques of the actors and associated extra-urban outreach. This is aligned with Martin Melosi's suggestion of an "ecosystem concept", which views the different facets of the urban environment as a system with multiple connections and interactions. Such "urban systems" include hinterlands and their intentional and unintentional

1 M.V. Melosi, *Rethinking the City-Building Process and Infrastructure: The Cultural Turn in American Urban Environmental History*, in "Informationen zur Modernen Stadtgeschichte", 1, 2015, pp. 17–29, here p. 17.

2 S. Barles / M. Knoll, *Long-Term Transitions, Urban Imprint and the Construction of Hinterlands*, in T. Soens et al. (eds.), *Urbanizing Nature. Actors and Agency (Dis) Connecting Cities and Nature Since 1500*, New York 2019, pp. 29–49; S. Barles, *Urban Metabolism*, in S. Haumann / M. Knoll / D. Mares (eds.), *Concepts of Urban-Environmental History*, Bielefeld 2020, pp. 109–124.

3 S. Barles / M. Knoll, *Long-Term Transitions*, p. 29.

https://doi.org/10.1515/9783111112756-003

transformation by the city[4]. Actors inside and outside the cities used techniques[5] and created infrastructures that organized and sustained the urban metabolism. These infrastructures were quite diverse and they could undergo significant transformations over time, with smaller simpler networks existing alongside or even within bigger and more complex systems[6].

This infrastructure was both stable and unstable and it usually involved areas outside of the city, which can be referred to as "hinterlands"[7]. Often there was a "plurality of hinterlands" and these could significantly evolve over time due to political interventions, crises, or economic and technological progress[8].

In an attempt to achieve a systemic perspective, this essay considers urban environmental infrastructures as being locked into the urban metabolism. Three aspects of premodern urban environmental infrastructure are discussed: 1) commercial networks supplying the cities with firewood and grain; 2) water infrastructures; and 3) socio-environmental infrastructures related to urban fires and flooding. These infrastructures are examined in three different cities in the eastern Alpine region: Salzburg, Linz, and Vienna. All three cities were centers of administration, trade, and transport, albeit of different sizes (cf. Tab. 1). Vienna and

Tab. 1: Inhabitants of Linz, Salzburg, and Vienna

Year	Linz	Salzburg	Vienna
1600	7.000	8.000	35.000
1650	9.000	9.000	50.000
1700	11.500	10.000	100.000
1750	17.000	12.000	175.000
1800	20.000	14.000	230.000

Source: Estimates based on G. Stöger, *Transformationen städtischer Umwelt*, p. 53; K. Klein, *Historisches Ortslexikon*, Wien 2016 (vols. on Salzburg and Vienna).

4 M.V. Melosi, *Humans, Cities, and Nature: How Do Cities Fit in the Material World*, in "Journal of Urban History", 36, 2010, 1, pp. 3–21, here p. 10.

5 As French sociologist Marcel Mauss suggested, "effective traditional acts", which can be understood in a broader and more comprehensive sense than the term "technology". Cf. S. Barles / M. Knoll, *Long-Term Transitions*, p. 29.

6 Cf. on the question of firewood supply: C. Zumbrägel, *Die vorindustriellen Holzströme Wiens. Ein sozionaturales großtechnisches System?*, in "Technikgeschichte", 81, 2014, 4, pp. 335–362.

7 S. Haumann / M. Knoll / D. Mares, *Urban-Environmental History as a Field of Research*, in S. Haumann / M. Knoll / D. Mares (eds.), *Concepts of Urban-Environmental History*, pp. 9–20.

8 S. Barles / M. Knoll, *Long-Term Transitions*, pp. 34f.

Linz were part of the Habsburg Empire, while Salzburg was the capital of the independent Prince-Archbishopric of Salzburg until the early nineteenth century. This paper is based on secondary literature and current research, so the different aspects of infrastructure are analyzed to different depths for the individual case studies and periods.

2 Commercial networks and the plurality of hinterlands

Energy was (and remains) an essential part of the urban metabolism[9]. As elsewhere in continental Europe, in the eastern Alpine region heat energy was based on firewood until the mid-nineteenth century. Cities needed large quantities of firewood for both domestic and commercial use[10]. Initially this was supplied from nearby forests or other easily accessible woodlands since transport costs were fundamental for the price of firewood[11]. For example in 1730s Linz, an Upper Austrian monastery transported firewood from the Alpine foreland south of Linz to its urban residence using rafts on the river Traun, with the rafts and logs costing about the same (23 Gulden/fl) as the transport and the tolls (nearly 24 fl)[12].

In Vienna there was a shift from local forests to other woodland already during the seventeenth century. The wood hinterland had expanded and by that time most of the firewood probably came from the Wiener Wald and more distant regions along the river Danube. The Danube became a central route for firewood, although substantial log floating was still active on smaller rivers[13]. In Linz the situation was quite similar. Like Vienna, the city of Linz did not own woodland and the inhabitants relied on firewood traders and local farmers. Up to the eighteenth century most of the firewood probably came from the local woods around

---

9 *Ibid.*, p. 38; P. Charruadas / C. Deligne, *Cities Hiding the Forests. Wood Supply, Hinterlands and Urban Agency in the Southern Low Countries, Thirteenth to Eighteenth centuries*, in T. Soens et al. (eds.), *Urbanizing Nature*, pp. 112–134.

10 D. Schott, *Energizing European Cities: From Wood Provision to Solar Panels – Providing Energy for Urban Demand, 1800–2000*, in T. Soens et al. (eds.), *Urbanizing Nature*, pp. 135–156; J. Radkau, *Das Rätsel der städtischen Brennholzversorgung im "hölzernen Zeitalter"*, in D. Schott (ed.), *Energie und Stadt in Europa. Von der vorindustriellen "Holznot" bis zur Ölkrise der 1970er-Jahre*, Stuttgart 1997, pp. 43–75.

11 P. Charruadas / C. Deligne, *Cities Hiding the Forests*, pp. 126–128.

12 G. Stöger, *Transformationen städtischer Umwelt. Das Beispiel Linz, 1700 bis 1900*, Wien 2021, p. 113.

13 D. Schott, *Energizing European Cities*, pp. 138–140.

the city, especially from the forested and sparsely populated Mühlviertel region north of the river Danube[14]. There is not much data or research on this, but the Danube and Traun rivers probably played a significant role in the supply of firewood to Linz before the eighteenth century, since there were already substantial trade networks that linked the upstream woodlands with the ever-growing city of Vienna and this wood also passed Linz[15].

Like Linz and Vienna, Salzburg also lacked its own "city forest", but it was surrounded by extensive woodlands, especially towards the South. Some of the larger urban institutions and the archbishop himself owned woodland (so-called "court woods", "Hofwälder"), or they received firewood as rent in kind ("Naturalabgabe"). The rest of the population relied on firewood sold by local farmers and traders, whose activities remained largely unregulated until the eighteenth century[16]. Accounting records make it possible to trace the firewood supply and identify the associated hinterlands over several hundred years for two urban institutions in the city of Salzburg, the municipal hospital ("Bürgerspital") and the brother-house ("Bruderhaus"). The earliest entries in the hospital's accounts (made in the 1470s) refer to wood purchased from Alpine areas towards the south, and the firewood was obviously transported to the city on the river Salzach via the city of Hallein[17]. Hallein had a high consumption of firewood due to its salt works, and early on it had a timber grill for collecting drifted logs[18]. This also emerges in the frequent use of the rather unusual measuring unit, the "Pfann" (pan), in the hospital's accounts up to the beginning of the seventeenth century[19]. There are also a number of entries that suggest the direct purchase of firewood at the salt works or at the timber grill[20]. At the same time the hospital received firewood from the vicinity of the city,

14 E. Koller, *Forstgeschichte Oberösterreichs*, Salzburg 1975, pp. 22f.

15 *Ibid.*, pp. 89f. and 171f.

16 R. Ebner, *An Nacht König für Seuberung der Cloaca. Grundbedürfnisse des Wohnens*, in R. Reith et al. (eds.), *Haushalten und Konsumieren. Die Ausgabenbücher der Salzburger Kaufmannsfamilie Spängler von 1733 bis 1785*, Salzburg 2016, pp. 121–133; C. Sonnlechner / V. Winiwarter, *Räumlich konzentrierter Verbrauch von Holz. Das Beispiel der Saline Hallein und der Stadt Salzburg vom 16. bis zum 19. Jahrhundert*, in W. Siemann / N. Freytag / W. Piereth (eds.), *Städtische Holzversorgung. Machtpolitik, Armenfürsorge und Umweltkonflikte in Bayern und Österreich (1750–1850)*, München 2002, pp. 55–77.

17 Archiv der Stadt Salzburg (City archive Salzburg, henceforth AStS), Archiv der städtischen Stiftungen (Stif) 92 (1478/79), fol. 180r.

18 *Ordentliche Beschreibung des Salzwesens im Erstift Salzburg*, Salzburg 1617; cf. C. Sonnlechner / V. Winiwarter, *Räumlich konzentrierter Verbrauch von Holz*.

19 *Ordentliche Beschreibung*, p. 58.

20 Cf. e.g. AStS, Stif 161, fol. 60r (27.3.1568); Stif 186, fol. 80v (21.11.1592).

which was probably not transported by water but on horse-drawn carts[21]. The wood hinterland of the brother-house appears similarly diversified. The surrounding woodlands and Hallein are frequently mentioned in the account books with the entries sometimes even noting water transport for the firewood ("Wasserholz"), but land transport from woodlands closer to the city appears to have been equally important during the sixteenth and seventeenth centuries[22]. The evidence thus suggests that there were parallel and sometimes intertwined networks of supply. There is no detailed information from these two institutions for the eighteenth century, but there is a household accounting book of a wealthy Salzburg merchant that offers interesting insights into firewood supply for the period from the 1730s to the 1780s. The household was the Spängler family, and they bought substantial quantities of wood and, unlike most other citizens at that time, they also stockpiled it, probably to save money. The Spängler family got their firewood directly from local farmers north-east of the city and only occasionally from the city's wood market. The supply infrastructure seems to have been quite stable because the same farmers are named repeatedly in the account books, sometimes even referring to them as "our farmers" ("unßern Pauern")[23]. The Spängler household's expenses for firewood were substantial. At the end of the 1740s, costs of around 65 fl were recorded annually, which was equivalent to 325 days of work for an unskilled laborer. By the end of the 1760s the annual costs for firewood had risen to around 130 fl, which was equivalent to 650 unskilled day wages[24].

It is interesting and revealing to study infrastructure and hinterlands from the perspective of long-term price data. In a recent research project, price data for the cities of Salzburg and Vienna was collected. The Salzburg data comes from the aforementioned accounting books kept by the municipal hospital and the brother-house, while for Vienna the accounting books of the municipal hospital were used[25]. This data is more relevant to large-scale consumers of firewood, but

21 AStS, Stif 136, fol. 65v (6.4.1545); Stif 185, fol. 82v (30.5.1591); Stif 185, fol. 82v (25.5.1591).

22 R. Reith / A. Zechner / E. Knapp, *Die Entwicklung der Preise für Lebensmittel und Verbrauchsgüter anhand der Rechnungsbücher des Bruderhauses St. Sebastian in Salzburg (1670–1800)*, in "Salzburg Archiv", 37, 2019, pp. 351–398, here pp. 387f.; AStS, Stif 781, fol. 51v (15.12.1567); Stif 858, fol 143 (19.1.1644).

23 R. Ebner, *An Nacht König*, p. 123; all expenses documented in these accounting books are accessible in a web-based database: Ausgabenbücher Spängler Online/Account Books Spängler Online (hereafter ASO), www.spaengler-haushaltsbuecher.at.

24 Own calculations based on ASO; the day wage is based on data provided by A. Zechner / E. Knapp / M. Adelsberger, *Prices and Wages in Salzburg and Vienna, c. 1450–1850*, in "Vierteljahrschrift für Sozial- und Wirtschaftsgeschichte", 108, 2021, 4, pp. 504–521 (Data supplement).

25 "Prices and Wages in Salzburg and Vienna, c. 1450–1850" funded by the Austrian Science Fund (FWF P 30241); cf. A. Zechner / E. Knapp / M. Adelsberger, *Prices and Wages*.

it does provide an overall view of long-term urban price changes (cf. Fig. 1). The prices correlate in an interesting way, steadily increasing from the sixteenth century until the mid-seventeenth century (almost doubling, which also affected other goods), then remaining stable until the beginning of the eighteenth century. From that point on the traces start diverging. In Salzburg the prices remained steady until the period of inflation of the Napoleonic wars of the 1790s, while in Vienna firewood prices grew steadily during the eighteenth century. Two features are noteworthy, a supra-regional convergence of prices for a long period of time, and a divergence of prices starting in the eighteenth century, albeit with some differences between hardwood and softwood[26].

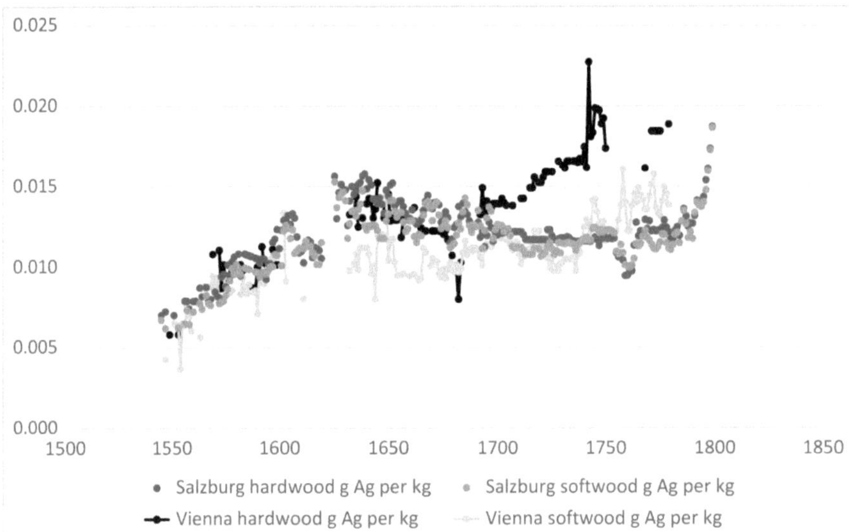

Fig. 1: Prices for firewood in gram silver, Salzburg and Vienna.
(A. Zechner / E. Knapp / M. Adelsberger, *Prices and Wages* – Data supplement).

These prices seem to reflect certain developments in the firewood supply infrastructure. First, the growing demand for firewood in Vienna from the late seventeenth century can be assumed to result from a substantial growth in population. Higher demand and higher prices led to an expansion of the wood hinterland, which involved the construction of a substantial infrastructure that included canals and tunnels. The woodlands also changed as a consequence of clear-felling with a transition

26 R. Reith / A. Zechner / E. Knapp, *Die Entwicklung der Preise*, p. 379.

towards coniferous forest[27]. There was a displacement towards more distant hinterlands. The firewood came mostly from the Mühlviertel region, other parts of Upper Austria and even from the Bayerische Wald, and to a lesser extent from the Schneeberg-Rax region[28]. During the second half of the eighteenth century these forest areas were increasingly used to provide firewood for growing cities like Linz and Vienna. A connection to the Danube by natural or artificial waterways was vital. On smaller rivers the firewood was drifted ("Trift") while on the Danube the logs were transported on boats and rafts[29]. The second observation emerging from the analysis of prices (and their overall stability) is an apparently regular supply of firewood. There are frequent mentions of wood shortages ("Holznot") in the sources, especially for the second half of the eighteenth century, but there are no suggestions that major firewood consumers (like breweries or brick makers) ever left the cities, with prices remaining remarkably stable for long periods of time, especially in Salzburg[30]. It thus appears that the wood hinterlands were capable of satisfying the growing demands of the cities. A third observation is that there were efforts by the city governments to control the supply of firewood, and this appears to have intensified during the second half of the eighteenth century, which was a phase of rising firewood prices (at least in Vienna). Regulation mostly regarded the officially controlled urban firewood markets, with increased pressure on traders (and buyers) to use these markets. City governments did not generally get directly involved in trade activities or subsidize firewood, except during brief periods of crisis. The liberalization of the firewood trade from the 1790s onwards followed the same philosophy, aiming to reduce prices but without playing an active role in the commercial network[31].

Another good statistic for assessing the daily urban metabolism was grain, which formed the basis of premodern diets. In all three cities grain came from multiple hinterlands, but Salzburg was probably more dependent on supra-regional imports. These grain hinterlands and markets have not been comprehensively studied, but information is available from a comparatively large number of sources regarding the 1770s famine. Starting from 1770 there were a number of

---

27 D. Schott, *Energizing European Cities*, pp. 138–140.

28 C. Zumbrägel, *Die vorindustriellen Holzströme Wiens*, pp. 341–353.

29 G. Stöger, *Transformationen städtischer Umwelt*, pp. 109–116; E. Koller, *Forstgeschichte Oberösterreichs*, pp. 91f. and 177f.

30 *Ibid.*; K. Brunner / P. Schneider (eds.), *Umwelt Stadt. Geschichte des Natur- und Lebensraumes Wien*, Wien 2005, pp. 176f.

31 C. Sonnlechner / V. Winiwarter, *Räumlich konzentrierter Verbrauch von Holz*, pp. 572–574; C. Zumbrägel, *Die vorindustriellen Holzströme Wiens*, p. 353; G. Stöger, *Transformationen städtischer Umwelt*, pp. 116f.

failed harvests, which caused rising grain prices and food shortages in many parts of western and central Europe. The crisis reached its peak during 1771 and 1772 and caused a drastic rise in mortality[32].

Despite the existence of local producers, during the second half of the eighteenth century Salzburg relied heavily on the import of grain from neighboring Bavaria[33]. A contract with Bavaria issued in 1766 even specified the quantity of grain that should be delivered annually to the salt workers in Hallein without taxes and tolls. Grain was normally the return cargo in the salt trade[34]. The accounting books of the Salzburg hospitals contain hints of connections with the grain hinterlands of Salzburg, but it is difficult to trace out an overall picture for the early modern period because it is not entirely clear whether the records refer to producers, traders, or transporters. However, the entries do indicate purchases from the city market, from the northern parts of Salzburg, and quite frequently imports from Bavaria and Upper Austria (and probably Hungary)[35].

It is possible to identify dependency on supra-regional hinterlands during the crisis of the 1770s and also the complete collapse of the supply infrastructure. The neighboring territories of Salzburg quickly halted grain exports, which disrupted the supply infrastructure and caused severe consequences. In 1771 the grain price in Salzburg almost tripled and the Salzburg government made costly and rather futile efforts to improve the supply and reduce prices. Prices returned to normal only in 1773 after a good harvest (cf. Fig. 2)[36]. As in other territories, the Salzburg government tried to import grain for the local market and to supply bakers. Already in 1771 the government was buying grain in Udine and Triest and bringing

---

32 D. Collet, *Die doppelte Katastrophe. Klima und Kultur in der europäischen Hungerkrise 1770–1772*, Göttingen 2019; D. Collet / D. Krämer, *Germany, Switzerland and Austria*, in G. Alfani / C.Ó Gráda (eds.), *Famine in European History*, Cambridge 2017, pp. 101–118; M. Vasold, *Die Hunger- und Sterblichkeitskrise von 1770/73 und der Niedergang des Ancien régime*, in "Saeculum", 59, 2008, 1, pp. 107–142; G. Stöger, *Transformationen städtischer Umwelt*, pp. 274–281.

33 H. Rankl, *Das Getreideland Altbayern um 1800. Produktion, Konsum, Binnen- und Außenhandel*, in F. Flachenecker / R. Kießling (eds.), *Wirtschaftslandschaften in Bayern. Studien zur Entstehung und Entwicklung ökonomischer Raumstrukturen vom Mittelalter bis ins 19. Jahrhundert*, München 2010, pp. 331–394, here pp. 374 and 377f.

34 *Ibid.*, pp. 378f.

35 R. Reith / A. Zechner / E. Knapp, *Die Entwicklung der Preise*, pp. 356–361; cf. e.g. AStS, Stif 780, fol. 45r (21.12.1566); Stif 780, fol. 45r (21.12.1566); Stif 781, fol. 53r (23.9.1567); Stif 795, fol. 60v (9.3.1581); Stif 96, fol. 111 (14.2.1495); Stif 96, fol. 111 (3.6.1495); Stif 142, fol. 89r (1.9.1551).

36 H. Rankl, *Das Getreideland Altbayern*, p. 345; G. Ammerer, *Von Franz Anton Harrach bis Siegmund Christoph von Schrattenbach – Eine Zeit des Niedergangs*, in H. Dopsch / H. Spatzenegger (eds.), *Geschichte Salzburgs*, vol. II/1, Salzburg 1988, pp. 245–324, here pp. 322f.; A. Zechner / E. Knapp / M. Adelsberger, *Prices and Wages* – Data supplement.

it to Salzburg despite the high transport costs[37]. In 1772 the archbishop requested a permit from the Austrian emperor to import a large quantity of grain directly from Hungary, which was approved after some negotiations[38].

The 1770s crisis is also documented in the accounting books from Salzburg. The brother-house bought its grain from the city and the estate warehouse, but the quantity of the most important grain (rye) was significantly smaller than in other years, which suggests it was being substituted[39]. It is hard to establish where and how the Spängler merchant family were procuring their grain. In their accounting book a local miller is mentioned frequently and there are numerous unspecified food bills, but there are also suggestions of stockpiling and substitution during this crisis (e.g. the family purchased rice from Italy). It is clear that this wealthy family was barely affected by the rising grain prices, considering that they used to spend about 1,500 fl a year on food during this period[40].

The price data available for Salzburg and Vienna indicates that the grain supply networks were supra-regional and greatly intertwined, although Viennese prices stayed lower and fell faster than in Salzburg (cf. Fig. 2). Overall, the crisis did not affect Linz and Vienna as badly as Salzburg. Unlike Salzburg, the other two cities were surrounded by highly productive grain farming areas and they were well connected to the Hungarian grain markets, which by then was a domestic market. Furthermore, the imperial court had established large storage facilities for grain in Vienna during the 1720s, with the aim of buffering shortfalls and stabilizing prices. There were objections to this practice because it was not required during "normal" harvests and it generated a steady and significant deficit. However, this stored grain was probably essential during the 1770s crisis and it appears to have lowered prices and improved the grain supply even outside of Vienna[41]. The city nevertheless still struggled, and was forced to rely heavily on (the habitual) imports from Hungary, which became more and more expensive as the crisis persisted[42].

As in Vienna, already in early 1771 Upper Austria made large-scale grain purchases from Hungary, which was not affected by the crop failures. Linz was supplied until 1773 with "state owned" grain from Vienna (and probably Hungary),

37 G. Ammerer, *Von Franz Anton Harrach bis Siegmund Christoph von Schrattenbach*, p. 323.

38 J. Kumpfmüller, "Die Hungersnot von 1770 bis 1772 in Österreich", unpublished PhD thesis, Wien 1969, pp. 38–40.

39 R. Reith / A. Zechner / E. Knapp, *Die Entwicklung der Preise*, pp. 361–363.

40 B. Pelzer-Reith, *Für 28 £ Kölbernes samt dem Kräb. Lebensmittelkonsum und Ernährung*, in R. Reith et al. (eds.), *Haushalten und Konsumieren*, pp. 179–203, here pp. 179f. and 191f.

41 J. Kumpfmüller, "Die Hungersnot von 1770 bis 1772", pp. 51–53.

42 *Ibid.*, pp. 54–60.

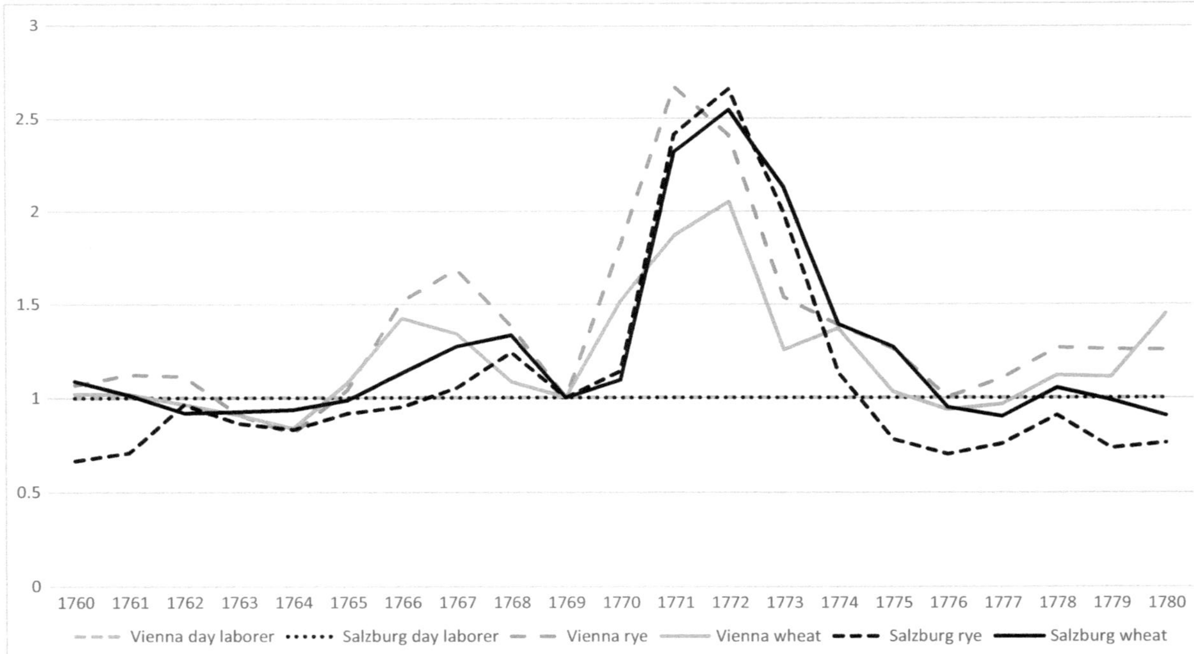

Fig. 2: Prices and wages in Vienna and Salzburg, 1760–1780. Index: 1769 = 1 (author's calculations based on A. Zechner / E. Knapp / M. Adelsberger, *Prices and Wages* – Data supplement).

and subsequent purchases in Hungary were negotiated by individuals and by the provincial government, even though transport along the Danube was expensive, slow, and somewhat risky[43]. These subsidized imports were vital to maintain the food supply, but they came at a significant cost and after the return to normal prices in 1773 the Upper Austrian estates estimated an expense of more than 500,000 fl, and their losses as roughly 110,000 fl[44].

3 Water – public and private infrastructure without a hinterland

Water flows were and remain an essential component of the urban metabolism, and water has been a frequent subject in recent urban environmental history, albeit more for the nineteenth century than the early modern period[45]. The supply of drinking water was especially important for city inhabitants, and so the following section will focus on this aspect without considering other urban water issues. In common with most premodern cities, the water infrastructures in Linz, Salzburg, and Vienna were largely privately owned and managed. The water infrastructure was decentralized, in Linz mostly based on ground-water wells with only a few urban buildings, like the castle or the assembly building, supplied by private networks of wooden water pipes. There were a number of public wells that used ground water or piped water[46]. The water infrastructure in Salzburg was similar, with numerous private groundwater wells and a small pipeline from a nearby hill supplying some houses and public wells in the eastern part of the city. There were other smaller private pipelines and a rather impressive canal ("Almkanal") dating back to the late medieval period and maintained (and constantly rebuilt) as a private project by a large inner-city monastery and the cathedral chapter. The canal linked a small river eight kilometers south of Salzburg with the inner city and it even included a tunnel. During the sixteenth century, the city government joined

---

43 *Ibid.*, pp. 54–60, 107 and 114; cf. G. Stöger, *Transformationen städtischer Umwelt*, pp. 278f.

44 J. Kumpfmüller, "Die Hungersnot von 1770 bis 1772", pp. 120–123.

45 S. Barles / M. Knoll, *Long-Term Transitions*, p. 39; M. Melosi, *Rethinking the City-Building Process*, p. 26; cf. E. Janssens / T. Soens, *Urbanizing Water: Looking Beyond the Transition to Water Modernity in the Cities of the Southern Low Countries, Thirteenth to Nineteenth Centuries*, in T. Soens et al. (eds.), *Urbanizing Nature*, pp. 89–111.

46 G. Stöger / L. Pichler-Baumgartner, *Water Modernity and Society in Linz, ca. 1700–1900*, in "UR Journal of Humanities and Social Sciences", 19, 2021, 2, pp. 52–76; cf. on the Netherlands E. Janssens / T. Soens, *Urbanizing Water*, pp. 91f.

this water project and it became a semi-public infrastructure supplying the western part of the city. The canal water was used mainly as process water for mills, irrigation, as well as powering a groundwater pump, but it was probably also used as drinking water[47]. Viennese drinking water also came primarily from private groundwater wells. There were some smaller, often private pipelines, but the importance of the groundwater wells did not decline until the nineteenth century[48].

It is reasonable to ask why these solutions remained so important until the establishment of modern, centralized water networks during the second half of the nineteenth century. These systems had emerged naturally, probably since the origins of the city. There were substantial financial and technological (and material) limits, with water pipelines being expensive to build and maintain. The conventional wooden pipes could not support high pressures and had to be replaced frequently[49]. An example was a well built in the 1650s in a central square in Salzburg. The intention was to connect it to a large karst spring six kilometers south of the city. The project was directed by the archbishop and also involved a Dutch hydraulic expert. Despite substantial investments the initial plan failed because the water pressure burst the wooden pipes. Finally, after further expensive blunders, a pumping station was constructed costing 5,000 fl, which at the time was equivalent to 25,000 day wages[50]. In contrast, the groundwater wells and minor pipelines were cheap and "functioning" systems. Groundwater could be found close to the surface in most areas of these cities, making it relatively easy to dig a well. The absence of sewers also made wells more practical, since a steady flow of water would have required the construction of a drainage system[51].

It is remarkable how financial investments by city governments in public water infrastructures remained so low during the early modern period. In Linz over a ten year period (1713 to 1722) an average of only about 130 fl per year was spent, while the total annual expenditure of the city at that time was around

47 R. Ebner / H. Weigl, *Das Salzburger Wasser. Geschichte der Wasserversorgung der Stadt Salzburg*, Salzburg 2014, pp. 13–38; H. Dopsch / R. Hoffmann, *Salzburg. Die Geschichte einer Stadt*, 2nd ed., Salzburg / Wien 2008, pp. 261f. and 325f.

48 G. Meissl, *Hochquellenleitungen und Unratsschiffe. Zur Geschichte der Wiener Wasserver- und -entsorgung vor 1914*, in S. Hahn / R. Reith (eds.), *Umwelt-Geschichte. Arbeitsfelder – Forschungsansätze – Perspektiven*, Wien / München 2001, pp. 157–179, here pp. 158f.; K. Brunner/ P. Schneider (eds.), *Umwelt Stadt*, p. 189; G. Haidvogl et al., *Wasser Stadt Wien. Eine Umweltgeschichte*, Wien 2019, pp. 214–218.

49 G. Stöger, *Transformationen städtischer Umwelt*, pp. 78f.

50 R. Ebner / H. Weigl, *Das Salzburger Wasser*, pp. 73–79; H. Dopsch / R. Hoffmann, *Salzburg*, p. 357.

51 G. Stöger, *Transformationen städtischer Umwelt*.

40,000 to 50,000 fl[52]. Investments in public water infrastructures were usually in response to specific needs or events. Two public wells in the main square in Linz were built (or rebuilt?) in the 1540s, probably as a response to a devastating city fire. These new wells served both the practical purpose of providing water for households and enterprises near the main square, for the weekly and seasonal markets held there, and for fire fighting[53]. They also played a symbolic role, as the main square of a baroque city could hardly be imagined without an impressive well. In eighteenth-century Linz, between eight and eleven wells maintained by the city can be reconstructed, supplying the inhabitants of the inner city and the suburbs. This is a relatively small number, but it is consistent with findings from other cities, and shows that cities played a limited role as water providers, at least during this period[54].

Most wells were located in backyards or gardens and they were private infrastructures not accessible to the public. Nevertheless, to some extent there was a "shared water infrastructure"[55], but this is quite difficult to identify. Sharing sometimes emerges in contracts. When a house was sold in Linz in the 1750s, the new owner pledged not to prohibit the use of the well by a neighboring household. More common was the sharing of work or maintenance costs, which in some cases was even noted in the land registers[56].

From a modern perspective it is interesting to investigate the water hinterland. Most premodern drinking water infrastructures did not rely much on a hinterland, mainly using on-site groundwater. Even piped water networks were generally supplied from a hinterland close to the city. In Linz the two public wells on the main square were supplied by a 3.5 kilometer pipeline, but the other pipelines were significantly shorter[57]. In Salzburg there was the abovementioned pipeline from a hill beyond city limits, and two more extensive projects, the canal and the failed pipeline from the mountainside. It is worth noting that the pipeline project was revived unsuccessfully several times, and its spring was finally used for the central water network built in the 1870s[58]. In all three cities more distant water hinterlands only began to evolve during the second half of the nineteenth century. This development was motivated by various factors, that included governmental efforts to improve sanitation after devastating cholera epidemics, improved financial resources (and

52 *Ibid.*
53 H. Kreczi, *Linz. Stadt an der Donau*, Linz 1951, pp. 28f. and 280.
54 G. Stöger, *Transformationen städtischer Umwelt.*
55 E. Janssens / T. Soens, *Urbanizing Water*, p. 96.
56 G. Stöger, *Transformationen städtischer Umwelt.*
57 *Ibid.*
58 R. Ebner / H. Weigl, *Das Salzburger Wasser*, pp. 80f. and 111–120.

availability of credit), and equally important the emergence of new materials and fossil fuels[59]. It is useful to briefly review the costs of water and waterworks. Wells were relatively cheap to build and cheaper to maintain than water pipes. This largely explains their ubiquity and extended persistence. It is difficult to find sources that reveal the costs for premodern in-house water. The eighteenth-century accounting books of the Salzburg merchant family record annual payments for the use of piped water in the house. The inner-city house was connected to a small pipeline from the hillside and there was a constantly running outlet on the ground floor. The cost was quite high, at 9 fl per year during the mid-eighteenth century, which is equivalent to 45 unskilled day wages[60]. The daily distribution was based mostly on invisible labor, with the water being carried from the well into the house, generally by female domestic workers. In Vienna (and perhaps elsewhere) there were also commercial water carriers, both females and males[61].

The premodern water infrastructure seems to have been relatively reliable. Pipelines were more prone to disruption than the groundwater wells since the pipes frequently became blocked and could freeze during winter. Sources from Linz note that many spring based supplies were not usable during the cold season (probably between November and April) because they were covered with straw. During this period the city water supply depended largely on the groundwater wells. The essential need for a daily supply appears to have encouraged redundant solutions, with many houses having two wells, and water pipelines often being supplemented with groundwater wells. Such dual infrastructures also reduced the risk of interruption during droughts or flooding[62]. The house of the Salzburg merchant Spängler had a groundwater well in its basement in addition to the connection to the water pipeline, and the household probably also used the water of a nearby public well[63]. This approach does not appear to have been widely questioned before the nineteenth century. There was premodern debate on water quality, and the larger scale water pipeline projects already mentioned also suggest some skepticism towards the use of groundwater, but we clearly lack focused research on that issue.

---

59 G. Haidvogl et al., *Wasser Stadt Wien*, pp. 219–224; G. Stöger, *Transformationen städtischer Umwelt.*

60 R. Ebner, *An Nacht König*, pp. 128f.

61 G. Meissl, *Hochquellenleitungen und Unratsschiffe*, pp. 190–193.

62 G. Stöger, *Transformationen städtischer Umwelt.*

63 R. Ebner, *An Nacht König*, pp. 128f.

4 Socio-environmental infrastructure

Socio-environmental infrastructure can be defined as societal answers to environmental risks that generated structures to reduce the vulnerability of the urban population[64]. This final section discusses two urban environmental risks, fire and flooding.

Fire posed a permanent risk for cities, since candles and oil lamps were used to illuminate houses and streets, and open fires were used daily in homes and by artisans. This omnipresence of fire represented an unpredictable hazard, although large-scale urban fires were quite rare (except during warfare). Nevertheless, they could cause enormous damage to cities and citizens, thus the residents developed a variety of measures and precautions, which can be conceived as a technical and social infrastructure. In the early years, sometimes even during the Middle Ages, the more prominent users of fire (like bakers, brewers, and blacksmiths) were located on (or moved to) the edge of town, which was probably also a reaction to the emissions they produced. There were rules regulating the use of fire and obliging preventive measures against the outbreak of fires. These rules, usually called "fire regulations" ("Feuerordnung"), already existed during the late medieval period and they became increasingly comprehensive during the early modern period[65].

Larger cities were more vulnerable than smaller ones and logically took earlier preventive measures. In Vienna the written fire regulations date back to the fifteenth century. These rules included regular fire safety checks by the city authorities, and required certain artisans (mostly building workers) to assist when fires broke out. There were building rules that were intended to reduce fire risk, like a ban on thatched roofs (and later on wooden shingles), the reduction of wood as a building material, and the construction of M-shaped roofs and firewalls[66]. As in the

---

64 E. Klinenberg, *Palaces for the People: How Social Infrastructure Can Help Fight Inequality, Polarization, and the Decline of Civic Life*, New York 2018, pp. 16–21; this notion can also be found (albeit more implicitly) in G. Bankoff, *The "English Lowlands" and the North Sea Basin System: A History of Shared Risk*, in "Environment and History", 19, 2013, 1, pp. 3–37 and M. Dobbie / R. Morgan / L. Frost, *Overcoming Abundance: Social Capital and Managing Floods in Inner Melbourne during the Nineteenth Century*, in "Journal of Urban History", 46, 2020, 1, pp. 33–49.

65 D. Garrioch, *Towards a Fire History of European Cities (Late Middle Ages to Late Nineteenth Century)*, in "Urban History", 46, 2019, 2, pp. 202–224; M.L. Allemeyer, *Fewersnoth und Flammenschwert. Stadtbrände in der frühen Neuzeit*, Göttingen 2007; G. Bankoff / U. Lübken / J. Sand (eds.), *Flammable Cities. Urban Conflagration and the Making of the Modern World*, Madison 2012.

66 S.C. Pils, *". . . damit nur an waßer khain menngl erscheine . . .". Vom Umgang der Stadt Wien mit dem Feuer in der frühen Neuzeit*, in M. Körner (ed.), *Stadtzerstörung und Wiederaufbau. Zerstörung durch Erdbeben, Feuer und Wasser*, Bern / Stuttgart / Wien 1999, pp. 173–186, here

case of drinking water, the fire regulations principally attributed private responsibility, with some limited supervision by the authorities (and the support of certain laborers, as already noted).

During the seventeenth century, probably in reaction to the threat of fire during war, the fire regulations were published more frequently and significantly expanded[67]. They began to include regular chimney sweeping, storage of fire-fighting equipment, and annual inspections by the urban authorities[68]. In Linz, the fire-fighting regulations even demanded the provision of a certain number of ladders, lanterns, hooks, hand pumps, and buckets for each house. In addition, filled tubs of water had to be kept in the attic, or in the home during winter. Accounting books (documenting the refilling of the tubs) and inventories (meticulously listing the equipment) indicate that these rules were widely obeyed[69].

Traditionally, night-watchmen were responsible for early detection of fires, with the support of tower watchmen, who raised the alarm when a fire broke out. In Vienna payments for tower watchmen are documented already in the mid-fifteenth century. As mentioned before, there were service duties for carpenters, masons, bearers, coach drivers, and (in Vienna) even barbers were responsible for providing larger water tubs. All these workers received a monetary compensation (and often a bonus) if they took part in fire-fighting operations. In Vienna the threat of a Turkish invasion led to an expansion of this infrastructure. Starting in the 1520s there was a permanent fire crier ("Feuerrufer") and three day laborers constantly on standby, and by the 1560s each city district had its own fire commissioner ("Feuerkommissar")[70]. There were similar systems in early modern Linz as well[71]. Over time some technical innovations were also introduced. The most significant were hoses and bigger fire pumps, which reached the eastern Alpine region in the late seventeenth century[72]. However, these pumps were few in number and they probably made little difference for larger fires, since they often also lacked reliable water supplies. In some cities, like Vienna, these pumps led to the formation of proto-fire brigades. By the 1720s four day laborers were employed permanently by the Viennese municipality to operate the fire pump[73].

---

pp. 176–178 and 183; G. Grüll, *Zur Geschichte der Brandverhütung und Schadensversicherung in Oberösterreich*, in "Jahrbuch des Oberösterreichischen Musealvereines", 111, 1966, pp. 355–398, here pp. 355f. and 361f.; R. Ebner, *An Nacht König*, p. 126.

67 S.C. Pils, "*. . . damit nur an waßer khain menngl erscheine . . .*", p. 183.

68 R. Ebner, *An Nacht König*, p. 125.

69 G. Stöger, *Transformationen städtischer Umwelt*; R. Ebner, *An Nacht König*, pp. 125f.

70 S.C. Pils, "*. . . damit nur an waßer khain menngl erscheine . . .*", pp. 177–182.

71 G. Grüll, *Zur Geschichte der Brandverhütung*, pp. 364f. and 379.

72 *Ibid.*, p. 366; S.C. Pils, "*. . . damit nur an waßer khain menngl erscheine . . .*", p. 183.

73 S.C. Pils, "*. . . damit nur an waßer khain menngl erscheine . . .*", p. 184.

It is hard to gauge the effectiveness of these infrastructures. During the early modern period there was just one large urban fire in Vienna (1627), and Salzburg does not appear to have experienced a major urban fire from the sixteenth to the beginning of the nineteenth century[74]. There were probably two large fires in Linz during the first half of the sixteenth century (1509 and 1542), and two war-induced fires in 1626 and 1741 (which only affected the suburbs of Linz). Apart from these there were no other major fires in Linz during the early modern period. Only in 1800 were large parts of the city destroyed by a major fire, which can be blamed on a combination of inadequate fire-fighting measures (or possibilities), and specific incendiary weather conditions (a long drought and strong winds). A small fire at the castle, perhaps caused by a carelessly emptied smoking pipe, caused damage totaling about 300,000 fl, burning down the castle, assembly buildings, and 58 houses[75].

An important and under-researched aspect of social infrastructure is social reciprocity and solidarity following fires. There was substantial local support, including accommodation of victims and monetary or non-monetary donations, as demonstrated by the fires in Salzburg and Linz mentioned above[76]. There was also supra-regional fundraising by institutions, extra taxes ("Brandsteuer") or tax reductions, with those affected being issued permits to collect alms ("Brandsammlung"), providing some relief before the advent of fire insurance[77]. All these infrastructures persisted into the second half of the nineteenth century, when the cities began to establish voluntary or professional fire brigades[78].

The risk of flooding was simultaneously both comparable and different. For cities situated close to large rivers (like Linz, Salzburg, and Vienna) floods were recurrent events[79]. As defined in recent research, this led to a certain "flood risk awareness" among the inhabitants, who developed a "risk culture" that was able

74 *Ibid.*, p. 183; however, large parts of Salzburg were destroyed by fire in 1818: cf. E. Marx (ed.), *"Die Flammen lodern wütend". Der große Stadtbrand in Salzburg 1818*, Salzburg 2018.

75 G. Grüll, *Beiträge zur Geschichte der Brände in Oberösterreich*, in "Jahrbuch des Oberösterreichischen Musealvereines", 110, 1965, pp. 267–299; G. Stöger, *Transformationen städtischer Umwelt.*

76 G. Stöger, *Transformationen städtischer Umwelt*; E. Marx (ed.), *"Die Flammen lodern wütend".*

77 M.L. Allemeyer, *Fewersnoth und Flammenschwert*, pp. 26f.; G. Grüll, *Zur Geschichte der Brandverhütung*, pp. 384–393.

78 O. Briese, *Für des Staates Sicherheit. Das Löschwesen im 19. Jahrhundert und die Gründung der ersten Berufsfeuerwehr Deutschlands in Berlin 1851*, Berlin 2018.

79 G. Haidvogl et al., *Wasser Stadt Wien*, pp. 160–171; G. Stöger, *Transformationen städtischer Umwelt*, pp. 290–298.

to cope with the recurrent ("normal") flood events[80]. The areas most exposed to flooding were usually avoided as settlement areas, or housed the lower classes[81].

Before its regulation during the second half of the nineteenth century the Danube had very variable fluvial dynamics, comparable to mountain rivers. The Danube regularly flooded Linz, although the city was on slightly raised ground and there were large floodplains downstream, so most floods only reached the outskirts of Linz. These low-lying areas were sparsely populated and the downstream floodplains were covered by alluvial forests and used extensively as meadows and pastures. The normal recurrent floods thus caused only minor damage, mostly affecting agricultural land and the bridge. The floods of the 1560s/70s and 1780s had a much more severe impact, since the spatial solutions could only cope with normal flood levels and even people accustomed to floods seem to have been surprised by the scale of these events[82]. The flood of June 1786 was described by contemporaries as being very sudden. A family living on the Danube island had to be rescued, and other inhabitants living close to the river remained in their houses despite the rising water and later had to be evacuated[83].

Before the nineteenth century there was no physical infrastructure in Linz against floods nor any regulations (in contrast with fire) that defined procedures in the case of flooding. Precautions fell within private responsibility, even more so than was the case for fire. The implementation of preventive infrastructures was possibly hindered by religious interpretations of extreme floods (as godly punishments for earthly sins), which were common up to the end of the eighteenth century[84]. The approach was realistic and pragmatic, given that the few measures undertaken by eighteenth century engineering, aiming to stabilize riverbanks and maintain water transport lanes, had been costly and of limited effect against such a powerful natural force[85]. At the time there was still an island in Linz, which served as a reminder of the river's power since it had been created by the extreme flood of 1572 when it cut off a section of the riverbank[86]. Moreover, there were "sharp

80 C. Rohr, *Urban Fringes: Conquering the Riverside and Lakeshores in the Nineteenth Century. Examples from Austrian and Swiss Medium-Size Cities*, in T. Soens et al. (eds.), *Urbanizing Nature*, pp. 241–260; G. Bankoff, *The "English Lowlands"*; cf. G. Haidvogl et al., *Wasser Stadt Wien*, p. 164.
81 M. Dobbie / R. Morgan / L. Frost, *Overcoming Abundance*, p. 35; G. Haidvogl et al., *Wasser Stadt Wien*, p. 167.
82 S. Hohensinner, *Historische Hochwässer der Wiener Donau und ihrer Zubringer*, Wien 2015, p. 9; cf. C. Rohr, *Urban Fringes*, p. 242.
83 G. Stöger, *Transformationen städtischer Umwelt.*
84 *Ibid.*, p. 296.
85 *Ibid.*; cf. G. Haidvogl et al., *Wasser Stadt Wien*, pp. 163f.
86 E. Neweklowsky, *Die Donau bei Linz und ihre Regelung*, in "Naturkundliches Jahrbuch der Stadt Linz", 1, 1955, pp. 171–226.

boundaries between the affected and protected", as Christopher Boone noted for nineteenth century Montreal[87].

Vienna was affected by flooding by the Danube and, more surprisingly, by the small Wien stream. For most of the year the Wien, which reached the suburbs of the city from the southwest, had little water, but torrential rainfall in the hinterland could cause severe floods. Contemporaries considered the Wien as the most dangerous, because its floods arrived more rapidly and sometimes completely unexpectedly. Nevertheless, until the nineteenth century the construction of flood prevention measures along the Wien were few in number and only localized[88].

As a consequence, when there were extraordinary flood events the affected city inhabitants had to rely mostly on social infrastructure in the form of collective and mutual help, much like the societal handling of urban fires. Help was improvised in each case, like the rescues of people surrounded by rising flood waters mentioned previously. Equally important was collective help after floods since the victims had often lost most of their belongings and even their homes. Support was provided in the form of donations in kind and money, mostly from local inhabitants, but there was also substantial regional and supra-regional help. Political-administrative functionaries or members of the imperial court donated as individuals, while the authorities themselves were only responsible for distributing the aid. In Linz the first civic charity activities (including stage plays, concerts, and publications) were introduced immediately after the devastating summer floods of 1786. These initiatives were recorded thanks to the mediality of such events, with announcements in newspapers or descriptions in other publications, thus they are traceable mostly from the mid-eighteenth century onwards[89]. As in the case of fire fighting, a more systematic infrastructure against flooding evolved during the nineteenth century. During the 1810s and 1820s numerous regulations were introduced for measures to take during floods (such as service duties and rewards for boat owners or alarm networks, and the systematic measuring of water levels) and after the mid-nineteenth century large scale hydraulic engineering started to transform the Austrian rivers, also aimed at providing active protection against flooding[90].

---

87 C.G. Boone, *The Political Ecology of Floods in the Late Nineteenth Century*, in S. Castonguay / M. Dagenais (eds.), *Metropolitan Natures. Environmental Histories of Montreal*, Pittsburgh 2011, pp. 133–147, here p. 146.

88 G. Haidvogl et al., *Wasser Stadt Wien*, pp. 163f.

89 G. Stöger, *Transformationen städtischer Umwelt*; cf. C.G. Boone, *The Political Ecology*.

90 G. Haidvogl et al., *Wasser Stadt Wien*, pp. 167–169; G. Stöger, *Transformationen städtischer Umwelt*.

5 Conclusions

Urban environmental infrastructure is (and was) essentially integrated into the urban metabolism, and therefore the study of infrastructure should not be confined to technical systems, but should also consider networks and supply zones, and how they are socioeconomically embedded. Likewise, it appears necessary to apply a broader definition of infrastructure that includes the aspect of social infrastructure, something that seems particularly relevant during the early modern period.

The role of a hinterland is central to infrastructures and networks. Some parts of the urban metabolism had multiple and parallel hinterlands that changed over time, while other networks were far more stable. Early on, the supply of firewood and grain was a generally stable and complex exchange infrastructure that expanded significantly in spatial terms. Especially during the eighteenth century these material flows started to span greater distances, but the "older", more local hinterlands nevertheless maintained their relevance in certain circumstances. Other infrastructures remained essentially without a supply hinterland, and up to the nineteenth century urban drinking water came mostly from inside the city or from its immediate surroundings.

Networks and supply systems evolved naturally as intertwined solutions that satisfied urban needs. They can sometimes be traced back to the Middle Ages or even earlier. This applies equally to the water supply and the socio-environmental infrastructure. Rules combined with social reciprocity and solidarity constituted social infrastructures that responded to environmental hazards like fires or floods, which helped to enhance the resilience of urban societies. The development of urban environmental infrastructures was limited by a deeply rooted private sense of responsibility and even more frequently by financial and technical-material limits. Not investing in infrastructure was a pragmatic and logical choice when the foreseen outcomes were doubtful or deemed unnecessary.

Many aspects of premodern urban environmental infrastructure have not yet been researched, with two issues deserving brief mention here. Not much is known about access to and sharing of infrastructures. What observations could be made about unequal access in relation to social and spatial issues? Infrastructural development is also poorly researched. Like the question of when and why (and by whom) were older systems and solutions declared outdated? And why (and for how long) did they persist alongside new infrastructures?

Claudio Lorenzini

From “Stues” to “Çates”

Infrastructures for Timber Transport in Friuli in the Early Modern Period

1 The other side of the coin

Adolfo di Bérenger, one of the founders of Italian forestry, described a *stua* (or as he called them, a *stuffa*) as follows:

> it is a bridge lock made from wood or heavy masonry, constructed at a suitable location to retain the uphill water of a gully or mountain stream, equipped with sluice gates (*scaricatoi*) and a larger gate designed so that it could be opened in a single action. This is closed a few hours before you want to float timber, and then opened (*la si batte*, you hit it) when the volume of water (known as *lagaccio*, ugly lake) is almost flowing over the top, so that this rushes out quickly to generate an artificial flood in the downstream watercourse, lifting up any timber lying in the stream bed and carrying it some miles downstream[1].

This is a clear technical summary of what these artificial barriers were and their function, published in his famous text, *Dell'antica storia e giurisprudenza forestale in Italia* (*The Ancient History and Law of Forestry in Italy*, 1859–1863). The passage is an extract from Chapter VI, *Governo del bosco* (Forest Management), making use of terminology alluding to a classic book that di Bérenger refers to continuously in this work. This was titled *Ilagogia*, the art of collecting and transporting timber.

> To the ancients there was no lack of adequate methods and means for overcoming the many obstacles that are generally faced when harvesting wood, techniques for extracting it

---

1 A. di Bérenger, *Dell'antica storia e giurisprudenza forestale in Italia*, Treviso / Venezia 1859–1963, pp. 505–506: “È una *chiusa* a ponte, di legname o di muro massiccio, costrutta in luogo opportuno a poter soprattenere le acque d'un borro o torrente, ed è fornita di portelle da scarico (*scaricatoi*) e d'una porta maggiore, costituita in modo da poterla d'un sol tratto disserrare. Chiusa questa, poche ore prima di voler fluitare, la si *batte* (apre) dopo che l'acqua rigurgitata (detta *lagaccio*) è quasi per *tracimare* il ponte, allo scopo che, sgorgando con impeto, generi una piena artificiale nel canale sottoposto, sollevi il legname giacente nell'alveo del medesimo, e lo trasporti ad alquante miglia di distanza”. This passage was also cited in A. di Bérenger, *Selvicoltura. Trattato scritto per uso degli agenti forestali, ingegneri e possidenti di boschi*, Napoli 1887, pp. 707–708. On its author see C. Lanzoni, Studii di archeologia forestale, o Dell'antica storia e giurisprudenza forestale *di Adolfo di Bérenger*, in “Quaderni della Rivista. Ricerche per la progettazione del paesaggio”, 3, 2006, pp. 138–155.

Translation: Gavin Taylor

https://doi.org/10.1515/9783111112756-004

> from steep valleys and canyons, collecting it from the cliffs and summits of mountains, and moving it from steep slopes where there were no viable roads or streams for floatation[2].

The land and water based forestry activities that di Bérenger goes on to describe after this premise proved that this problem had always been central to the "management" of forests and they were the outcome of an extended domestication of forest resources by humans, in order to efficiently exploit them, continuously and increasingly.

Artificial barriers like the *stue* were essential when watercourses had inadequate flow rates or seasonal discontinuities that prevented free floatation, and by nature could not be navigated with rafts. Across the Alpine area considered here, and for mountain areas in general, this condition was always the rule rather than the exception. Needless to say, these were complex systems to construct and use, generating considerable expenses that substantially increased the already high costs of wood transport. However, they were necessary expenses since otherwise many areas of forest would have remained unexploitable.

Di Bérenger describes these systems not long before they disappeared. The introduction of aerial transport for logs using steel cables (cable-ways) from the side of the *stue*, and the arrival of trains from that of the raft (the *çates* in the title), rendered these systems economically unviable, reducing them to obsolescence within a few decades[3]. In the Friuli mountains, in the upper basin of the Tagliamento River the transport of timber on rafts was no more than a memory by the start of the 1920s, while the floatation of loose logs down to the sawmills still persisted, with more or less all being transported by hydraulic energy[4].

The essay by Graham Hollister-Short, *The Other Side of the Coin: Wood Transport Systems in Preindustrial Europe* published in 1994 is among the first and few overviews within what has become an extensive literature on the history of forestry.

---

2 A. di Bérenger, *Dell'antica storia e giurisprudenza forestale in Italia*, pp. 498–499: "Agli antichi non mancavano modi e mezzi appropriati a vincere i tanti ostacoli che generalmente si oppongono alla condotta del legname, massime per estrarlo dal fondo delle valli e dei burroni, raccoglierlo sulle balze e vette dei monti, e trarlo fuori fra mezzo i dirupi, dove mancano strade carreggiabili e torrenti fluitabili".

3 See M. Agnoletti, *From the Dolomites to Venice. Rafts and River Driving along the Piave River in Italy (13th to 20th Centuries)*, in "Journal of the Society for Industrial Archeology", 21, 1995, 1, pp. 15–32 and, by the same author, *Commercio e industria del legname fra XIX e XX secolo nell'Italia nord-orientale: aspetti tecnici e scelte imprenditoriali*, in G. Fontana / A. Leonardi / L. Trezzi (eds.), *Mobilità imprenditoriale e del lavoro nelle Alpi in età moderna e contemporanea*, Milano 1998, pp. 31–45; M. Agnoletti, *Storia del bosco. Il paesaggio forestale italiano*, Bari / Roma 2018, pp. 143–152.

4 O. Marinelli, *Monti ed acque*, in G. Marinelli, *Guida della Carnia e del Canal del Ferro*, new ed. by M. Gortani, Tolmezzo 1924–1925, pp. 7–23, here p. 23.

It considers the technological problem of timber transport in the modern period, in which water played a decisive role[5]. Its eloquent title could be interpreted as follows: in a market like timber, which offered great benefits for anyone who could control it, transport costs represented an independent variable that often diminished profits for the timber trade. As will be discussed later, this involved watercourses flowing down and flooding between the mountains and the risks involved in using them to transport a material that was as bulky as it was valuable were considerable. Nevertheless, they had to be used if you wanted to avoid transport along tracks that were often unusable by wheeled carts, and above all in order to speed up delivery[6].

Only the use of water made wood a commodity for remote delivery, and the intelligent use of water led to the creation of infrastructural systems that enabled extraction and transport of timber from the mountains down to the plains. These systems were consolidated over the course of the late medieval and persisted up until the appearance of trains. While transport on rafts declined after the arrival of railways in the second half of the 1800s, the same was not the case for traditional log extraction systems, like waterways and artificial air and ground channels. An example were the *risine* (called *lisses* and/or *plàncjes*, in Friuli), which were artificial channels constructed with the logs themselves as they were felled, and then moistened with water to create a downhill slipway. Along with free floatation along minor watercourses, all these techniques persisted until the 1960s.

The upper basin of the Tagliamento River is the focus of the present study. Its three main tributaries, from west to east, are the Degano, But, and Fella rivers. The latter did not rise in Venetian territory but in the lands of the Holy Roman Empire (Imperial dominions), running first down the Valcanale/Kanaltal valley under the jurisdiction of Bamberg Abbey, and then down Canale del Ferro. Like much of the territory considered here, the latter was under the dominion of the Republic of Venice. Finally, the Fella joined the Tagliamento River at the village of Amaro. The wood originating from these valleys was mainly for construction (spruce, silver fir, and larch), extracted from both Imperial and Venetian forests.

5 G. Hollister-Short, *The Other Side of the Coin: Wood Transport Systems in Preindustrial Europe*, in "History of Technology", 16, 1994, pp. 72–97. Also see M. Devèze, *Flottage et transport du bois sur les fleuves européens à l'époque moderne (Consequénces pour le développement économique)*, in A. Vannini Marx (ed.), *Trasporti e sviluppo economico. Secoli XIII–XVIII*, Firenze 1986, pp. 181–189 and E. Johann, *Transportation of Wood Out of the Forest (Along Short Distances)*, in "International Journal of Wood Culture", 1, 2021, 1/3, pp. 1–32.

6 Floatation and wood extraction systems in general that made use of water contrasted with the nature of transport of people and goods due to their slowness: F. Braudel, *Civilization and Capitalism, 15th–18th Century*, vol. 1: *The Structure of Everyday Life. The Limits of the Possible*, London 1983, pp. 424–425.

The other two main tributaries and the main river, running down valleys of the same names, also carried firewood, like beech[7]. It was impossible to construct *stue* on any of these rivers due to both the width of the river beds and the lack of rock walls for anchoring a barrier. This was necessary on various minor tributaries, two of which will be discussed here: the Lumiei and the Chiarsò rivers.

The context for the present discussion was briefly outlined above with anticipations of some conclusions that could be reached regarding the history of timber transport in the Friuli mountains during the modern period. The picture that emerges can serve as an unchanging and unchangeable backdrop, in which significant transformations are only observed from the beginning of the second half of the 1800s. This was the time of the industrialization of the main river of the region, involving both the drainage and irrigation of plain, and exploitation of the mountain basin to generate hydroelectric energy in the early decades of the 1900s.

The perspective is from the side of the coin of transport, which threatened profitability, creating insecurity for timber merchants. The winning side of the coin was the vastness of market demands. This gives some insight into all the paradigms, also historical, that viewed forests as "omnipresent" resources, as Fernand Braudel has called them, to the extent that these societies and the period are defined, with Werner Sombart, as an "age of wood". Accepting these observations simply as 'given' creates the risk of confirming what seems obvious, without assessing continuity and discontinuity in the 'management' of forests, and without considering the other side of the coin, with the possibility of glossing over history[8].

There were many aspects to the 'bad' side of the coin. One of these was an important component of the infrastructure conceived for timber extraction, the *stue*. Opening these dams for the transport of logs did not always have beneficial effects, neither upstream nor especially downstream of each individual *stua*, to the extent that the merchants, who often built the *stue* and/or were entitled to use them, and local communities who owned the forests (and sometimes even the *stue*) and rented them to the merchants, could not always maintain peaceful

7 For a full description of transport systems in the Venetian area in the modern period, see A. Lazzarini, *Le vie del legno per Venezia: mercato, territorio, confini*, in M. Ambrosoli / F. Bianco (eds.), *Comunità e questioni di confini in Italia settentrionale (XVI–XIX sec.)*, Milano 2007, pp. 97–110 (now under the title *Le vie del legno per Venezia*, in A. Lazzarini, *Boschi e politiche forestali. Venezia e Veneto fra Sette e Ottocento*, Milano 2009, pp. 195–208). For the Friuli area see C. Lorenzini, *Praticare il bosco, praticare le acque. Appunti sul trasporto del legname*, in F. Bianco et al. (eds.), *Il Tagliamento*, Verona 2006, pp. 395–399; on the forestry economy see in its entirety F. Bianco, *Nel bosco. Comunità alpine e risorse forestali nel Friuli in età moderna (secoli XV–XX)*, Udine 2001.

8 C. Lorenzini / G. Bernardin, *Assenti più o meno illustri: "Comunità alpine" e il bosco. Il caso delle Alpi orientali*, in "Histoire des Alpes / Storia delle Alpi / Geschichte der Alpen", 18, 2013, pp. 179–195.

relations. This was frequently a specific consequence of the management of these dams, with these infrastructures representing true engines for conflicts.

Graham Hollister-Short’s essay of 1994 discussing the transport of timber was comparative over a European scale. The studies on this theme in the eastern Alps were first conducted by historians, geographers, ethnographers, and linguists largely starting in the 1960s[9]. The same years witnessed the establishment (elsewhere) of the historiographic perspectives that led to the development of environmental history[10], which includes the retracing of timber transport infrastructural systems. In the same decades many Alpine regions and especially Friuli experienced a surge in depopulation and there was a decline in the ‘traditional’ practices of

9 Quoting only a few titles, for the Friuli area: A. Feruglio, *Il disboscamento e il trasporto del legname in Friuli*, in “In alto”, 33, 1922, 4/6, pp. 49–54 and 34, 1923, 1/3, pp. 12–20 (now in A. Feruglio, *Scritti di geografia e geologia*, vol. 1: *La prima attività scientifica (1912–1926)*, ed. by F. Micelli / F. Vaia, Tavagnacco 2000, pp. 90–97); L. Peressi, *La “menada” in Valcellina*, in “Ce fastu?”, 55, 1979, pp. 177–200 (now, as a book, Barcis 2003); A. Simonetti, *L’antica tecnica della fluitazione del legname mediante l’utilizzo di chiuse. Le “stùis di Tralbe” a Moggio Udinese*, Pontebba 1993; A. Martinis, *La fluitazione in zattere. Una tecnica tradizionale per il trasporto del legname in Friuli fino al primo decennio del Novecento*, in “Ce fastu?”, 84, 2008, 2, pp. 177–198; A. Martinis / P. Piussi / T. Ribezzi, *Il trasporto del legno. Tecniche tradizionali*, Udine 2017. For the Venetian area see G.B. Pellegrini, *Appunti sulla terminologia della fluitazione nell’Italia nord-orientale*, in G. Moretti (ed.), *Lingua, storia e vita dei laghi d’Italia*, Rimini 1984, pp. 51–85 (now with a *Post Scriptum*, in D. Perco (ed.), *Zattere, zattieri e menadàs. La fluitazione del legname lungo il Piave*, Castellavazzo 1988, pp. 217–245) and various ethnographic authors in G. Caniato (ed.), *La via del fiume. Dalle Dolomiti a Venezia*, Verona 1993; G. Caniato / M. Dal Borgo (eds.), *Dai monti alla Laguna. Produzione artigianale e artistica del Bellunese per la cantieristica veneziana*, Venezia 1988; D. Perco (ed.), *Zattere, zattieri e menadàs*; L. Corrà, *La fluitazione sul Piave*, in M. Cortellazzo (ed.), *La civiltà delle acque*, Milano 1993, pp. 73–93; R. Asche / G. Bettega / U. Pistoia, *Un fiume di legno. Fluitazione del legname dal Trentino a Venezia*, Ivrea 2010. A review of anthropological approaches to the study of forest resources is provided in P. Clemente / N. Breda / V. Lappiccirella-Zingari, *Between Nature and Culture: The Contribution of Anthropology to Environmental Study*, in M. Agnoletti / S. Anderson (eds.), *Methods and Approaches in Forest History*, Wallingford 2000, pp. 183–194.

10 J.R. McNeill, *The State of the Field of Environmental History*, in “Annual Review of Environment and Resources”, 35, 2010, 1, pp. 345–374.; P. Warde / L. Robin / S. Sörlin, *The Environment. A History of the Idea*, Baltimore 2018. For a summary of historical-environmental developments in Italian historiography, especially from the economic perspective, see G. Alfani / M. Di Tullio / L. Mocarelli, *Storia economica e ambiente: un’introduzione*, in G. Alfani / M. Di Tullio / L. Mocarelli (eds.), *Storia economica e ambiente italiano (ca. 1400–1850)*, Milano 2012, pp. 7–18; L. Mocarelli, *L’ambiente in una prospettiva storico–economica: l’Italia dell’età moderna*, in “Storia economica”, 20, 2017, 2, pp. 499–510; G. Bonan, *Storia e ambiente: scambio ineguale e mercato storiografico*, in “Annali dell’Istituto storico italo–germanico in Trento”, 46, 2020, 2, pp. 15–31 (*Storia ambientale: Nuovi approcci e prospettive di ricerca/Environmental History: New Approaches and Research Perspectives* ed. by G. Bonan / K. Occhi).

the mountain economy. The professions associated with forestry were among the most affected, if not in terms of jobs then certainly from a cultural perspective. Ethnographers who have dealt with these issues have observed the traditional ways of exploiting forests as relics of a laborious but valued past, from the primary work in the forest all the way down the wood processing chain.

Concentrating on the *stue* in this area, the focus of the study started from ethnography[11]. Historical research into these constructions, and the wood production chain in general, started later, which raises the issue of sources[12]. The historiography of forestry resources in the eastern Alpine area is without doubt among the best developed in Italy. As is well known, the driving force was the presence of Venice, which was the final destination for a substantial part of the timber produced in these areas up until the late medieval. Basically, Venice was constructed on top of wood, in the form of ground consolidation piles, while the two major industries of the *Arsenale* shipyards and glassworks needed constant regular supplies of wood. Venice was among the first state in Europe to develop a protectionist policy for its forests[13]. As the attention of historians shifted progressively from the main site of consumption to the production areas, they realized that there was a lack of specific sources for investigating what had been a well consolidated production chain from the late medieval onwards. For example, there are almost no family archives of wood merchants, who normally financed the construction of the *stue*, and there are few and scattered sources regarding the village communities that held the rights for exploitation of the forests and water resources in these areas (and on the subject of interest, the faculty to permit the construction

11 V. Fabbroni Grillo, *La stùe di Ramàz*, in "Ce fastu?", 53, 1977, pp. 141–151; L. Peressi, *La "menada" in Valcellina*; A. Nicoloso Ciceri, *Las càlas*, in "In alto", 107, 1989, pp. 22–26; A. Simonetti, *L'antica tecnica della fluitazione del legname*.

12 For these aspects see K. Occhi, *Exploiting the Alps. Wood Supplies and Waterways in Early Modern Europe*, in "Annali dell'Istituto storico italo-germanico in Trento", 46, 2020, 2, pp. 33–67, pp. 37–38. Studies on specific local Friuli rivers basins, with historical documentation, are provided by D. Molfetta, *Gli opifici idraulici e la fluitazione del legname nell'Alto But*, Tolmezzo 1986; N. Screm, *Il trasporto del legname dei tempi andati nella Valle d'Incarojo. Strutture ed attrezzi per le fluitazioni*, Udine 1990; A. Simonetti, *L'antica tecnica della fluitazione del legname*.

13 On these aspects, which are only briefly mentioned here, the literature is very extensive. As a minimum reference, A. Lazzarini, *Boschi e politiche forestali*; R. Vergani, *Venezia e la Terraferma: acque, boschi, ambiente*, in "Ateneo veneto", 197, 2010, pp. 173–193; K. Appuhn, *A Forest on the Sea. Environmental Expertise in Renaissance Venice*, Baltimore 2009. For an overview of the relationship between Venice and watercourses, see D. Gasparini, *"Acque patrizie". Venise entre terre et eau à l'Époque moderne*, in P. Fournier / S. Lavaud (eds.), *Eau et conflits dans l'Europe médiévale et moderne*, Toulouse 2012, pp. 87–106 (now in D. Gasparini, *Dalla campagna alla tavola. Sistemi alimentari della Terraferma veneta in età moderna e contemporanea*, Verona 2020, pp. 286–306).

of a *stua*). This significantly conditioned the research, including studies into the systems of transport, making it necessary to refer to indirect sources like the records of public notaries, legal documents, and even rarer accounting records.

2 The timber production chain in the Friuli mountains in the modern period: an envirotechnical system

The section of the timber production chain downstream of the *stue* in the Friuli Alps can be illustrated with a small example, an argument between a wood merchant and the owner of a field where the timber, felled in a forested area above, had to transit before being put into water for transport to the plain.

In 1633 felling was underway in the forest of Rio Simon near Moggio, a community of Canale del Ferro on the right bank of the Fella torrent. Pietro Fortino, known as 'Vinago', and his brothers from Villanova, a village a bit further north, was the 'driver' responsible for extracting the felled logs. He had been assigned this task by the timber merchant, Biagio Motis from Udine. In November of that year Giovanni Zanotto from Ovedasso, a village lying below the forest, obtained a ruling from the judge of the Abbey of Moggio to suspend the activity. Some of the logs had been stacked on the fields of Raunis that belonged to him, between the village and the forest, and others were to be added, further ruining the fields. Stacking logs on a field compromised the possibility of producing fodder for a number of years, which is what happened. Giovanni Zanotto requested and obtained suspension of the extraction operations until he was compensated for the damage.

The merchant pressed his operator to resume immediately, stating that he would settle all damages requested by the owner of the field. Clearly, interrupting the timber extraction process would have generated even higher costs for him. However, this did not suffice and the interruption was extended to the point that the merchant became irritated with his driver and denounced him, requesting that he make good the damages the merchant had suffered. A year later the legal case was still underway. In a long memorandum for the judge, Pietro Fortino tried to list all the damages suffered as a result of not being able to continue with timber extraction. Since Giovanni Zanotto was still impeding the transit of timber through his field, Fortino had to return to Resiutta, close to his home, with his entire team of workers and 10 pairs of oxen, where he waited in the village inn for news. In the following April it appeared that work could resume, so Fortino and his team of men and animals headed back to the forest, but they were again stopped, resulting in 30 days of residence in the inns of Moggio and Resiutta for the workers and 11 pairs of oxen. In July everything appeared to be in order and they prepared to resume work in a nearby village, Roveredo, where they had to stay for 20 days because Giovanni Zanotto continued to oppose their transit "with arms and with stones". At this point, Pietro Fortino resorted to cunning and distracted Giovanni Zanotto in the inn while an effort was made to move at least some of the logs, but in vain.

The extended passage of time had rotted the wooden bridges and compromised the roads they had prepared for transport, the maintenance of which was the responsibility of the log drivers. And that was not all. They had purchased hay for the animals and stashed it in the forest where the logs had to be dragged, and it too had rotted. Pietro Fortino had to sell off some of the oxen they had to help cover the many expenses that were accumulating. In January 1635 the issue was still not resolved[14].

This episode reveals various important aspects of the infrastructure required for the exploitation of forests in these areas, applicable for the entire modern period and even beyond. These can be listed schematically as follows.

a. First of all the legal aspects. The forest in question belonged to the community of Moggio, who had rented it to the merchant Biagio Motis a few years previously. This was the rule in almost all the Friuli mountain territories including the Republic of Venice. Based on the specific legislation for collective resources applied by the Venice Republic, the forests were almost entirely the property of the state but conceded for use to the village communities. The latter were allowed (or tolerated) to rent them out, sometimes earning conspicuous economic returns[15]. The duration of rentals varied according to the extension of forest and wood varieties. Partly as a consequence of the infrastructures required in order to exploit them, the rental periods were never less than one year and normally extended to two or three decades, on one hand to provide the necessary time for renewal of forest growth, and on the other hand to enable the merchants to spread out their investments over time[16].

---

14 Archivio di Stato di Udine (ASU), *Giurisdizione di Moggio*, b. 44, fasc. *Processus ser Petri Furtini de Villa Nova cum heredibus q. domini Blasii Motis de Utino*. During the legal procedure, the merchant Biagio Motis had already died and his heirs acted on his behalf.

15 S. Barbacetto, *"La più gelosa delle pubbliche regalie". I "beni* communali" *della Repubblica veneta tra dominio della signoria e diritti delle comunità (secoli XV–XVIII)*, Venezia 2008.

16 G. Bonan / C. Lorenzini, *Montagne condivise, montagne contestate. Le risorse d'uso collettivo delle Alpi orientali (secoli XVI–XIX)*, in "Histoire des Alpes / Storia delle Alpi / Geschichte der Alpen",

b. Each stage in the timber production chain, from the selection of trees for felling to transport of the timber on rafts, required organized teams of specialized workers, who were employed for substantial periods ranging from a few months to two or three decades[17]. As already noted, their work could be conditioned not only by the seasons but also by the infrastructures prepared for timber extraction, like wooden bridges.
c. Alongside the teams of workers, it was essential to have animals for dragging the logs during the initial felling and handling stages. These were mainly oxen and horses, which, like the men, always needed to be fed. The presence of snow and ice was not necessarily an obstacle for timber extraction and so these operations, including the use of animals, were also conducted during the winter. When the waterways were not too far from the forests, and when the use of animals alone was too risky and difficult, artificial channels had to be created in wood and stone for sliding the logs downhill, either on the ground or in the air (the *plàncje* and *lisse* already mentioned)[18].
d. The dispute between the owner of the field and the haulers (*foderatori, menàus* in the Friulian language, those who conduct the *menàda*, able to move – *menâ* – the logs out of the forest) involved integrated systems of infrastructure, both artificial and natural. In this specific case, to reach the Raunis field the logs were (almost certainly) floated down the Rio Simon, the torrent running down the valley where the forest was being cut. To achieve this they would have used the Rio Simon *stua* at 950 meters, the operation of which is testified up until 1947[19]. Both before and after the *stua*, the logs would have been dragged by animals and accumulated in a place suitable for their transport by water on the main mountain rivers. The Raunis field at about 600 meters was in fact close to the Fella mountain torrent, which could have been used to transport the logs to the sawmills for subsequent transport on rafts.

24, 2019, pp. 87–103; G. Bonan / C. Lorenzini, *Common Forest, Private Timber: Managing the Commons in the Italian Alps,* in “Journal of Interdisciplinary History”, 52, 2021, 1, pp. 1–26.

17 For a full description of these aspects in the Tyrolese area between the sixteenth and the seventieth century, see K. Occhi, *Boschi e mercanti. Traffici di legname tra la Contea di Tirolo e la Repubblica di Venezia (secoli XVI–XVII),* Bologna 2006, pp. 77–109.

18 G. Ferigo, *Boscadôrs, menàus, segàz, çatârs. La filiera del legno nella Carnia del Settecento,* in F. Bianco / A. Burgos / G. Ferigo, *Aplis. Una storia dell’economia alpina in Carnia,* Tolmezzo 2008, pp. 15–80, pp. 31–36 (now in G. Ferigo, *Morbida facta pecus . . . Scritti di antropologia storica della Carnia,* ed. by C. Lorenzini, Udine 2012, pp. 381–431).

19 A. Simonetti, *L’antica tecnica della fluitazione del legname,* p. 77.

e. When extraction was halted it was November, just before the first snows arrived. An effort was made to resume between April and May in the spring when the snow was melting and the Simon and Fella torrents were beginning to swell. Even in July the water level was sufficient for floatation, although transport on rafts was more problematic. The seasonal nature of the different stages in the production chain always has to be taken into account. Furthermore, the felling operations, especially for beech trees, had to be synchronized with the phases of the moon. Trees had to be cut under a waning moon to avoid sap remaining in the trunk and accelerating decay[20].

All the elements that emerge directly or indirectly from the story of the log driver Pietro Fortino, the merchant Biagio Motis, and the owner of the field Giovanni Zanotto in the 1630s are components of the *envirotechnical system* that is established between forests and water.

As already noted, sliding channels like the *risine* can represent an extension of the hydrographic network, just as the *stue* become a means, disruptive as it might be, for regulating water flow to the advantage of timber transport. The resulting interweaving of ecological and technological systems is an *envirotechnical regime*, in which the institutions and actors involved in the timber production chain play a critical role in maintaining its continuity[21].

A simple storage area for the accumulation of timber before flotation is an important component in this scheme, but if this is a field that becomes ruined and unusable for its main purposes, then the result is conflict, compromising the operation of the entire system. This minor case also reveals a wider conflict between animal farming and the timber trade, which was central to a long and complicated debate about the legitimacy of grazing animals in the forest during the second half of the 1700s[22]. Often, though not in this specific case, the powerful influence of the commercial investments, which directly contributed to the construction of the infrastructures, imposed the adoption of one system or another[23].

---

20 G. Bonan / C. Lorenzini, *Selvicoltura e pratica forestale nell'area alpina orientale (secoli XVIII–XIX). Gli sviluppi di una scienza ibrida*, in "Histoire des Alpes / Storia delle Alpi / Geschichte der Alpen", 26, 2021, pp. 125–143.

21 G. Bonan, *Le acque agitate della Patria. L'industrializzazione del Piave (1882–1966)*, Roma 2020, pp. 30–32; G. Bonan, *An Alpine Energy Transition: The Piave River from Charcoal to "White Coal"*, in "Environmental History", 25, 2020, 4, pp. 687–710, here pp. 696–697.

22 B. Vecchio, *Il bosco negli scrittori italiani del Settecento e dell'età napoleonica*, Torino 1974, pp. 37–41; G. Bonan, *The State in the Forest. Contested Commons in the Nineteenth Century Venetian Alps*, Cambridge 2019, pp. 102–109.

23 M. Lorenzini, *Infrastructure Financing in the Early Modern Age. The Beginning of a 'Little Divergence'*, in Y. Cassis / G. De Luca / M. Florio (eds.), *Infrastructure Finance in Europe: Insights*

However, it is always important to bear in mind the other side of the coin, water transport had to deal with the difficult features of these rivers and torrents. By its very nature, the hydrographic basin of the Tagliamento River was undoubtedly among the most tormented of the eastern Alpine region.

3 The Tagliamento River: characteristics

The Fella torrent is navigable for rafts starting from Chiusaforte, the village of Pietro Fortino, at the considerable distance of at least 30 km from the source. Its waters were used to transport timber produced both in the Venetian territories, and imported from the nearby Valcanale inside the Imperial realm. Like all the tributaries of the Tagliamento, the Fella is a mountain torrent prone to flooding (Fig. 1).

The Friuli area differed from the other forested zones serving the Venetian Lagoon in that the Tagliamento was a much more difficult river to navigate, even with rafts, than the Adige, Brenta, and Piave rivers, which were the three main transport axes for the timber trade. Its course from the mountains down to the sea, especially after the mountains give way to the plain, is shorter than the other rivers, which results in a braided, ramified, discontinuous watercourse, despite the width of the river bed. One consequence of this was that well into the 1800s there were still no bridges to ensure transit, with instead only boats or barges positioned at key points in the Friuli transport system, the geography of which was strongly conditioned by this factor[24]. From the perspective of transport, even the main river could be considered more like a mountain torrent. Some contemporary descriptions of the river and its basin help to reveal the characteristics, demands, and the positive features attributed to the Tagliamento.

The Bologna inquisitor, geographer and historian Leandro Alberti, wrote in his *Descrittione di tutta Italia* (1550):

> The main Tagliamento River [. . .] flows out from Monte Mauro above the district of Forni, where there is a wonderful fountain that has the power to harden the bark of timber like stone, along with any grass and leaves that fall into it. The river descends from the Alps,

into the History of Water, Transport, and Telecommunications, Oxford 2016, pp. 61–80. On the relationship between regional development and infrastructure in the Alpine area, see the essays in U. Pfister (ed.), *Regional Development and Commercial Infrastructures in the Alps. Fifteenth to Eighteenth Centuries*, Basel 2012.

24 A. Fornasin, *Tra Vienna e Venezia. La viabilità dalla Patria del Friuli in età moderna*, in “Studi veneziani”, 38, 1999, pp. 15–36 (now in A. Fornasin, *La Patria del Friuli in età moderna. Saggi di storia economica*, Udine 2000, pp. 127–154).

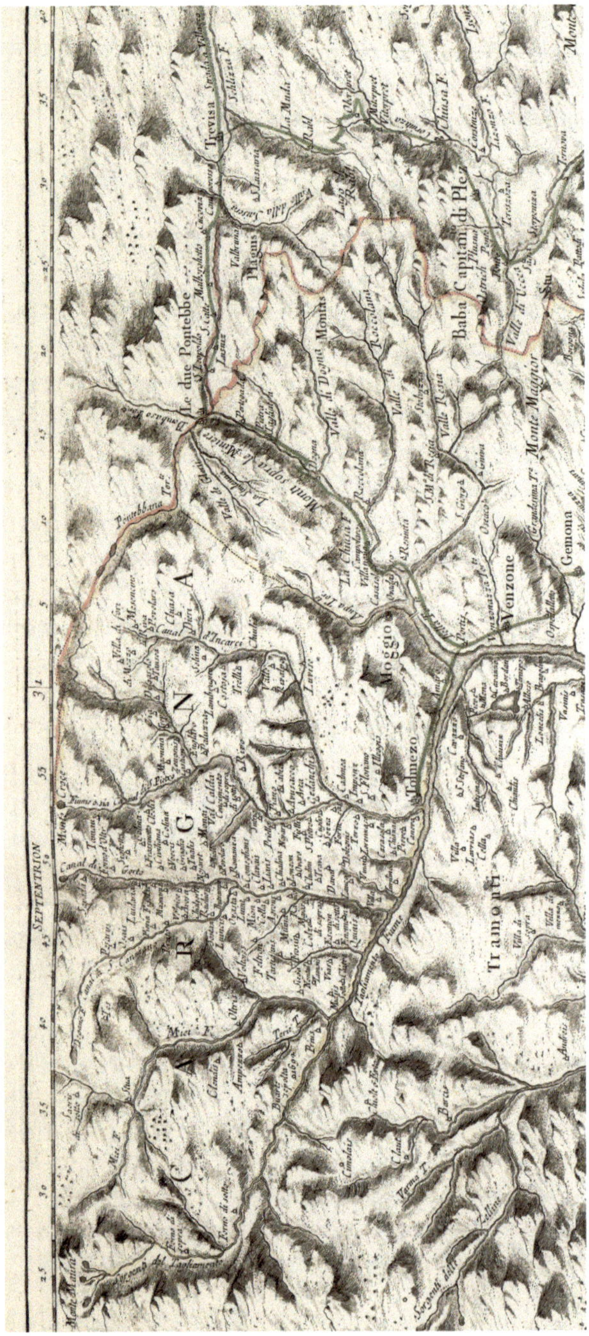

Fig. 1: The mountain basin of the Tagliamento River in the map by Tiberio Maieroni and Giovanni Antonio Capellaris, *Le Friul dressé sur la carte recemment rectifiée par les ordres des messieurs les sept députés de la ville de Udine capitale de la ditte Province*, à Venise, par P. Santini, 1778 chez M. Remondini. © David Rumsey Map Collection, David Rumsey Map Center, Stanford Libraries.

> joined by the following rivers. The But, Degano, and the Fella, having passed through the narrow jaws of the Alps it is intersected by the river Idra, which rises in the territory of Gemona, and then the Arzino, and the increase in water level is so great that it can easily be navigated. There are about 750 landing 'stages', from its source (which is in the Carnia mountains, as already noted) to the mouth, through which it enters the sea[25].

At the beginning of August 1683 a noble pilgrim departed Frattina Castle on the plain lying to the right of the Tagliamento River, heading towards Sauris. In the high Lumiei Valley he reached the banks of the river on Spilimbergo hill, on the high plateau, where a boat transfer would help him to cross, and saw:

> A lovely view of mountains, hills, castles, and the vast river bed of the Tagliamento, which emerging from between two hills . . . forms its own Dardanelles on the Hellespont. A wild torrent that swallows all the turbid waters of the Carnia and other mountains. It could be called the great merchant of the Julian Alps, a wealthy dealer of the most valuable trees from those high cliffs, outstanding plunderer of the snow slopes stripping countless woods, who marches ahead of his armies cutting and devouring the mountains, earning his terrible name, and marching on, loaded with so much booty, with giant strides lawless and unrestrained across much of the lands of Friuli, loaded with laurels and trophies, he enters the murky waters of the Adriatic Sea[26].

---

25 L. Alberti, *Descrittione di tutta Italia . . . nella quale si contiene il sito di essa, l'origine, et le signorie delle città, et de i castelli, co i nomi antichi, et moderni, i costumi de' popoli, le condittioni de i paesi*, in Vinegia, Domenico de' Farri, MDLVII, fol. 432r. "Il Taiamento maggiore . . . esce di monte Mauro sopra la contrada Fornio, ove si vede una maravigliosa fontana che ha possanza di far doventar la scorza de i legni posti dentro pietra, e similmente l'herbe, et foglie che in essa cascano. Scende adunque questo fiume dall'Alpi, nel quale entrano gl'infrascritti fiumi. Il Buti, Decano, et il Felle, passate le strette foci delle Alpi vi sboccano in esso il fiume Idra, che nasce nel territorio di Glemona, et poscia l'Argino, et tanto s'ingrossa per l'acque che vi entrano, che facilmente si può navigare. Annoveransi circa 750 stadij, dal principio d'esso (ch'è ne' Carni, com'è detto) alla bocca, per la quale entra nel mare". The first edition dates back to 1550; regarding the author and his famous Italian description: M. Donattini (ed.), *L'Italia dell'inquisitore. Storia e geografia dell'Italia del Cinquecento nella* Descrittione *di Leandro Alberti*, Bologna 2007. The Arzino torrent, which was also usable for floating timber, joins the river at Flagogna, helping to make the lower Tagliamento more navigable.

26 F. Bianco, *Comunità di Carnia. Le comunità di villaggio della Carnia (secoli XVII–XIX)*, Udine 1985, p. 94: "una bellissima vista di montagne, colli, castelli, il vastissimo alveo del Taiamento, ch'uscendo fra due colli [. . .] mostra il suo sito de' Dardanelli su l'Hellesponto. Horrido torrente, che bevendo tutte l'acque torbide della Cargna, et altre montagne, si può chiamar superbo mercante dell'Alpi Giulie, rico condottier degl'arbori più preciosi di quei alti diruppi, predator superbo delle nevi spoglie di tante selve, che marchiano alla testa de suoi eserciti andar tagliando e divorando i monti ha preso il suo terribile nome, e caminando gonfio di tante prede, con passa da gigante per molto la Patria del Friul senza freno e senza legge, carico di palme e trofei entra mare torbido nell'Adriatico".

Vincenzo Formaleoni was a traveller and cartographer from Piacenza. In his wide-ranging *Topografia veneta* (1787) he described the Tagliamento starting from the region in which it rises, Carnia, which was:

> a barren mountainous landscape. However, there are abundant forests, from which the Republic of Venice derives large quantities of timber for the construction of boats and galleys. It is drained by numerous torrents rising in the Julian Alps, which enclose the Province. The largest are the *Degano*, *Pontaiba*, and *Lumiei*, all flowing into the *Tagliamento*, which also runs through Carnia in the north. Along this river, which initially runs very fast, structural timber is transported to the Caorle lagoons in Dogado, and from there it travels along canals to the Venetian lagoon[27].

These few examples offer a glimpse of a few constants and peculiarities. The first is the abundance of water accumulated in the Tagliamento, fed by cold, fast running tributaries, not really ideal characteristics for transporting timber. The second is the symbiotic association between the waterways and forests. Leandro Alberti noted that a characteristic of the spring water was to harden tree bark, which could be considered an action that helped to conserve the timber immersed in it, something of commercial value. Vincenzo Formaleoni noted the sterility of the mountain soil in contrast with the quantitative abundance of forests, whose timber could be used in the Venetian Lagoon thanks to the steeply flowing waters of the Tagliamento. The noble pilgrim considered the river capable, on a par with the Hellespont, of dividing two different regions, also based on its name ('tagliamento' means 'incision'). He explicitly personified the Tagliamento as an arrogant, rich merchant devouring the mountain forests.

27 V. Formaleoni, *Topografia veneta ovvero Descrizione dello stato veneto. Secondo le più autentiche relazioni e descrizioni delle provincie particolari dello Stato marittimo, e di Terraferma*, Venezia, presso Giammaria Bassaglia, 1787, tomo IV, p. 203: "un paese montuoso, e poco fertile. Abbonda però di boschi, dai quali la Repubblica di Venezia ritrae gran quantità di legname per la costruzione delle navi, e delle Galere. È bagnata da molti torrenti che nascono dalle Alpi Giulie in mezzo alle quali la Provincia è serrata. I maggiori sono il *Degun*, la *Pontaiba*, ed il *Lumejo*, tutti confluenti del fiume *Tagliammo*, che bagna anch'esso la Carnia a mezzodì. Per mezzo di questo fiume, che nella sua origine è rapidissimo, si trasportano i legnami da fabbrica nelle lagune di Caorle nel Dogado, e di la per canali di navigazione fino a quelle di Venezia". Formaleoni was also the author of one of the first treatises on Venetian hydrography: *Saggi idrografici sulle acque dello Stato veneto*, Venezia 1780. About him see M. Infelise, *Formaleoni Vincenzo Antonio*, in *Dizionario biografico degli italiani*, Roma 1960–2020, vol. 46: 1997, pp. 22–26.

4 "Stue"

Di Bérenger established that the height of a *stua* was between 8 and 22 meters. This is a big range which depends on the flow rate and steepness of the waterway to be dammed. The definition probably also included what were referred to as *stuetti*. These dams were similar in all respects to *stue* but of smaller dimensions.

In the Friuli mountains, there does not appear to have been widespread use of stone and timber *stue* or *stuetti*. Instead they were made by closely interweaving logs arranged longitudinally and transversally to the flow of water, forming a barrier as thick as 6 meters at the bottom and 5 meters at the top. When the intermeshing was imperfect, stones and especially moss was applied on the upstream side to make them completely waterproof[28].

The tree trunks had to be anchored to rock sidewalls from the base to the top. This was the prerequisite for setting up a *stua*.

A gate was created (called a *bocje*, or 'mouth' in the Friulian language) at the midpoint between the two walls of the *stua*. This was opened to allow the timber to exit, possibly multiple times a day depending on the water flow rate and the size of the dam. At the bottom a second much smaller gate was opened to allow water to escape and facilitate the delicate operation of closing the main gate. Both these opening mechanisms were activated using a long tree trunk attached to them and controlled from the top of the *stua*, fixed in place with iron nails.

When the gate was opened the timber inside the dam started floating out. Once the logs had gone, the gate was closed again. To help secure the gate, a stairway was created descending inside the *stua* down to the gate position. It is likely that *stuetti* did not have this feature.

Without going into the other constructional aspects of a *stua*, we will move on to what happened after the gate was opened.

The *stue* were structures that enabled what is defined as 'assisted' floatation. They modulated the flow of water and facilitated the descent of logs, but opening a *stua* did not eliminate the need for continuous assistance for the downstream movement of timber. Since the watercourses on which they were constructed were between rocks with narrow stream beds, the logs could easily become tangled together, jam, and stop moving downstream. Dedicated driving teams were employed to liberate the logs using pike poles with special metal tips (known as *anghîrs*) and

---

28 Also for the following see V. Fabbroni Grillo, *La stùe di Ramàz* and G. Ferigo, *Boscadôrs, menàus, segàz, çatârs*, pp. 36–42.

in extreme cases they even had to descend the rocks using ropes. However, at least some of the logs, "tended to naturally line the banks of the river forming sidewalls that could [. . .] facilitate the flow of the timber that followed"[29].

As soon as the watercourse widened, other teams of workers arranged trestles along the edges of the stream bed on which more logs were arranged to form walls and direct the flow. These operations were also essential to limit the dispersion of the timber, not an unusual event which required the logs to be marked with the symbols of the owners. A third work team was dedicated to recovering stray logs[30].

The arrival of the timber in proximity to the sawmills concluded this delicate stage of forest extraction and initial downhill transport of the timber using water.

When the gates were opened, the exit of the timber from the *stue* generated a force on the downstream banks and bed that was capable of destroying anything it encountered, and compromise the preceding timber. The joiner Fulgenzio Schneider (1864–1941) had possibly seen the large *stua* of Sauris in operation on the Lumiei torrent, or he might have heard old people recounting its effects. "To fill up the water capacity", he wrote, "took an entire week, forming a substantial lake, which then drained out in three hours after the opening of two enormous gates, which when opened made the ground tremble and even caused windows to rattle in the houses in Maina", the habitation immediately upstream of the *stua*[31].

On 9 August 1683, the noble pilgrim who was travelling from Frattina to the famous sanctuary of Saint Oswald of Sauris, arrived at the *stua* that functioned as a bridge to reach the village, comparing it to the name itself of the torrent it was designed to dam:

> The Stuffa river, running deep through the San Marco forest, is crossed over a wooden bridge and the water below, which has cut deeply into the rocks of the two mountains, meeting after a drop of 100 or more feet, makes such a noise exiting its prison that it terrifies anyone looking down from the bridge.

29 V. Fabbroni Grillo, *La stùe di Ramàz*, p. 151.

30 In comparative terms see G. Corazzol, *A margine di una scheda perduta*, in M. Rech / S. Turrin (eds.), *Bòt e tàie*, Seren del Grappa 2014, pp. 119–137.

31 F. Schneider, *Raccolta di antiche tradizioni ed avvenimenti fino ai giorni nostri di Sauris*, Sauris 1992, p. 34. He did however note that "this form of floatation was only suited to beech wood cut to short lengths for burning", due to the risk of splitting the logs along the narrow watercourse. Regarding this author see D. Isabella, *Schneider Fulgenzio Carlo, falegname, intellettuale popolare e memorialista*, in C. Scalon / C. Griggio / G. Bergamini (eds.), *Nuovo Liruti. Dizionario biografico dei friulani*, vol. 3: *L'età contemporanea*, Udine 2011, pp. 3103–3105.

> They say that timber is used to block the gap and stop the river where the two mountains meet causing the water to build up above forming a lake, and in this way the ingenuity of man is able to carry away all the timber accumulated in the water[32].

At the time the *stua* was in the hands of the Perarolo merchant, Francesco Zuliani, resident in Venice. Along the Lumiei he "organizes infinite amounts of processed timber, sending it down with the first freeze in the valleys involved"[33].

Previously, in 1603 and 1604, a substantial part of the extensive forests of the community of Ampezzo, which extended towards Sauris, were leased for 15 years to the Venetian patrician Giacomo Michiel[34]. In order to extract the timber, he was obliged, "at intolerable expense", to construct "buildings and *stue*", the same described by Fulgenzio Schneider and by the pilgrim. Unfortunately, "due to the notorious floods of the rivers and streams of the Carnia, and the abundant snowfall, ice, and rain", with the addition of the action of "malign men" who did not support his ends, the large quantities of timber that had been cut were in "obvious danger of rotting"[35]. This testimony was written on 10 October 1606, just three years after the signing of the leases. The investment for the realization of these infrastructures could only be paid for with substantial capital, as might be available to members of rich families like the Michiel[36]. But not even their wealth

---

32 F. Bianco, *Comunità di Carnia*, p. 95: "Il fiume Stuffa, alle radici del bosco di San Marco, si passa sopra un ponte di legno e l'acqua al di sotto, che ha apperto durissimi i macigni delle due montagne che s'uniscono con la caduta di 100 e più piedi, fa tanto rimbombo nell'uscir da quelle carceri che fa terror a chi guarda da quel ponte. Dicono che con legnami chiudono et arostano il fiume all'unir delle montagne e fano ritroceder l'acqua che forma un lago di sopra e così fanno uscir con l'industria d'homeni tutto il legname radunato in quell'acqua". On the sanctuary, see A. Tilatti, *La parrocchia di Sauris: le chiese, gli uomini, i santi*, in D. Cozzi / D. Isabella / E. Navarra (eds.), *Sauris Zahre. Una comunità delle Alpi carniche*, Udine 1998, vol. 1, pp. 63–90.

33 F. Bianco, *Comunità di Carnia*, p. 95. There is some mention of Francesco di Grazioso Zuliani and his family in P. Da Ronco, *La famiglia Zuliani Porta di Ferro*, in "Archivio storico di Belluno Feltre e Cadore", 13, 1941, 74, p. 1271.

34 Archivio di Stato di Venezia (ASV), *Provveditori sopra beni comunali*, b. 471, Libro V, *Denuncie de beni comunali dalla parte di Udine e della Carnia*, fol. 408–410. On 12 November 1603 there was a request to extend the lease on the forest of Andris for another nine years beyond the six already agreed on 8 November 1603, because, "a term of six years would be very short in order to cut and extract the timber from those forests"; fol. 411–412, 17 December 1604, a lease on the forests of Cervia and Mernon for 15 years for 1,000 ducats.

35 ASV, *Provveditori sopra beni comunali*, b. 471, Libro V, *Denuncie de beni comunali dalla parte di Udine e della Carnia*, fol. 416r., letter from Giacomo Michiel to the officials in charge of common property, 10 October 1606.

36 For a comparison with the commercial affairs in the basin of the Cellina torrent by another patrician family, Giustinian, see F. Bianco, *Nel bosco*, pp. 40–44 and, by the same author, *Le terre del Friuli. La formazione dei paesaggi agrari in Friuli tra XV e XIX secolo*, Mantova / Verona 1994, pp. 109–110.

could do anything against excess rainfall, the effects of extremely cold winters, and possibly the negligence of their workers.

Due to its location this *stua* was one of the nerve centres for timber production in the upper Tagliamento valley (Fig. 2).

Fig. 2: The Lumiei torrent (indicated/referred to as "Mei F[iume]") and its confluence in the Tagliamento. At Sauris, the indication of the *Stua* (detail of the map by Tiberio Maieroni and Giovanni Antonio Capellaris). © David Rumsey Map Collection, David Rumsey Map Center, Stanford Libraries.

Being able to identify exactly who owned it would provide a clear picture of the timber market for the entire valley, one of the richest in resources of the Friuli mountains. Just two more cases will be described here.

At the beginning of September 1717 a dispute was underway for the use of the *stua*, between the Venetian merchant, Fabiano Marsili, and the log driver, Giovanni Battista Luca of Ampezzo. The former was the owner and he was demanding payment for use of the facility; the latter required that the *stua* be renovated before he would pay for its use. An attempt to reconcile them was made by Giovanni Pietro

Veritti of Terzo, in Carnia, but without success. A second attempt was entrusted to Giacomo Pante, of Feltre. Luca had to pay Marsili 260 lire for 800 logs passing through the *stua*. In compensation for the renovation work on the same, Marsili was to concede the cost of transit of other logs cut by Luca, 350 for Count Pietro Domini from Sauris, and 150 for the Nigris family of Ampezzo[37]. The Veritti and Pante families were also wood merchants.

Just less than thirty years later, on 15 October 1751, the *stua* was owned jointly by the Nigris family and the Fornara family of Portis, again wood merchants. On the same day an effort was made to draw up an estimate of what remained of the *stua* in order to carry out renovation work requested by Lorenzo Dall'Asta, a merchant from Venice, and his business partner, Antonio Benedetti, a merchant from Ampezzo. The three experts called on to draft the estimate were all outsiders: Giovanni Battista Zuzzi from Resiutta in Canale del Ferro, Giovanni Battista Bianchi from Cibiana, and Giovanni Manarin from Longarone the latter two both from the Cadore region[38].

In the examples described, the *stue* belonged to merchants and this appears to have been normal. The *stue* sometimes needed repairs between the end of one lease and the beginning of the next. The capital required for constructing and maintaining such infrastructures was beyond the means of local communities, but they did own the forests and the use of waterways had to be negotiated and agreed with them.

There are some documented cases of *stuetti* owned by local communities or other public institutions, like churches. The *stua* of Ramaz on the Chiarsò torrent in the Incaroio valley (like the one on the Lumiei) was among the largest and probably most enduring structures in the Tagliamento basin. Its operation was definitively compromised only during the World War I. At least from the 1730s it was owned by the Calice family of Paularo, the most important merchants in the valley[39]. Around the second half of the 1700s the upper basin of this river also had at least another fifteen *stuetti* along the minor torrents that flowed into the

37 ASU, *Archivio notarile antico* (*Ana*), b. 59, Bernardo Bernardis di Ampezzo, fasc. 3, on 7 and 8 September 1717 (no. 202). The size is the section of spruce log to be converted into planks of about 4 meters in length.

38 ASU, *Ana*, b. 60, Giovanni Sburlino di Ampezzo, *Instromenti dal 1736 sino 1756*, dated 15 October 1751. Overall, C. Lorenzini, *La valle del Lumiei. Comunità, risorse forestali e mercanti fra Sei e Settecento*, in M. Ambrosoli / F. Bianco (eds.), *Comunità e questioni di confini in Italia settentrionale (XVI–XIX sec.)*, Milano 2007, pp. 128–143.

39 Archivio Calice, Paularo, b. 2, *Famiglia Calice, secoli XVII–XX*, fasc. 10, *Carte relative alla stuva di Ladino*; R. Valesio Calice, *La famiglia Calice. Dalla valle d'Incaroio al mondo*, Udine 1995.

Chiarsò, before reaching the waters of the But torrent[40]. Three of these *stuetti* were upstream of Ramaz (Figs. 3 and 4).

Tab. 1 summarises some of the structural and institutional details of these infrastructures. It reveals just how narrow the bed of the torrent was at Ramaz, little more than 2 meters, and the impressive scale of the *stua* structure, at 15 meters in height and 27 meters in width. In some cases the dimensions of the *stuetti* were comparable, although most were smaller, of heights less than 14 meters and averaging around 7 meters. The distances from the Chiarsò torrent were important: the shortest was 1.3 kilometers and the longest was over 5 kilometers. Ramaz was 18 kilometers from Cedarchis, the settlement where the Chiarsò flowed into the But. This meant that logs extracted using the Cordìn *stuetto* travelled a total of about 23 kilometers to get there.

The fee for transit of logs through the *stuetti* was paid to the communities or institutions, like the church of Santa Maria Maggiore of Dierico, which owned the forests being cut.

Finally, this scenario dating back to the second half of the 1700s helps to demonstrate how much the pressure on these forests (and thus also on the waterways) had increased to satisfy a continuous and growing demand.

On 2 March 1577 the merchant Gabriele Vando of Sacile, a citizen of Udine, made an agreement with three woodcutters from Sappada, Mattia Solero and the brothers Giovanni and Benedetto Benedetti, for the construction of a *stua* between Collina Piccola and Chiaula Tumieçina in the upper But valley. The agreement stipulated that they would maintain the *stua* operational throughout the entire period of the lease contract, for which the merchant would pay them the (substantial) sum of 600 ducats. The timber to pass through the *stua* comprised 4,000 logs, which had to be driven to Tolmezzo making use of the But torrent. If the timber caused damage this was to be paid half by the drivers and half by the merchant. Similarly, the construction of bridges and repair of roads damaged by the timber was again payable half each. It was strictly forbidden to allow others to use the *stua*[41].

40 N. Screm, *Il trasporto del legname dei tempi andati nella Valle d'Incarojo*. The data derive also from field surveys and should be treated with caution. The results obtained by comparing them are in any case indicative.

41 ASU, *Ana*, b. 6593, Gio Domenico Salamonio, *Processi*, fol. [1]–[2]r. (this document was indicated to me by Agostino Peressini: my thanks to him). Vando worked in the iron market. In the same year, obtained in concession the mine of Timau: G. Ferigo, *Morbida facta pecus . . . Aspirazioni e tentativi di Riforma nella Carnia del Cinquecento*, in "Almanacco culturale della Carnia", IV, 1988, pp. 7–73 (now in G. Ferigo, *Morbida facta pecus . . .*, pp. 3–77, here p. 65). On 27 December 1583 he agreed with the brothers Giovanni Angelo and Evangelista Ruffini, from Bergamo, for the construction of a oven *alla bresciana* (Brescia style) in Venzone: ASU, *Ana*, b. 6376, Federico Buiatti di Udine, fasc. XIII, fol. 155v.–157r.

Fig. 3: The *stua* of Ramaz, drawing by Filippo Giuseppini (1811–1872). Biblioteca civica di Udine 'Vincenzo Joppi', Archive of the writer Caterina Percoto (1812–1887), Ms. 4109, *Miscellanea di scritti altrui*, fasc. 3, *Disegni di F. Giuseppini.*

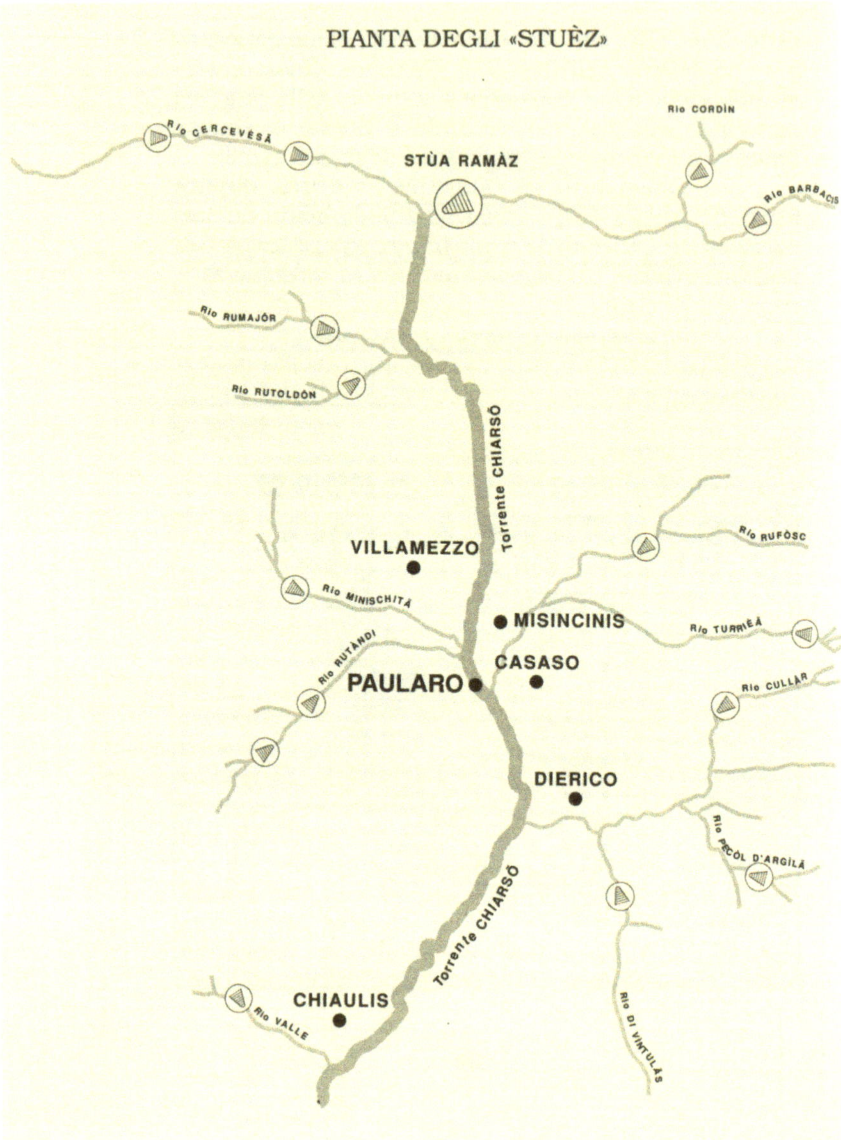

Fig. 4: Relocation of the *stuetti* and the *stua* of Ramaz in the upper Chiarsò torrent in the reconstruction by Nazario Screm, *Il trasporto del legname dei tempi andati nella Valle d'Incarojo. Strutture ed attrezzi per le fluitazioni*, Udine 1990, p. 60.

Tab. 1: Dimensions and distances of the *stua* of Ramaz and the *stuetti* of the upper Chiarsò torrent, in the Incario valley, 1718–1773

			width		height	distance	‘transit’ (*pedaggio*) payable to; when
			base	top			
		Ramàz	2.3	27	15		
1	s	Cordìn	5.3	15.5	4.2	4,850	Municipality of Rivalpo, 1769
2	s	Barbàcis	3	17.5	6.2	5,350	Municipality of Rivalpo, 1768
3	s	Cercevèsa	4	19.5	7.8	2,300	Santa Maria maggiore di Dierico, 1769
4	b	Cercevèsa	4.2	14.5	5.5	3,950	Santa Maria maggiore di Dierico, 1773
5	s	Rumajôr	3	20	14	1,650	Municipality of Ligosullo, 1769
6	s	Rutoldôn	2.5	16	10	1,300	
7	s	Turrièä	3.5	16.5	7	4,950	Municipality of Paularo, 1768
8	s	Rofòsc	5.3	17.5	8.5		
9	s	Minischitä	3.8	15	8	2,350	Municipality of Paularo, 1772
10	s	Rutàndi	4.3	20.5	4.5	2,250	
11	b	Rutàndi	4.3	12	5.5	3,550	
12	s	Cullâr	6	22	18	4,050	Santa Maria maggiore di Dierico, 1766
13	s	Pecol d’Argìlä	4	16.5	6.5	3,700	Santa Maria maggiore di Dierico, 1768
14	s	Vìntuläs	9.5	16.5	6	2,400	Santa Maria maggiore di Dierico, 1771
15	s	Valle	4	14	8		Municipality of Rivalpo, 1718

Source: N. Screm, *Il trasporto del legname dei tempi andati nella valle d'Incarojo.*
Abbreviation: s: *stuetto*; b: *botàc*, which was a barrier smaller than a *stuetto* and circular in shape.
Note: all measurements are in metres.

The inclusion of this clause, in addition to indicating the economic burden on the drivers, suggests that the risk of causing damage was high. Among the greatest expenses sustained by communities lying alongside the major torrents was the construction of *roste*, artificial protections in stone and wood. Timber in the streams was a common hazard that the *roste* had to counter. In order to assist the flow of logs, a *stua* had to compromise the constant flow of water, and consequently the use of water to power mills and saws downstream were affected[42]. While conflicts with merchants was incessant in this respect, their interests also converged, since the larger the areas of forest leased out, the greater the income for the community.

Contracts are indicators for the growing interest of merchants in these forests and the need for them to set up infrastructures in order to exploit them. The evidence available for a chronology of the spread of *stue* in the Friuli area, suggest

42 C. Lorenzini, *Spazi “communi”, comuni divisioni. Appunti sui confini delle comunità di villaggio della Carnia, secc. XVII–XVIII*, in “La Ricerca folklorica”, 53, 2006, pp. 41–54; G. Corazzol, *Piani particolareggiati. Venezia 1580–Mel 1659*, Seren del Grappa / Feltre 2016, pp. 75, 117, 211–212.

that the Canale del Ferro valleys were among the first to have these barriers during the middle of the 1500s, with western expansion into Carnia coming later. A comparison with other river basins, like for example the Piave, where the presence of *stue* and barriers for the accumulation and sorting of logs (like the *cidoli*) is attested from the end of the 1200s[43], provides a further demonstration of the unamenable nature of the Friuli mountain waterways. Only the growing demand for timber, together with improving technical skills in the construction of *stue* and *stuetti*, ultimately enabled profitable exploitation.

Finally, the area of Collina Piccola and Chiaula Tumieçina, where Gabriele Vando's *stua* was constructed, are areas scattered with Alpine meadows, the summer grazing areas where the communities took their animals. The same names were used to refer to meadows and forests together (as in this case) and sometimes the same was true for watercourses, as in the case of Rio Simon.

This overlapping toponymy for forests, meadows, and waterways raises a question. In the examples collected here, in addition to reservoirs, dams, and logs under transport, animals also appeared on various occasions. Oxen and horses assisted timber extraction and it was thanks to their strength that the timber could be moved to the reservoirs created by the *stue*[44]. The skill-set required to raise these animals thus falls within the envirotechnical system applied for the transport of timber.

Merchants sometimes leased meadows together with forests in order to provide summer pastures for the animals, saving on the cost and work of supplying fodder. This led to a sectorial integration, forests and meadows, and the development of the technical and business skills to exploit them adequately[45].

This scenario had direct consequences on the work market. Complex operations like the construction, maintenance, and operation of a *stua* required unusual

---

43 K. Occhi, *Exploiting the Alps*, pp. 54–55. For an example of a late *stua* facility, in the important Cansiglio public forest, see A. Lazzarini, *La trasformazione di un bosco. Il Cansiglio, Venezia e i nuovi usi del legno, secoli XVIII–XIX*, Belluno 2006, pp. 87–95 (but also see A. Lazzarini, *Uomini, tecniche, organizzazione: il trasporto del legname dal bosco del Cansiglio a Venezia tra XVIII e XIX secolo*, in "Archivio storico di Belluno, Feltre e Cadore", 70, 1999, 306, pp. 16–35). For the previous period in the Friuli context, D. Degrassi, *Water, Wood, Minerals: The Resources of Friuli and their Use Between the XIIIth and XVth Centuries*, in P. Štih / Ž. Zwitter (eds.), *Man, Nature and Environment Between the Northern Adriatic and the Eastern Alps in Premodern Times*, Ljubljana 2014, pp. 74–85.

44 G. Corazzol, *Piani particolareggiati*, pp. 15–39.

45 C. Lorenzini, *Monte* versus *bosco, e viceversa. Gestione delle risorse collettive e mobilità in area alpina: il caso della Carnia fra Sei e Settecento*, in G. Alfani / R. Rao (eds.), *La gestione delle risorse collettive nell'Italia settentrionale, secoli XII–XVIII*, Milano 2011, pp. 95–109. On the theme of integration between waterways and forests, M. Di Tullio / C. Lorenzini, *La ricerca della sostenibilità. Economia, acqua, risorse e conflitti nell'Italia settentrionale (secc. XV–XVIII)*, in *Gestione dell'acqua in Europa (XII–XVIII secc.)*, Firenze 2018, pp. 165–185.

skills. In the Carnia region, as emerged in some of the cases examined, these skills were not always available locally and generated a movement of specialized personnel from bordering Alpine areas: Cadore and Bellunese, the Canale del Ferro, and the valleys of the Friuli Alpine foothills[46]. This aspect of work organization can be interpreted in different ways. The high mobility of this sector could lead to the movement of work teams between Alpine regions, even over long distances, engaged for specific tasks, over short terms or for multiple years within the same sector. The merchants are known to have owned multiple homes in these areas right through the modern period in order to better monitor and coordinate all the elements in the production chain[47], and these can be understood in the light of the territorial mobility of their workforce. In this way, the movement of these individuals helps us to understand what a *socio-environmental regime* might consist of.

46 G. Ferigo, *Da estate a estate. Gli immigrati nei villaggi degli emigranti*, in G. Ferigo / A. Fornasin (eds.), *Cramars. Emigrazione, mobilità, mestieri ambulanti dalla Carnia in età moderna*, Udine 1997, pp. 133–152 (now in G. Ferigo, *Le cifre, le anime. Scritti di storia della popolazione e della mobilità in Carnia*, ed. by C. Lorenzini, Udine 2010, pp. 293–315); G. Ferigo, *Boscadôrs, menàus, segàz, çatârs*.

47 On these aspects: G. Corazzol, *Cineografo di banditi su sfondo di monti. Feltre, 1635–1642*, Milano 1997, pp. 231–232; K. Occhi, *Resources, Mercantile Networks, and Communities in the Southeastern Alps in the Early Modern Period*, in M. Bellabarba / H. Obermair / H. Sato (eds.), *Communities and Conflicts in the Alps from the Late Middle Ages to Early Modernity*, Bologna / Berlin 2015, pp. 165–178; K. Occhi, *Economie alpine e risorse forestali: la prospettiva storica*, in M.A. Denzel et al. (eds.), *Oeconomia Alpium I: Wirtschaftsgeschichte des Alpenraums in vorindustrieller Zeit. Forschungsaufriss, -konzepte und -perspektiven*, Berlin / Boston 2017, pp. 123–136.

Astrid Mignon Kirchhof, Yaroslav Koshelev, Florian Manthey,
Anna-Katharina Pelkner, Judith Schein, Christiane Uhlig

Uranium Stories

Making the Wismut Narrative Visible

1 Introduction

Wismut was a cover name for the Soviet Union's largest and most important enterprise on German soil, namely the Soviet (later Soviet-German) Joint Stock Company Wismut (S(D)AG Wismut), founded in 1947, which mined uranium in the German Democratic Republic (GDR) for the Soviet Union (USSR) over more than four decades[1]. In response to the atomic bombs dropped on Hiroshima and Nagasaki by the United States of America and for the political balance of power in the Cold War, the Soviet Union needed uranium to keep up in the nuclear arms race. By the end of the GDR, half a million people at Wismut had produced 231,000 tons of enriched uranium[2]. On the one hand, many people found work above and below ground through the mining operations, and they were usually very well paid. On the other hand, those working and living in the region were exposed to an increased risk of illness due to radiation and environmental degradation (Fig. 1)[3]. Only after production ceased in 1990 did one of the greatest environmental disasters on earth become fully apparent[4].

1 On May 10, 1947, Wismut was founded as a branch of the State Soviet Joint Stock Company of the Non-ferrous Metal Industry, "Wismut". Cf. R. Karlsch, *Uran für Moskau. Die Wismut – eine populäre Geschichte*, Berlin 2007, p. 54.

2 *Ibid.*, p. 234, and Wismut GmbH, *Chronik der Wismut (CD–Rom)*, 1, Chemnitz 2010 [1999], p.1. The atomic bombing of Hiroshima and Nagasaki by the US in August 1945 accelerated the Soviet nuclear project. On August 20, 1945, Stalin ordered the construction of the atomic bomb. Cf. R. Karlsch, *Uran für Moskau*, p. 43. The uranium industry was part of the reparations that the Soviet Union imposed on defeated Germany (*ibid.*, p. 46).

3 J. Schütterle, *Kumpel, Kader und Genossen. Arbeiten und Leben im Uranbergbau der DDR. Die Wismut AG*, Paderborn 2010, pp. 157–162.

4 Wismut GmbH is funded by the German government as an institutional grantee. Of the sum invested up to the end of 2020, 3.2 billion (47%) will go to Saxony and 3.6 billion (53%) to Thuringia. Cf. Wismut GmbH, *Die Finanzierung der Wismut*, https://www.wismut.de/de/wismut_finanzierung.php, last accessed June 10, 2021.

https://doi.org/10.1515/9783111112756-005

Fig. 1: Thuringia, tailings, uranium mining. Photo by Jan Peter Kasper, 1990, (Wikimedia Commons by the German Federal Archive), access number: Bild 183-1990-1109-004, https://commons.wikimedia.org/wiki/File:Bundesarchiv_Bild_183-1990-1109-004,_Th%C3%BCringen,_Abraumhalten,_Uranbergbau.jpg.

Infrastructures, the subject of this volume, play a key role in the sustainability challenges of the twenty-first century related to growing populations, increasing material and energy demands, environmental changes, and changing societal values[5]. This article refers to infrastructure systems involved in the redevelopment of the Wismut uranium mining operations[6]. Although these technological systems include specialized knowledge and expertise based in institutions, informal knowledge systems for operation and maintenance, and a broader system of governance and regulatory policy, this project report focuses on the retrospectives of contemporary witnesses who remember and reflect on the redevelopment that started 30 years ago. Infrastructure relies on environmental influences to function, it channels and protects society from environmental impacts, and affects environmental

5 J. Zbigniew Grabowski, *Removing Dams, Constructing Science: Watershed Restoration Through a Socio-Eco-Technical Systems Lens*, dissertation published online 2018, p. 7, https://www.proquest.com/openview/43ee4cf607212bb4a5334dba392d920d/1?pq-origsite=gscholar&cbl=18750, last accessed July 28, 2021.

6 On power generation in general, see M.Z. Jacobson / M.A. Delucchi, *A Path to Sustainable Energy by 2030*, in "Scientific American", November 2009, pp. 58–65.

systems. Consequently, the goals for long-term infrastructure sustainability are set by attitudes towards technology and appropriate human-nature relationships. This is achieved both through societal willingness to pay for infrastructure systems – which in the case of Wismut amounted to 6.8 billion by the end of 2020 – and through societal awareness and desire for certain types of systems. In the following, we present the Wismut Heritage Contemporary Witnesses Project, discuss the 1989 caesura that led to the redevelopment of uranium mining in unified Germany, and propose initial analytical approaches to the landscape redevelopment narrated as a success story.

2 Memory repositories and memory traces: an interview project on uranium mining in the GDR

In 2018, the German Mining Museum in Bochum was commissioned by Wismut GmbH to develop an implementation concept[7] for future handling of the heritage of uranium ore mining in Saxony and Thuringia. The safeguarding of contemporary testimony was considered "a particularly urgent task in the context of the Wismut heritage, since the number of witnesses capable of providing information is continuously decreasing due to age"[8]. The interview-project described in this article started thirty years after the end of the GDR and was motivated by the ever decreasing number of living contemporary witnesses. "Uranium Stories. Memories of Wismut, the largest mining company in the GDR" was dedicated to the cinematic documentation of the subjective memories of people who worked in the Wismut complex, still work there, or whose lives were profoundly affected by Wismut. The Saxon Academy of Sciences in Leipzig was put in charge of the overall project. In cooperation with the Chair of Recent and Contemporary History at Humboldt University in Berlin, the historian Astrid Mignon Kirchhof was entrusted with coordinating the two-year interview project. The team consisted of Yaroslav Koshelev and Florian Manthey, both historians, the social scientist Anna-Katharina Pelkner, the

7 The following institutions were involved in the preliminary work for this commission: the German Federal Ministry for Economic Affairs and Energy (BMWi), the Thuringian Ministry of Finance (TFM), the Saxon Ministry of Finance (SMF), Wismut GmbH, and the Bergbautraditionsverein Wismut e.V. (BTV). See: S. Brüggerhoff et al., *Umsetzungskonzept Wismut-Erbe*, Bochum 2019, p. 4.
8 *Ibid.*, p. 32.

social/visual anthropologist Judith Schein, and Christiane Uhlig, a human geographer. In November 2018, the project was started with the objective of holding 50 high quality filmed interviews with former and current Wismut mining employees for later research use, for public or media applications, and for documentaries or exhibitions (see Fig. 2). In addition to mining employees who worked underground or are now involved in regional redevelopment, contemporary witnesses were also interviewed from the spheres of education, personal care, health, commerce, technology, art, and science, along with family members of Wismut employees.

The plan was to start interviewing witnesses in spring 2020, but the Corona pandemic and subsequent lockdown in March 2020 delayed this schedule. After relaxation of the Corona regulations, the first interviews were conducted in the fall of the same year in Saxony and Thuringia – each involving one interviewer and two technicians to manage the sound and filming. A further lockdown subsequently made travel impossible again, and from November 2020 the interviews were conducted online. It was impossible to visit contemporary witnesses in person until spring 2021. Overall, about one third of the interviews were conducted in person and two thirds online, with each interview averaging two to three hours. The interviews were then key worded and described with a set of criteria.

Fig. 2: Historical objects of a Wismut employee during the interview, image by Wismut Heritage Witnesses Project, 2020.

In addition to the filmed interviews[9], existing source materials and data about Wismut were also recorded. The database contains written interviews (so-called "profiles") and a wealth of digital materials like home-made films and photographs of contemporary witnesses, as well as motion pictures and documentaries about Wismut[10]. Further memory traces were collected from written interviews with Russian-speaking witnesses conducted in earlier projects[11]. The project also published its own blog[12] with an average of 400 visitors per month, while also broadcasting television, radio, and podcast reports[13].

---

9 All interviews are digitally keyworded and linked on the database. See: https://wismut.saw-leipzig.de/content/de/bestaende/zeitzeugen-interviews.

10 These include documents, personal film recordings of contemporary witnesses, as well as publications and multimedia interviews with contemporary witnesses, photographs and Wismut films.

11 Thanks to the Russian Traditions Association, which has been doing extensive work on this since 2008, we currently have 131 written interviews and reports (approx. 700 pages) available in Russian.

12 Blog: https://wismut.hypotheses.org/. Profiles as well as TV, radio, and podcast contributions about the project are available here.

13 Interview for the history magazine MDR Zeitreise about uranium mining in the GDR and the current Wismut Heritage Contemporary Witnesses Project (May 4, 2021). Participation in the radio report on the Wismut-Erbe final conference on MDR Kultur (May 4, 2021). Radio interview with the broadcaster F.R.E.I., 96.2 MHz, about the Wismut Heritage Contemporary Witnesses Project "Visualized Contemporary Witnesses and Multimedia Memory in Wismut – 30 years later": https://www.radio-frei.de/index.php?iid=7&ksubmit_show=Artikel&kartikel_id=8802, (broadcast date May 1, 2021). Organization and participation in the discussion panel on the occasion of the final conference of the Wismut Heritage Contemporary Witnesses Project of the Saxon Academy in Leipzig, moderated by Alexander Roth, broadcast on the MDR Kulturwerkstatt program (live stream April 29, 2021), https://www.google.com/url?sa=t&rct=j&q=&esrc=s&source=web&cd=&cad=rja&uact=8&ved=2ahUKEwj3odS19vj7AhVyRfEDHcPEA6oQwqsBegQICBAG&url=https%3A%2F%2Fwww.youtube.com%2Fwatch%3Fv%3D5hern1B-uPs&usg=AOvVaw3cbgkY277AqS4k0h4qm16H. Interview about uranium mining, GDR history and experiences with contemporary witnesses in the time of the pandemic with Martin Fischer from "Citizenship – A Podcast About Life in the GDR", episode: *Surface Mining. For the Construction, Dismantling, and Renovation* (broadcast date April 10, 2021), https://www.staatsbuergerkunde-podcast.de/ueber-tage/. Newspaper interview about the preservation of the Wismut legacy with Tina Puff from the "Ostthüringische Zeitung", (March 5, 2021).

Press publications by Humboldt University on the Wismut Heritage Contemporary Witnesses Project *Visualized Contemporary Witnesses and Multimedia Memory in Wismut – 30 Years Later*, (November 2020 and March 2021), https://www.hu-berlin.de/de/pr/nachrichten/november-2019/nr-19116-3 and https://www.hu-berlin.de/de/pr/nachrichten/maerz-2021/nr-2133. TV reports with an interview about the Wismut Heritage Project on Mitteldeutscher Rundfunk (MDR) in the "MDR Aktuell" program (September 10, 2020), https://cloud.saw-leipzig.de/s/3S7eDjmBpRpkCSz and in the "Sachsenspiegel" program (October 8, 2020), https://cloud.saw-leipzig.de/s/qYwogmkg3qQFKz5.

The interviews can be accessed on a website that is being developed by a second research group within the overall Wismut Heritage Research Project[14]. Prospective users of this online archive will be able to research a wide range of information and topics relating to Wismut in all its historical complexity. The online archive will provide historical sources, scientific texts, empirical reports and studies, and photographs, together with interviews with contemporary witnesses in order to reveal and clarify any connections between cultural, technical, medical, and environmental history, as well as relevance for political and social science. The use of the website opens up the possibility of interactively discovering social and cultural aspects of East German environmental and mining history. The Centre for Contemporary History (ZZF) in Potsdam has kindly agreed to archive the generated project data and to keep it up to date technically[15]. However, this is an interim solution and a long-term archiving solution – given the financial resources – still has to be found.

3 Methodology and oral history in the interview project

Oral history entered German historical scholarship in the 1970s and became well established over the course of the 1980s, with extensive ongoing discussions about the opportunities and limitations of this methodology. Proponents argue that one of the greatest opportunities of oral history is to reveal minority perspectives "from below", offering historical authenticity[16]. Critics point out the "subjectivity" of the sources, and question the reliability of human memory and the construction of life stories and historical images[17]. Martin Sabrow, for example, emphasizes that contemporary witnesses are a valuable historical source, but

14 The research environment was developed under the direction of Lisa Ellmers, project coordinator of project A of the overall Wismut Erbe Forschung Project.

15 The person responsible for long term archiving of the Wismut material at the Center for Contemporary History is Olaf Berg: olaf.berg@zzf-potsdam.de.

16 On the topos of historical authenticity Cf. M. Sabrow / A. Saupe (eds.), *Historische Authentizität*, Göttingen 2016.

17 On the citation Cf. J. Obertreis, *Oral History – Geschichte und Konzeptionen*, in J. Obertreis (ed.), *Oral History. Basistexte*, Stuttgart 2012, p. 7. On the methodology of oral history again, among others, D. Wierling, *Oral History*, in M. Maurer (ed.), *Neue Themen und Methoden der Geschichtswissenschaft*, Stuttgart 2003, pp. 81–151; R. Breckner, *Von den Zeitzeugen zu den Biographen. Methoden der Erhebung und Auswertung lebensgeschichtlicher Interviews*, in J. Obertreis (ed.), *Oral History*, pp. 131–151; L. Niethammer (ed.), *Lebenserfahrung und kollektives Gedächtnis.*

that the "breath of immediacy emanating from the contemporary witness is an illusion. We know that memories cannot be recalled as directly as the person speaking suggests. Narratives become smoother over the years, acquire new meaning, gain dramatic quality. Again, we often remember not so much the event itself, but more the last time we talked about it"[18].

Fig. 3: Astrid Kirchhof in an interview with Gisela Gründel, image by Wismut Heritage Witnesses Project, 2020.

Contemporary witnesses thus not only provide information about the past, but also about how we deal with and perceive the past (see Fig. 3). Historiography could pick this up and ask, for example, which narratives are used in interviews and how they change over time. Insights are provided below about the decision-making process for how the "Wismut-Erbe-Zeitzeug:innen" project would utilize the methodological repertoire of oral history.

Die Praxis der Oral History, Frankfurt a.M. 1985; M. Sabrow / F. Bösch (eds.), *Die Geburt des Zeitzeugen nach 1945. Geschichte der Gegenwart*, Göttingen 2012, vol. 4.

18 M. Sabrow, quoted in F. Dame, *Der Sinnlosigkeit des Leidens einen Sinn geben*, in "Die Welt", February 18, 2016, online, https://www.welt.de/regionales/nrw/article152390610/Der-Sinnlosigkeit-des-Leidens-einen-Sinn-geben.html, last accessed May 27, 2021.

3.1 Methodological foundations of oral history in practice

The historian Dorothee Wierling identifies three different interview types: first, the expert interview; second, the thematic interview; and third, the biographical interview. An expert interview primarily enquires about the expertise and factual knowledge of the interviewee, while a thematic interview, according to Wierling, focuses on a specific subject. The third type, instead, addresses the entire biography of the interviewee. Wierling explains that "the separation between the different categories of interviews [. . .] is artificial"[19], which also became apparent in the Wismut interview project, since the interview types could hardly be separated with a sharp line, as Wismut was and remains an identity-forming factor across the system and is closely interwoven into the life stories of the interviewees.

It was not uncommon for the interviewees to state that Wismut not only had a strong impact on the working lives but also a profound influence on the private lives of the employees. This also becomes obvious in literature, which often refers to Wismut as a "state within the state"[20] as it had its own medical supplies, food shops and offered a comprehensive cultural program for its employees. In summary, it can be stated that the biographical narratives of the interviewees cannot be separated from their work expertise and activities at Wismut. Therefore, the life stories of the interviewees and the memories of their working experiences at Wismut correlate with each other.

3.2 The guidelines: interview structure and question horizons

The structure of the interviews was oriented towards the established methodological preliminary work of the sociologist Roswitha Breckner. She identifies three interview stages: "the entrance narrative (1), the so-called 'internal inquiry section'

---

19 D. Wierling, *Oral History*, pp. 109–111.

20 See, among others, R. Karlsch, *Uran für Moskau*; by the same author, *Sonderzone und Leistungsregime. Uranerzbergbau durch die SDAG Wismut – ein „Staat im Staat"*, in P. Kaiser (ed.), *Arbeit! Ostdeutsche Arbeitswelten im Wandel 1945–2015*, Dresden 2015, pp. 102–108. The latter item is also available online: R. Karlsch, *Urangeschichten der Wismut S(D)AG. Erinnerungen an den größten Bergbaubetrieb der DDR*, https://Wismut.hypotheses.org/die-Wismut, last accessed May 27, 2021. Historian Sabine Loewe-Hannatzsch takes a contrary view: "Since the environmental burdens and effects of uranium ore mining extended far beyond the so-called 'Wismut area' and a large number of actors at the state, district, municipal, and company levels were confronted with the environmental problem, made decisions, and had detailed knowledge of the burdens, the construct of the 'state within the state', which dominates the literature, is difficult to sustain". Cf. S. Loewe-Hannatzsch, e-mail correspondence with Astrid Kirchhof on June 9, 2021.

(2), and finally the external inquiry section (3)". Following the work of cultural anthropologist Edmund Ballhaus, a fourth action-oriented phase (4) is added in the Wismut question guide[21]. In this fourth phase, the contemporary witnesses were given the opportunity to present objects such as photographs, documents, or uniforms. The first question of the interviewer (1), reveals the above-mentioned interweaving of biography and Wismut as a company: "Please tell me your life story and what role Wismut played in it and still plays today!"[22]. In order not to interrupt the interviewee's narration and thus disrupt the flow of the story, follow-up questions to the initial narrative followed in the subsequent second internal inquiry section (2). To establish some degree of comparability of the interviews, in the next step the interviewees were asked to answer the same list of questions (3).

Questions were asked about the early and rebuilding years, the development of mining operations, wages, bonuses and standard of living, social life at Wismut, the company as an economic factor, accident and health protection, the dissolution of the enterprise, the experience of the *Wende-Zeit*, the redevelopment of post-mining landscapes and occupational activities in reunified Germany.

The challenges of this section were to identify topic families that could be of interest for future research. These were explored in exchanges with the commission members[23] of the "Wismut legacy", targeting topics like identity, modernity, gender, environment and nature conservation, health, domination, and personal as well as structural caesura and continuities (4). In the fourth phase of the interview further stories and emotions were retrieved from the memories of the interviewees through interaction with objects, bringing to light additional social, political, and cultural values[24]. In this final interview phase, contemporary witnesses who had given previous interviews on the topic of Wismut were asked about their earlier and present statements, in order to reveal any variability in the memories and attitudes of interviewees.

---

21 R. Breckner, *Von den Zeitzeugen zu den Biographen*, p. 136. Contentwise congruent, but with differing terminology also in D. Wierling, *Geboren im Jahr Eins. Der Jahrgang 1949 in der DDR. Versuch einer Kollektivbiographie*, Berlin 2002, p. 21.

22 For interview guidelines, see the Appendix.

23 Members of the commission: Carsten Drebenstedt, Norbert Frei, Andreas Hochhaus, Sebastian Lentz, Martin Sabrow, Hans Wiesmeth.

24 See, among others, E. Ballhaus, *Rede und Antwort. Answer or Speech? Interviewformen im kulturwissenschaftlichen Film*, in J. Wossidlo / U. Roters, *Interview und Film. Volkskundliche und Ethnologische Ansätze zu Methodik und Analyse*, Münster et al. 2003, pp. 11–49.

3.3 Who was interviewed? The diversity of narratives

The Wismut Heritage Contemporary Witnesses Project intended to collect a vast range of diverse memories. In order to embrace the full breadth of narratives, a wide variety of professions, genders, and ages were included. In addition to mining-specific professions, like team leaders and hewers, other professions were included, with educational personnel, health and nursing services or medical professionals, art and cultural workers, scientists, skilled artisans, service workers, administrative and ministry employees, athletes, and technical specialists (see Fig. 4). The interviews also included children of Wismut employees and local residents affected by mining, along with Soviet employees. For reasons of data protection, it was not possible to proactively search for interview partners and instead calls for participation were published in various media to which interested contemporary witnesses could respond.

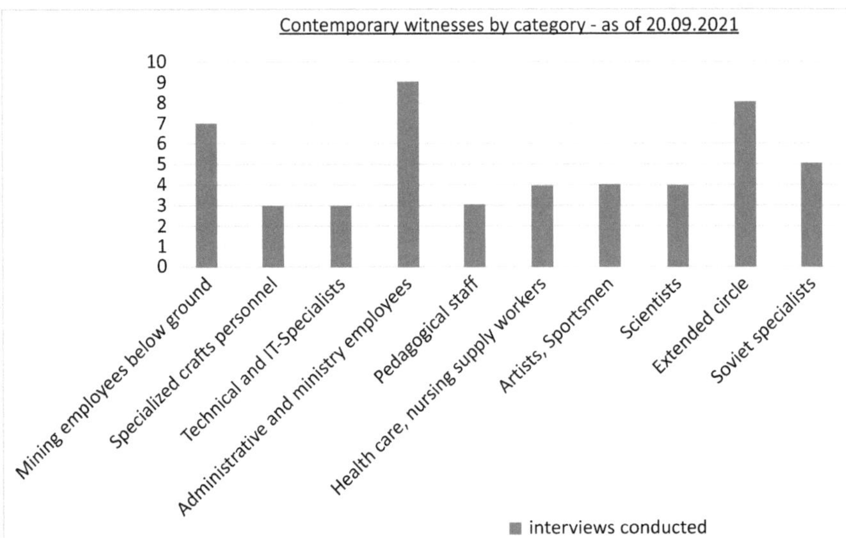

Fig. 4: Categories of contemporary witnesses.

4 Wismut in the Federal Republic post 1990: flourishing landscapes through infrastructural re-cultivation and redevelopment? First analytical approaches

In 1987, the GDR government decided to close mining operations that had become unprofitable and to initiate a structural change in the company. Laid off Wismut staff were given the opportunity to transfer to other nationally owned companies and to the former auxiliary Wismut companies specialized in the development and production of mining-specific equipment and machinery. The environmental and process engineering section was also extended. At the end of 1990 ore mining came to an end and SDAG Wismut was dissolved the following year. In this process, the shares that the Soviet Union held in the company were transferred to the Federal Republic, which thus became the sole owner of the Wismut mining enterprise. Wismut GmbH, as a company of the Federal Ministry of Economics and Technology, took over the decommissioning, custody, redevelopment and reclamation of the mining areas[25]. Some 1,500 km of open pits, 311 million m^3 of tailings, and 160 million m^3 of radioactive sludge[26] were the legacy.

Among other topics, interview questions addressed this decommissioning and redevelopment phase. The research interest was therefore directed not only towards Wismut within the GDR, but also the far-reaching economic, social, and environmental transformation processes after the fall of the Berlin Wall.

4.1 Saving jobs and layoff practice

Looking at the transformation of Wismut from the perspectives of economics and social history, some contemporary witnesses observed that the transformation of Wismut SDAG into a federal German company was a painful process for many employees, dividing the former workers into winners and losers.

---

25 Wismut GmbH, *Die Finanzierung der Wismut*, online, https://www.Wismut.de/de/Wismut_finanzierung.php, last accessed June 10, 2021. See also R. Karlsch, *Uran für Moskau*, pp. 202–230; Wismut GmbH, *Ein Generationenprojekt und seine 25-jährige Erfolgsgeschichte*, in "Dialog. Mitarbeiterzeitschrift der Wismut GmbH", 90, 2016, 6, p. 6.

26 See the podcast about life in the GDR. Astrid Mignon Kirchhof in conversation with Martin Fischer, *Staatsbürgerkunde, vom Leben in der DDR: Übertage. Vom Aufbau, Abbau und Umbau.* (April 10, 2021), https://www.staatsbuergerkunde-podcast.de/ueber-tage/, last accessed June 29, 2021.

Gerd Schneider (2:34:32):

> Well, the hewing activities, who knows how long they would have lasted? It had been decided that the Soviet Union would slowly withdraw. [. . .] Everything had already been decided. [. . .] That was no secret. [. . .] That was already foreshadowed by the fact that the enterprises were merged. [. . .] [The] division manager was replaced because he was supposedly no longer appropriate. [. . .] He was my neighbor here in the house. And then a new area manager came [. . .]. 'Oh', he says, patting me on the back, 'we're pulling the cart out of the mud now! Now everything will be better in terms of work'. Yes, but it didn't get better. Then he quit, too, got a fat severance pay, that I saw by chance[27].

This quotation illustrates various economic and sociopolitical consequences of the period of upheaval. For example, the witness mentioned that the uranium mining company was already in decline before 1989 and that workers were well aware of it. By mentioning the "losers of German reunification", who lost their jobs at Wismut, it becomes clear that social hardships could not be softened even if foreseen (see Fig. 5). The non-transparent personnel policy, which was also mentioned, probably led to even more uncertainty among the employees.

Martina Runge, another witness, described the psychosocial consequences of these changes and explained that, in her estimation, there was more cohesion among employees in GDR times:

Martina Runge (1:26:29):

> [. . .] We had a colleague who was very unstable. She also drank a bit. [. . .] And in GDR times, for example, [. . .] she was supported in the team[28]. It gave her support. [. . .] After the reunification [. . .] she was [. . .] part of the second wave of dismissals. She was fired. And she later committed suicide. Because she suddenly lost her grip. [. . .] She drank herself to death[29].

---

27 Interview conversation between Astrid Mignon Kirchhof and Gerd Schneider. G. Schneider, Interview on September 16, 2020, https://wismut.saw-leipzig.de/content/de/bestaende/zeitzeugen-interviews/interview-mit-schneider-gerd/2020-09-16-schneider-gerd-1080p.mp4, last accessed September 29, 2021.

28 Here "work group" means the company work collective. A possible follow-up research topic could focus on the strong identification of GDR workers with their workplace collectives, especially in large GDR enterprises. Many contemporary witnesses describe the cohesion in the company in a positive sense, like a family that spends a large part of its free time together, in which joy and sorrow are also shared inside the workplace.

29 Interview conversation between Astrid Mignon Kirchhof and Martina Runge. M. Runge, Interview on March 10, 2021, https://wismut.saw-leipzig.de/content/de/bestaende/zeitzeugen-interviews/interview-mit-runge-martina/2021-03-10-martina-runge.mp4, timecode: 1:26:29, last accessed September 29, 2021.

Fig. 5: Schmirchau, Wismut, Protest against shutdown. Photo by Jan Peter Kasper, 1990. The image was provided to Wikimedia Commons by the German Federal Archive, access number: Bild 183–1990-0907-020, https://commons.wikimedia.org/wiki/File:Bundesarchiv_Bild_183-1990-0907-020,_Schmirchau,_Wismut,_Protest_gegen_Schlie%C3%9Fung.jpg.

It could be argued that Runge primarily blames the elimination of the "welfare" dimension of the socialist system for personal turning points during and after the "Wende". Here, an analytical link could be made to a suggestion by the historian Konrad Jarausch, who characterized East Germany with the neologism of "care dictatorship" in order to "bring the contradictory character of the GDR, which consisted of both emancipatory aspects and dictatorial practice, into a concise denominator"[30]. Other historians concluded that the GDR failed not because of its economic decline, but because of the abandonment of the fundamental premise of the German Democratic Republic, which always included a promise to be a social state[31]. In an interview with the German TV station Mitteldeutscher

30 K. Jarausch, *Fürsorgediktatur. Version 1.0*, in "Docupedia-Zeitgeschichte" (11/2/2010), https://docupedia.de/zg/F%C3%BCrsorgediktatur, last accessed June 15, 2021.
31 M. Sabrow, *Der Konkurs der Konsensdiktatur. Überlegungen zum inneren Zerfall der DDR aus kulturgeschichtlicher Perspektive*, in K. Jarausch / M. Sabrow (eds.), *Der Weg in den Untergang. Der innere Zerfall der DDR*, Göttingen 1999, p. 103.

Rundfunk (MDR), Kirchhof stated that the almost exclusively positive memories of the witnesses about Wismut were surprising. Contrary to the expectation that issues linked to uranium mining, like environmental degradation and disease, would be critically berated in the interview, the dominant narrative was instead of Wismut as a caring employer that brought prosperity and privilege to the region[32].

Similarly positive statements were recorded for the 1989/1990 turning point, which the interviewees did not perceive as particularly drastic, unlike the prevailing narratives of GDR history[33]. One reason for this could be the aforementioned way that the project researchers established contact with the interviewees. It was the interviewees who proactively expressed interest in participating in the interview project and, as they themselves stated, they wanted to correct the rather negative prevailing perception of Wismut through their positive narratives. It is also the case that many people tend to idealize their lives in retrospect, partly to avoid questioning their lifelong achievements. It might therefore be assumed that the positive portrayals were due to a strong identification of the interviewees with their employers. Cultural products of the (positively associated) Erzgebirge mining industry, such as candle sticks with mining motifs, and mining parades that still occasionally take place, also indicate a cultural identity with the traditional mining industry in the region. Interviewees frequently expressed their pride in having been part of Wismut, identifying themselves as "Wismuters": they praised the social cohesion and local community, saying that they felt special. Many of the interviewees are also proud to be part of the succeeding redevelopment company, Wismut GmbH. This is remarkable since the redevelopment work was essentially the inversion of the former mining work: the dismantling, closure, and elimination of the (visible) traces of uranium mining, and consequently the disappearance of the company they had strongly identified with[34]. Identity is, however, an unclear concept, because instead of embracing a plurality of identifying elements it is often used in a very simplified way. The identity of an individual is already far too complex to be captured as a singularity, and this is even more radically true for collectives, in which the identity of each individual is modulated by their role, and the expectations of individual, social, regional, and national derivation,

---

32 H. Schade, *Geheimsache Wismut. Zeitzeugenprojekt*, MDR Zeitreise, (April 5, 2021): https://www.mdr.de/geschichte/ddr/wirtschaft/wismut/erbe-forschung-konferenz-uran-bergbau-100.html, last accessed June 20, 2021.

33 Martin Sabrow at the event "Immer noch Geheimsache? Sprechen über die Wismut heute". Cf. M. Sabrow, in *Sächsische Akademie der Wissenschaften zu Leipzig: Immer noch Geheimsache? Sprechen über die Wismut heute*, Mittweida / Leipzig 2021: https://youtu.be/5hern1B-uPs, timecode: 1:26:40, last accessed September 23, 2021.

34 *Ibid.* Timecode: 1:27:36.

all elements that do not remain unchanged during a lifetime[35]. It could therefore be assumed that identification with the employer provides an important but not sufficient explanation, with the economic aspect also contributing significantly to personal assessment of the turning point after the Berlin Wall came down. An important question therefore is whether the (former) Wismut employees continued to have jobs in the succeeding company in their home region. This would mean that no job-related move was necessary, something that would have greatly disrupted their lives. All of the contemporary witnesses interviewed during the project had found subsequent employment. For example, Hans-Georg Fischer, a hewer, later a blasting hewer and team leader, worked in underground and surface redevelopment after Wismut's transformation into a limited liability company in 1991. In the following quotation, he interconnects the different activities:

Hans-Georg Fischer (1:28:16):

> So you see . . . I would actually have to say two [things]. When you were an underground miner, you were still young, you still had verve, and so on and so forth. Well, while working in the redevelopment of the mines, I had a tearful eye, yes, because you understand that it's over and that it was actually a good time. But the removal of the uranium dump with the large machinery was also a lot of fun[36].

The fun that Hans-Georg Fischer alludes to in the quote refers to the enjoyment of getting to know a new area of mining with the possibility of handling large machines. He also expresses a certain feeling of mining honor through being able to reduce environmental damage thanks to his new work.

4.2 Establishing a redevelopment infrastructure for Wismut

On October 3, 1990, the Federal Republic of Germany became a shareholder of SDAG Wismut. An intergovernmental agreement between the Federal Republic of Germany and the USSR sealed the Soviet Union's withdrawal from the company on May 16, 1991. The last Soviet executive, Valentin Nasarkin, left the company nine months later. All Soviet shares were transferred to Germany without compensation,

---

35 H. Moller, *Erinnerung(en), Geschichte, Identität*, in "Politik und Zeitgeschichte", 48, 2001, 28: https://www.bpb.de/apuz/26151/erinnerungen-geschichte-identitaet?p=all, last accessed August 31, 2019. See also A. Assmann / H. Friese (eds.), *Identitäten*, Frankfurt a.M. 1998, vol. 3.

36 Interview conversation between Astrid Mignon Kirchhof and Hans-Georg Fischer. H.-G. Fischer, Interview on September 9, 2020 in Gera, https://wismut.saw-leipzig.de/content/de/bestaende/zeitzeugen-interviews/interview-mit-fischer-hans-georg, timecode: 1:28:16, last accessed June 3, 2021.

and both sides agreed to waive any sharing of the cleanup costs[37]. Planning and initial work began immediately for decommissioning and safeguarding the facilities, along with redevelopment and land reclamation. A continuation of mining activities had previously been ruled out for economic reasons. Under the "Wismut Law" passed by the German Parliament, the mining company was transformed into a corporation under German law. The Federal Republic of Germany became the sole owner of the shares within a limited liability company created on December 20, 1991. Responsibility for company shares was transferred to the Federal Ministry of Economics (BMWi). Since then, Wismut GmbH has been tasked with cleaning up the legacy of uranium ore mining. Environmental activist Michael Beleites called this transformation the "Wismut metamorphosis", referring to Wismut's seamless transition from a Soviet nuclear project to West German environmental remediation company[38]. However, some redevelopment activities were already part of Wismut SDAG's regular work before 1990. For example, excavated mine workings were backfilled, waste rock piles revegetated and sludge ponds cleaned up[39]. Beleites argues that this work was not motivated so much by the environmental awareness of the actors, but more often carried out with a view to economic gain. In an interview, Dr. Rudolf Daenecke, who played a leading role in drawing up the first landscape restoration concepts, recalled the practice of the 1960s:

Dr. Rudolf Daenecke (1:50:58):

> [W]e [were] already disposing of sludge in a village pond in Gera [. . .] in the 60s [1960s]. But not [. . .] because we observed environmental protection back in the 60s [1960s]. But mainly because the sludge had wonderful uranium mineralizations. [. . .] So economic motives were behind it at that time[40].

Starting in the 1980s, Wismut SDAG was increasingly confronted with the negative consequences of its work by the growing East German environmental movement. In particular, the abovementioned activist Michael Beleites created a basis for subsequent public environmental criticisms of Wismut SDAG's operations

37 M. Meissner, *Schichtende. Kontroversen um Rückbau und Sanierung*, in R. Boch / R. Karlsch (eds.), *Uranbergbau im Kalten Krieg. Die Wismut im sowjetischen Atomkomplex*, Berlin 2011, vol. 1, pp. 361–366 and 370–373.

38 M. Beleites, *Altlast Wismut. Ausnahmezustand, Umweltkatastrophe und das Sanierungsproblem im deutschen Uranbergbau*, Frankfurt a.M. 1992, pp. 75ff.

39 S. Geyer, Interview on June 6, 2021 in Aue-Bad Schlema: https://wismut.saw-leipzig.de/content/de/bestaende/zeitzeugen-interviews/interview-mit-geyer-siegfried, last accessed June 17, 2021.

40 R. Daenecke, Interview on January 21, 2021 in Berlin, Bad Schlema, https://wismut.saw-leipzig.de/content/de/bestaende/zeitzeugen-interviews/interview-mit-daenecke-rudolf, timecode: 1:50:58, last accessed June 17, 2021.

with his investigative and widely read study *Pechblende*[41]. According to Rudolf Daenecke, the ongoing protests of opposition groups prompted Wismut SDAG to contact environmental activists in the 1980s and to make environmental issues increasingly relevant within Wismut:

Dr. Rudolf Daenecke (1:51:46):

> There were [. . .] environmental departments [. . .] established in the general management, but then also in the plants. [. . .] And a number of measures were actually introduced. [. . .] So that [. . .] at the end of 89 [1989] [. . .] I had a first contact for example with Mr. Beleites. [. . .] And [we] always then [. . .] ultimately after the turnaround, [. . .] tried to find a common denominator [. . .] for the ideas and initiate redevelopment progress[42].

Future research projects should look at the (proto)civil society dimension of environmental activism and, with the help of this methodological approach, more closely examine the influence of environmental groups on Wismut redevelopment practices in the 1980s[43].

During reunification, some media also described the Wismut region with headlines such as the "valley of tears and tailings piles" in which the "houses radiate"[44]. The historian Rainer Karlsch, however, considers statements like these to be "sensationalism"[45], as examination showed that most waste rock piles were no longer radioactive or only slightly so. There was a total of 48 waste rock piles containing 311 million cubic meters of low radiation waste. Other less hazardous features that also required redevelopment included mine buildings and workings that needed to be cleaned of pollutants to avoid contaminating the groundwater. The mine was partially backfilled and finally flooded, involving the construction of dams and barriers. The Ronneburg pointed cone dumps were completely removed, while others

---

41 M. Beleites, *Pechblende der Uranbergbau in der DDR und seine Folgen*, Lutherstadt Wittenberg 1988.

42 R. Daenecke, Interview, timecode: 01:51:46.

43 The discussions revolve around the question of whether a definition of civil society based on Western liberal societies can also be applied to real socialist states. The public component, which cannot be attested in the full discursive sense in real socialist states, proves to be problematic. Cf. among others K. Jarausch, *Aufbruch der Zivilgesellschaft – Zur Einordnung der friedlichen Revolution von 1989*, in "Totalitarismus und Demokratie", 3, 2006, 1, pp. 25–46. Jarausch operates with Jürgen Kocka's definition of civil society, see: J. Kocka, *Zivilgesellschaft in historischer Perspektive*, in "Forschungsjournal Neue Soziale Bewegungen", 16, 2016, 2, pp. 29–37. On the scope of the East German environmental movement, see: A.M. Kirchhof, *For a Decent Quality of Life. Environmental Groups in East and West Berlin*, in "Journal of Urban History", 41, 2015, 4, pp. 625–646.

44 Interview conversation between Astrid Mignon Kirchhof and Oliver Titzmann. O. Titzmann, Interview on April 1, 2021, https://wismut.saw-leipzig.de/content/de/bestaende/zeitzeugen-interviews/interview-mit-titzmann-oliver/2021-01-04-titzmann-oliver.mp4, last accessed September 29, 2021.

45 R. Karlsch, *Uran für Moskau*, p. 213.

remained partially in place, were leveled, integrated into the landscape, and revegetated. The residual radiation was contained by covering the tailing piles.

Therefore, no widespread environmental hazards were identified, with only a few large dangerous sites. These were 14 industrial tailings ponds, used for treating wastewater, and comprising a volume of 160 million cubic meters. The heavily contaminated areas of the site were those used for mining, interim storage, processing, and transport of uranium ore[46]. It should be mentioned, however, that the Ordinance on Nuclear Safety and Radiation Protection (VOAS) dating from GDR times still applied in reunited Germany. Regulations on mining liabilities did not exist in the Federal Republic and so, in order to avoid a redevelopment standstill, the Unification Treaty stipulated that the Wismut redevelopment should be carried out provisionally according to the GDR Radiation Protection Law[47]. On January 11, 2000, an appeal was filed (but later dismissed) before the Federal Constitutional Court, in which nine plaintiffs criticized this regulation. Today the guideline values for radon content have been adjusted[48].

Siegfried Geyer was responsible for redevelopment below and above ground. He reported that redevelopment expertise could only be developed on the basis of existing redevelopment practices, communicating to the responsible German authorities:

Siegfried Geyer (0:58:30):

> So, there was an immense amount of work [. . .]. After all, new authorities were founded [. . .]. These were people who had never had anything to do with mining. [. . .] Now an operating plan went to the LfULG [State Office for Environment, Agriculture and Geology] and it didn't take long at all, then you get a letter back with a hundred questions [. . .] Well, there were questions to which you, as an experienced miner, just shook your head. [. . .] In the beginning, it was extremely complicated[49].

---

46 *Ibid.*, pp. 213–214 and pp. 217–218.

47 Statement by Ulrich Rieger in the interview with Astrid Mignon Kirchhof. U. Rieger, interview on June 22, 2021, https://wismut.saw-leipzig.de/content/de/bestaende/zeitzeugen-interviews/interview-mit-rieger-ulrich/2021-06-22-rieger-ulrich.mp4, last accessed September 29, 2021.

48 See *AGURMINE: Ein Reader anlässlich der Wander-Ausstellung. Uran – oder das Recht auf Leben? Ein SchülerInnen-Studierenden Projekt zum Thema Uranabbau und den Folgen*, Marburg 2004, p. 48, https://www.gruene-tuttlingen.de/fileadmin/gruene-tuttlingen/texte/Uranabbau.pdf, last accessed June 30, 2021. See also: Le Monde diplomatique / Nuclear Free Future Foundation / Rosa-Luxemburg-Stiftung / Bund für Umwelt und Naturschutz Deutschland (eds.), *The Uranium Atlas. Facts and Figures About the Raw Material of the Nuclear Age*, Berlin 2020, p. 31, https://www.rosalux.de/fileadmin/rls_uploads/pdfs/sonst_publikationen/URANATLAS_final.pdf, last accessed June 30, 2021. See also: Federal Office for Radiation Protection: wismuth cohort study, https://www.bfs.de/DE/bfs/wissenschaft-forschung/projekte/wismut/wismut.html, last accessed January 20, 2023.

49 Interview conversation between Astrid Mignon Kirchhof and Siegfried Geyer. S. Geyer, Interview on June 11, 2021, https://wismut.saw-leipzig.de/content/de/bestaende/zeitzeugen-interviews/

Redevelopment of the devastated landscapes in the early 1990s was thus not only associated with novel technical challenges, but also with complex regulatory negotiations that were necessary for the creation of new guidelines and concepts. Experts even traveled to Canada and the United States to learn from their redevelopment practices. Wismut found its own solutions applying the latest technologies based on foreign expertise and adapted to the local geological and climatic conditions. In the opinion of the witnesses interviewed in this project, a comprehensive reclamation project was created over time, becoming an international model because no other country had undertaken a reclamation project equal to that of the Federal Republic of Germany[50]. This proclaimed role model status – even on a global level – perhaps induces certain inherent failures in the process to fade into the background in the perception of contemporary witnesses. Possible follow-up research could start here and examine the actual pioneering work, together with any possible transfer of knowledge to other countries in more detail[51].

In general, the redevelopment of Wismut is often simply assumed to have been a success by contemporary witnesses and researchers alike[52]:

Oliver Titzmann (0:48:59):

> Because what the redevelopment company has achieved in the region is indescribable. And many things, especially in Bad Schlema, the rebirth of the Schlema spa, would be completely unthinkable without the Wismut Redevelopment Company. Thus, from my point of view, the Wismut redevelopment operation must also be rated very very positively [. . .][53].

After restoring the area, the second step was recultivation and "cosmetic" redevelopment (see Fig. 6), as Oliver Titzmann explained in the same interview.

---

interview-mit-geyer-siegfried/2021-06-11-interview-mit-geyer-siegfried.mp4, timecode: 00:58:30, last accessed September 29, 2021.

50 U. Rieger, Interview on June 22, 2021.

51 On technical and environmental knowledge transfer between communist and capitalist countries, see: L. Coumel, *Building a Soviet Eco-Power while Looking at the Capitalist World. The Rise of Technocratic Environmentalism in Russian Water Controversies, 1957–1989*, in A.M. Kirchhof / J. McNeill (eds.), *Nature and the Iron Curtain. Environmental Policy and Social Movements in Communist and Capitalist Countries 1945–1990*, Pittsburgh 2019, pp. 17–35.

52 Historian Rainer Karlsch, for example, describes the redevelopment of Wismut as a unique success: "Three decades is a long period of time. And in these three decades, nowhere in the world has such a densely populated area been renaturalized, as far as that is possible at all, as the Wismut areas have been renaturalized in Saxony and Thuringia. It is an extraordinary achievement that has been brought about with a lot of money, with a lot of effort". Cf. R. Karlsch, *Die Zukunft des Wismut-Erbes. Ein interdisziplinäres Forschungs-Forum der Sächsischen Akademie der Wissenschaften zu Leipzig*, https://youtu.be/5hern1B-uPs, timecode: 01:14:42 ff, last accessed June 30, 2021.

53 O. Titzmann, Interview on April 1, 2021.

Fig. 6: Ronneburg – Schmirchauer Höhe. Photo by André Karwath, 2007, Wikimedia Commons CC BY-SA 2.5, https://commons.wikimedia.org/wiki/File:Ronneburg_-_Schmirchauer_H%C3%B6he_(aka).jpg?uselang=de.

Oliver Titzmann (02:30:37):

> Step number two was cosmetic redevelopment. So not just making the slag heap wider, but how to shape it? Do we want to plant pretty shrubbery or trees there? Do we want to build a golf course on the former devastated landscape or a spa park, or should we create hiking trails? That was the next step to be taken. And the third step, which also has to be considered, is how can the land be used economically? Leaving all the dump materials and dump landscape as unproductive land in the middle of a densely populated region is not an option. So, you have to think about options for subsequent use. Golf offers a sports option, and hiking trails offer recreational opportunities for leisure time activities. Or a spa park, which has become a necessary part of spa facilities. So, you also had to keep an economic use in mind. Hazard prevention, cosmetic – yes cosmetization (sic!) – the cosmetic design of the whole and long-term subsequent use were the three big steps for me that were taken in the region over the last 30 years[54].

The spa park mentioned by Titzmann refers to the Schlema spa and health resort, which was rebuilt after the fall of the Berlin Wall thus resuming a tradition established in the nineteenth century. At the beginning of the twentieth century, radon springs were tapped in the Oberschlema Marx-Semler-Stolln, and the location developed into a world-famous radium spa after the First World War. Bad Schlema was able to resume this tradition after reunification, building a modern hotel where people are treated with radon once again. In the same year, 1992, a "Kurgesellschaft Schlema mbH" was established, laying the foundation for a future spa complex. In the following years the Schlema Valley was the most ambitious infrastructure project in the region. Restructuring measures were especially intense in the district of Oberschlema and a spa park with terrain paths, water features, and lookout

54 *Ibid.*

points was created with earth mounds and infills. The spa finally opened for business in 1998.

Discussing the Wismut redevelopment success story, the historian Sabine Loewe-Hannatzsch observed that research has failed so far to provide a conclusive explanation for how Wismut was able to metamorphose from being considered an environmental polluter to an environmental savior virtually overnight. It is fair to say that not only the redevelopment but also the active Wismut period in the GDR has not been subjected to adequate critical analysis[55]. She underlines how the narrative of the Wismut redevelopment as a success story requires further investigation, cross-checking the statements of contemporary witnesses against archival documents. Another relevant question is whether the uranium mining areas and their redevelopment represented a fortunate special case in the history of East German transformation.

5 A preliminary conclusion

The interview excerpts analyzed here relate primarily to the transformation of Wismut from a mining business to a redevelopment enterprise, which occurred as a result of the collapse of the GDR. The profound social, economic, and environmental changes that accompanied this transformation affected Wismut's workforce, the region (Thuringia and Saxony), and the local inhabitants as a whole. The interviews revealed the marked turning points in the biographies of Wismut employees, but with a predominantly positive balance regarding both the former work context and later redevelopment scenario. The large-scale infrastructural developments resulting from the newly created Schlema spa and health resort were certainly decisive in this respect. The literature also describes overburdened infrastructure systems[56] that reveal unforeseen weaknesses[57], suggesting the possibility of a generalized systemic failure[58]. But despite this, the redevelopment of Wismut

55 S. Loewe-Hannatzsch, Lecture, "New Perspectives on Dealing with Environmental Problems in Uranium Ore Mining in the GDR", in Berlin-Brandenburg Environmental Colloquium on June 9, 2021.

56 M. Gross, *Ignorance and Surprise: Science, Society, and Ecological Design*, Cambridge MA 2010. C. Perrow, *Normal Accidents Living with High-Risk Technologies*, Princeton NJ 1999.

57 E. Klinenberg, *Adaptation: How Can Cities Be "Climate-Proofed"*, in "New Yorker", January 7, 2013, pp. 32–37. T. Comes / B. Van de Walle, *Measuring Disaster Resilience: The Impact of Hurricane Sandy on Critical Infrastructure Systems*, Brussels 2014.

58 S. Rinaldi / J. Peerenboom / T. Kelly, *Identifying, Understanding, and Analyzing Critical Infrastructure Interdependencies*, in "IEEE Control Syst. Mag.", 21, 2002, 6, pp. 11–25.

appears to be inscribed in the memory of the contemporary witnesses as a success story, and it is similarly conceived in academic research[59].

The positive narratives of the interviewees were surprising for the project team, who assumed that the environmental destruction, risk of disease from radioactive contamination, and cutbacks due to the annexation of the GDR to the Federal Republic would have induced a sense of alienation among the interviewees. One explanation for the mismatch between these prior assumptions and the actual views expressed could be that, for reasons of data protection, it was not possible for the researchers to access the employee records held by Wismut and choose specific cases for interview. This would have made it possible to find interview subjects who hold less positive views of uranium mining in the GDR. Among those interviewed in this study, no one had remained unemployed and only one person had a relative who became seriously ill.

Negative views of Wismut were therefore rare, with instead a predominantly strong identification with the former employer and pride in having been part of the Wismut empire. This pride did not diminish when Wismut SDAG had to close down and the employees found work in Wismut's redevelopment company. This suggests that the close ties to the mining tradition of the region, which were repeatedly emphasized, were not the only decisive factor for the positive narratives, and that Wismut itself is also remembered favorably. There are several reasons for this. While the Russian contemporary witnesses viewed Wismut's uranium mining as a guarantor for equilibrium in the Cold War, the German interviewees referred to the uranium mining company as a caring and social employer whose wages and employee medical care were considered exemplary.

The issue of a 'darker' side of Wismut is an area of research that still needs to be explored. This would also include medical studies into the course of diseases and the Wismut health system. It would be interesting to investigate the positive narratives and binding power of a state socialist project 30 years after its demise. Other future research projects could focus on the transnational history of Wismut, and, for example, the interaction of Soviet Wismut employees with their German colleagues.

The transfer of knowledge to and from other countries should also be scrutinized. A further subject for study could be the "master narrative" of Wismut uranium mining, whose main protagonist is the German male miner working underground. Previously marginalized actors in mining could be incorporated into a corrected or supplemented common narrative. The redevelopment of Wismut has

59 R. Karlsch, *Die Zukunft des Wismut-Erbes*, https://youtu.be/5hern1B-uPs, timecode: 01:14:42 ff, (as of 6/30/2021).

also been little researched to date. In this context the role of environmental activists in civil society and their influence on Wismut's remediation measures in the 1980s should be of interest to historiographers. Last but not least, the artistic legacy of the many visual artists who worked for Wismut awaits reappraisal. The eyewitness project presented here is intended as another piece in the mosaic of research into the multifaceted history of Wismut.

Appendix: Interview Guide – Wismut Heritage Witnesses Project

[Entrance Narrative]

Please tell me your life story and what role Wismut played in it and still plays today!

[Follow-up questions]
If not already recounted during the "Entrance Narrative":
1. Tell us how you grew up.
2. Describe your first points of contact with Wismut.
3. What were your reasons for joining Wismut?

[caesura]: Are there any decisive experiences that have remained in your memory ("classic" [1953, 1961, 1989, etc.] as well as private ones)?

[Own position]
Tell us about the time of the *Wende* and the *Wiedervereinigung*.
How did you see yourself and how did you deal with the different developments and positions? How did you feel as a new FRG citizen?

[Factual questions]
How do they assess the following facts:
1. Was the number of employees dismissed after 1990 justified?
2. Is your pension adequate for your work at Wismut?
3. Do you think the federal government is providing sufficient funding for the cleanup?

[Sentiments]:
1. Could you please describe the mood and atmosphere at the time you started working at the plant?
2. What time would you describe as the heyday of operations and how did that feel to you personally?
3. Could you please describe the mood and atmosphere during the final phase of operations?

[State in the state]:
It is widely suggested that Wismut was a "State within the state".
1. What can we understand from this?
2. Please explain it to me.
3. How did you perceive this?

[*Wende*]:
1. At what point did you notice that something was changing in the company and that things were starting to transform? What changes were on the horizon up to the *Wende*?
2. What were the first signs, how did it become noticeable?
3. How did you experience this time? How did you experience the change from SDAG to GmbH?
4. What changed for you?
5. How did it continue for you personally?

[Illness]
Mining is also associated with hazards.
1. Was and is the issue of occupational disease present?
2. Were there and are there people in your circle of acquaintances who fell ill because of their work at Wismut?
3. Do they feel supported enough by the Federal Republic of Germany?
In the case of recognition of an occupational disease:
What is your financial support for illness?
Tell us about the process up until your illness was recognized as an occupational disease!

[Environment & Sanitation]
What impact did the plant restructuring and remediation plan have on your work and on you personally?
Please describe what it changed for you and how you felt about it.

[Role/Presence of the SED]
1. What role did the SED, and mass organizations such as the FDJ or DSF, play in your life? How present were they in Wismut?
2. Could you describe the role of the SED in your everyday (working) life?
3. How would you assess your political self-image at that time?

[Work]
Tell us about your work.
What did a normal working day look like for you, from getting up to going to bed?

[Soviet specialists and Relations]
How did you perceive Soviet colleagues or superiors? What presence did they have in the workplace, and in the public sphere, and what was your experience of the Society for German-Soviet Friendship?

How would you describe the contacts? Did they extend into your private sphere as well?

[Identity / Belonging / Modernity]
Wismut – what did it mean to you then? What does it still mean to you today? What has left a special mark on you? What made you get up every morning and go to Wismut and do your work?
Did your relationships with immediate workmates outlast Wismut? Were they aware that it was a special situation?

[Conclusion]
Is there anything else you'd like to share that we haven't talked about yet?

[Items]
Do you have objects and mementos related to Wismut that are important to you? Show us and say something about what they mean to you personally.

III. The Multiple Scales of Enviro-Technical Systems

Giacomo Parrinello

Water as Infrastructure and the Scalar Mismatch

1 Introduction

In 2003, during a heat wave that killed tens of thousands across Europe, the basin of the Po River experienced a major drought. The discharge of the Po reached record lows, with cascading effects for agriculture and energy production. Distress was particularly acute in the delta, where seawater penetrated far inland with resulting contamination of groundwater and irrigation intakes. Thermoelectric power plants located along the Po River lacked cooling water and had to cut energy distribution to customers. The water shortage led to a call for hydroelectric energy producers to release water from hydroelectric reservoirs, ironically at the very same time that energy consumption was peaking as a result of the heat wave increasing use of air conditioning. It was the worst possible moment to release stored water[1].

The 2003 episode (like many that followed) starkly revealed something easily overlooked: how much the physical infrastructure of social and economic life depends on *predictable* water flows. Water itself is an indispensable infrastructural component for agricultural production, energy generation, and urban water supplies, just as much as pipes, cables, and concrete. Without water, the existing agricultural, energy, and urban infrastructure could not exist or operate. In a very practical sense, and for the multiple economic and social activities that depend on it, water *is* infrastructure. But it is also much more, it is also part of natural processes operating on multiple scales, from river systems to the global climate. The multiple existence of water is the focus of the present essay.

It is difficult to define infrastructure despite numerous attempts to do so. The literature of Science and Technology Studies and anthropology emphasizes infrastructure's role in enabling movement, circulation, exchange, and formation of relationships[2]. This extends the concept of infrastructure beyond the conventional

1 A. Massarutto / A. de Carli, *I costi economici della siccità: il caso del Po*, in "Economia delle fonti di energia e dell'ambiente", 2, 2009, pp. 124–143; D. Musolino / C. Vezzani / A. Massarutto, *Drought Management in the Po River Basin*, Italy, in A. Iglesias / D. Assimacopoulos / H.A.J. Van Lanen, *Drought: Science & Policy*, Chichester 2018, pp. 201–215.

2 Some influential examples are S. Leigh Star, *The Ethnography of Infrastructure*, in "American Behavioral Scientist", 43, 1999, 3, pp. 377–391; P.N. Edwards, *Infrastructure and Modernity: Force, Time, and Social Organization in the History of Sociotechnical Systems*, in T.J. Misa / P. Brey / A. Feenberg

https://doi.org/10.1515/9783111112756-006

idea of "hardware" by incorporating institutions and social relations, but without excluding its purely material aspects. Regardless of how infrastructure is defined, pipes, canals, and hydroelectric power plants certainly always qualify since they enable water circulation, make exchanges and interactions possible, and establish relationships between people, environments, and activities.

Water itself is incorporated into and becomes part of these infrastructures. From the perspective of envirotechnical scholars like Sara Pritchard and others, (any) infrastructure is neither natural nor technological. It is a hybrid configuration of environment and technology, in which the environment is always an active part[3]. I adopt this perspective here, drawing especially on Ashley Carse's important article, *Nature as Infrastructure*[4]. In his discussion of the Panama Canal and its watershed, Carse does not set out another version of concepts such as ecosystem services or natural capital. His aim was instead to investigate how historical actors have incorporated certain natural processes into infrastructural development, managing or excluding them, and what the consequences were of such inclusions and exclusions. Here the phrase "water as infrastructure" similarly aims to focus on ways in which water as a *natural substance* has been incorporated into technical hydraulic infrastructure. In other words, how natural water processes are *manufactured* into water as infrastructure, or to use the anthropologist Andrea Ballestero's phrase, how it is "infrastructuralized"[5].

Making water into infrastructure is a matter of scale. While many scholars often conflate "scale" with "level" or "size", human geographer Nathan Sayre distinguished scale as *level*, from scale as spatial and temporal *relations* "between (processes at different) levels"[6]. At a certain level of observation, one can always see multiple processes occurring on multiple scales. These processes, in turn,

(eds.), *Modernity and Technology*, Cambridge MA 2003, pp. 185–225; B. Larkin, *The Politics and Poetics of Infrastructure*, in "Annual Review of Anthropology", 42, 2013, 1, pp. 327–343.

3 See S.B. Pritchard, *Confluence: The Nature of Technology and the Remaking of the Rhône*, Cambridge MA / London 2011. For a broader overview of envirotechnical scholarship see M. Reuss / S.H. Cutcliffe (eds.), *The Illusory Boundary Environment and Technology in History*, Charlottesville 2010; D. Jørgensen / F.A. Jørgensen / S.B. Pritchard (eds.), *New Natures: Joining Environmental History with Science and Technology Studies*, 1st ed., Pittsburgh 2013.

4 A. Carse, *Nature as Infrastructure: Making and Managing the Panama Canal Watershed*, in "Social Studies of Science", 42, 2012, 4, pp. 539–563. See also A. Carse, *Beyond the Big Ditch: Politics, Ecology, and Infrastructure at the Panama Canal*, Cambridge MA 2014.

5 A. Ballestero, *The Underground as Infrastructure? Water, Figure/Ground Reversals, and Dissolution in Sardinal*, in K. Hetherington (ed.), *Infrastructure, Environment, and Life in the Anthropocene*, Durham 2019, pp. 17–44., esp. p. 22.

6 N.F. Sayre, *Scale*, in *A Companion to Environmental Geography*, ed. by N. Castree et al., 1st ed., Chichester UK / Malden MA 2009, p. 101.

condition what is observed at any given level. The hydrology of a watershed, for example, depends simultaneously on local, regional, continental, and planetary climatic processes. It also depends on processes occurring on multiple temporal scales, be these seasonal, annual, over decades, centuries, or millions of years of geological time. Such scales together constitute the material reality of watershed hydrology. However, they are not automatically visible to observers, they depend on active choices by the observer and have their own political implications[7].

This understanding of scale can be fruitfully applied to envirotechnical analysis. For water to function well as part of an infrastructure, it needs to be predictable and controlled. Clearly no hydroelectric plant can generate energy without an adequate water supply from a river or lake. This involves tasks familiar to scholars of Science and Technology Studies: classification, standardization, and knowledge accumulation[8]. These processes occur at the scale of social institutions. The flow of water in rivers or lakes is on different scales, the multiple spatial and temporal scales of climatic, geological, and hydrological processes. In brief, the spatial and temporal scales of hydrological processes do not match the scales of infrastructure. There is a structural gap between them: a scalar mismatch.

The modern history of infrastructure like aqueducts, irrigation canals, and hydropower plants is characterized by efforts to resolve the disparity between the excess scales of hydrological processes and the scales of infrastructure. As such, it is an example of what Deborah Coen calls a "history of scaling"[9]. Predictability, and thus knowledge about water, is at the center of these scaling efforts. Knowing how much water will be available at a given time is what enables hydraulic infrastructures to operate, and it makes it possible to scale infrastructures to match the scale of hydrological processes. Much of this paper will be concerned with prediction technologies and their role in converting water into infrastructure. These technologies are sometimes highly successful, but history is also

7 This latter distinction is what Sayre frames as the "ontological" and the "epistemological" moments of scale. See N.F. Sayre, *Ecological and Geographical Scale: Parallels and Potential for Integration*, in "Progress in Human Geography", 29, 2005, 3, pp. 276–290, https://doi.org/10.1191/0309132505ph546oa; N.F. Sayre, *Scale*. For a case study on scale and its politics see N.F. Sayre, *The Politics of Scale: A History of Rangeland Science*, illustrated ed., Chicago 2017.

8 G. Bowker / S.L. Star (eds.), *Sorting Things Out – Classification & Its Consequences*, Cambridge MA 1999; M. Lampland / S. Leigh Star, *Standards and Their Stories: How Quantifying, Classifying, and Formalizing Practices Shape Everyday Life*, Ithaca / London 2009; P.N. Edwards, *A Vast Machine: Computer Models, Climate Data, and the Politics of Global Warming*, Cambridge MA 2010.

9 D.R. Coen, *Climate in Motion: Science, Empire, and the Problem of Scale*, Chicago 2018, pp. 16–20. On scaling and the water cycle see S. Dry, *Waters of the World: The Story of the Scientists Who Unraveled the Mysteries of Our Oceans, Atmosphere, and Ice Sheets and Made the Planet Whole*, Chicago / London 2019.

characterized by persistent difficulty in matching scales and prediction failures. Overall, effective scaling has proven to be elusive.

I investigate these issues in the Po River basin, the region I have mentioned in relation to drought. I am currently writing a book on this major European watershed, analyzing the transformation of the river system during the transition to a capitalist economy and the creation of a modern state during the nineteenth and twentieth centuries. The present text draws on this project[10]. In the following, the focus will be on the implementation of knowledge about water in agricultural infrastructures in the nineteenth century, and then in energy infrastructures in the twentieth century, before discussing more recent examples of scalar mismatching.

2 Water for agriculture

At the turn of the nineteenth century, the lower basin of the Po was home to one of the wealthiest agricultural areas in Europe, based on a close integration of farming and livestock, and including the processing of dairy products, such as butter and *grana* cheese. The famed British agronomist Arthur Young observed during a trip to Italy that this integrated farming system was possible thanks to intensive irrigation: "water, clover, cows, cheese, money, and music! These are the combinations that string Italian nerves to enjoyment and give lessons of government to northern politicians"[11]. Using a water intensive irrigation technique known as *marcite*, farmers were able to produce fresh fodder year-round, with up to four harvests between December and April. This provided them with a significant advantage over other European competitors, who had to nourish their cattle with less appetizing and less nourishing dry fodder. Thanks to this food regime, farmers on the plain could feed a large population of high-yield milk cows. This large well-nourished cow population not only produced significant quantities of milk, it also generated large quantities of fertilizing manure. Crop rotation included rice, which benefitted from the abundance of water and manure. Water flows were the foundation for the entire agricultural ecology of the plain, and if Arthur Young can be believed, for its political system.

10 I am also drawing on preliminary findings of this project published in G. Parrinello, *Charting the Flow: Water Science and State Hydrography in the Po Watershed, 1872–1917*, in "Environment and History", 23, 2017, 1, pp. 65–96; G. Parrinello, *Systems of Power: A Spatial Envirotechnical Approach to Water Power and Industrialization in the Po Valley of Italy, ca. 1880–1970*, in "Technology and Culture", 59, 2018, 3, pp. 652–688.

11 A. Young, *Travels in France & Italy during the Years 1787, 1788 and 1789*, London 1915, p. 240.

Knowledge of river flow patterns was a long-standing concern in the valley. One aspect regarded the construction and maintenance of flood protection infrastructures. Farmland had expanded over the centuries to occupy wetlands and floodplains, and it required protection from flood waters, mostly based on embankments. Flood protection infrastructure needs to work with water as much as against it. The main purpose of an embankment is to contain the flow of water and this requires a knowledge of how high the river can potentially rise. In the nineteenth century, the main strategy was based on previous flood crests. Embankments had to be higher than the highest recorded flood crest. Here history was an absolute reference, providing a temporal scale of hydrological processes over as many decades or centuries as the historical records documented. The spatial scale instead covered solely the section of the river to enclose within the embankments. What happened upstream or downstream was not a concern[12].

In the case of irrigation canals, the issue was different. The point of interest was not exceptional crests, but average discharge: how much water did the river *usually* carry. Both issues of flood crests and discharge were long-standing concerns in the region and the focus of intellectual efforts dating back as far as the seventeenth century[13]. In the nineteenth century estimating river discharge gained in importance. During this century, the high-yield irrigated agriculture described above intensified and expanded across the plain, thanks to a series of new irrigation schemes including the Pavia canal in lower Lombardy, the Cavour Canal in Piedmont, and the Villoresi Canal in upper Lombardy. The increasing demands of such schemes led to a perception of water resources as increasingly scarce, in spite of an abundance of water in the region. Knowing how much water was effectively available in rivers could indicate the feasibility and profitability of any new infrastructures involving already highly exploited rivers.

The method developed and promoted by nineteenth-century European hydrologists was based on the notion of *mean discharge*. As discussed by Fréderic Graber in his study of the *Canal de l'Ourq* in Paris, at the turn of the century hydrologists and engineers debated the usefulness of calculating the average state of a river as one option among others[14]. The value of such an approach gained consensus in the

12 For an example of a collection of historical flood crest records, see P. Paleocapa, *Degli effetti del Castagnaro, diversivo dell'Adige, e delle conseguenze che avrà la sua totale e perpetua chiusura (1835)*, in *Memorie d'idraulica pratica*, Venezia 1859, pp. 90–135.

13 See for instance B. Castelli, *Della Misura Delle Acque Correnti*, 3rd ed., Roma 1660. On early modern Italian water science in context see C. Maffioli, *Out of Galileo: The Science of Waters 1628–1718*, Rotterdam 1994.

14 F. Graber, *Paris a Besoin d'eau: Projet, Dispute et Délibération Technique Dans La France Napoléonienne*, Paris 2009.

following decades, and an 1846 paper reviewing recent measuring efforts in Italy, France, and Germany by the hydrologist and engineer Elia Lombardini provided a synthesis of this approach[15]. By plotting together enough discharge measurements, it would be possible to calculate monthly, seasonal, and annual river discharge averages. Lombardini called this method "river statistics" (*la statistica dei fiumi*) and it would enable prediction of river behavior for successful integration of their flow into hydraulic infrastructures.

This method differed from using historical records of flood crests in two important ways. The scale considered was no longer a section of river, but increasingly a whole river system (even if the measurements were taken at selected points). Secondly, the temporal scale was considerably shorter. There was no need to accumulate centuries of extreme levels, a few decades of observations would be adequate to establish the mean discharge rate. A few decades later, Francesco Brioschi, mathematician, hydrologist and first head of the Politecnico di Milano, would provide estimates of the discharge of the Po River based on measurements performed at only two points on the river, and over a span of just three years. Brioschi considered these results as provisional, but nevertheless remained convinced that a limited series of observations and measurements, like those he had taken, could be used to establish the average hydrological regime of the Po River. This would be of great advantage for all manner of hydraulic projects, from irrigation canals to flood protection infrastructures[16].

The shortcomings of river discharge estimations also had serious practical implications for hydraulic infrastructure. The Cavour Canal provides a summary example. This canal is a major irrigation infrastructure, conceived in the 1840s and constructed by a British joint stock company between 1863 and 1866, with the purpose of transporting water from the Po to irrigate the fields of eastern Piedmont[17]. The project was designed by state engineer Carlo Noé in the 1850s and was based on the assumption that the Po River had enough water to provide a flow of 110 m^3/s to the canal. This forecast was included in the contract signed by the new Italian government with the British investors who would build the

15 E. Lombardini, *Importanza degli studi sulla statistica dei fiumi con cenni intorno a quelli finora intrapresi: memoria dell'ingegnere Elia Lombardini.letta nei giorni 16 juglio e 6 agosto 1846 All'I.R. Instituto Lombardo di Scienze, Lettere ed Arti*, Milano 1854.

16 Ministero dei Lavori Pubblici, Commissione Brioschi, *Idrometria Del Po-1878-79-80 Relazione Provvisoria*, Roma 1898. The present author discusses the history of these measurements in G. Parrinello, *Charting the Flow*.

17 L. Segre, *Agricoltura e costruzione di un sistema idraulico nella pianura piemontese (1800–1880)*, Milano 1983.

canal[18]. However, this assumption proved to be incorrect. As soon as the canal was completed and inaugurated, it became clear that the river did not have enough water to supply a flow of 110 m^3/s, and the infrastructure could not function as foreseen.

This hydrological error had major economic and political consequences. The company had much less water to sell than foreseen, which compromised its profitability. More importantly, as a result of this shortfall, the Italian government refused to pay its promised financial contribution to the British investors, which amounted to no less than 6% interest on the invested capital. This played a significant role in leading the company to bankruptcy, with the Italian state assuming the management of the canal, in contradiction to the *laissez-faire* economic policy of the ruling majority. In order to compensate the lack of water supply, the state had to build a subsidiary intake from another river[19], but even this proved inadequate and the canal continued to have problems of flow rate well into the twentieth century. This failure was still very much in mind when Brioschi conducted his "hydrometric" experiments on the Po in 1878–1880. In the late 1880s, Brioschi's calculations of the Po River's "mean discharge" rate led him to question the feasibility of another major irrigation canal from the Po, further contributing to the demise of the project[20].

3 Water for energy

The issues of predictability and the scale on which it could be most successfully achieved became even more important at the turn of the twentieth century, on the advent and rapid growth of hydroelectricity. Local hydroelectric generation based on dynamos was already relatively common in the 1870s. However, the development of long-distance transmission in the early 1890s opened up a new era. Hydroelectric energy was no longer limited by the "geographic inflexibility" that characterized mechanical hydropower, but could now be consumed far away

18 "Concessione per La Costruzione Di Un Canale d'irrigazione Da Derivarsi Dal Po a Chivasso a Beneficio Dell'agro Vercellese e Casalese, Novarese Lomellino, e Colla Simultanea Cessione Dei Canali Demaniali Derivati Dai Fiumi Dora Baltea e Sesia". Progetto Di Legge Presentato Alla Camera Il 9 Giugno 1862 Dai Ministri d'agricoltura, Industria e Commercio, e Delle Finanze (Pepoli e Sella), in *Atti Del Parlamento Italiano. Sessione Del 1861–62 (VIII Legislatura) Raccolti e Corredati Di Note e Di Documenti Inediti. Documenti – Volume Terzo*, Torino 1878, pp. 1866–1875.

19 E. Benazzo, *Canale sussidiario Cavour. Testo*, Torino 1870.

20 F. Brioschi, *Studio Di Progetti d'irrigazione Autorizzato Dalla Legge 28 Giugno 1885, n. 3901 (Serie 3a). Seduta Del 26 Giugno 1888*, Roma 1888.

from the point of generation. This finally made it possible to exploit remote rivers to power urban infrastructures and factories.

The first long-distance commercial hydroelectric power plant in Italy was inaugurated in Tivoli, near Rome, in 1892, but the hydroelectric energy sector developed mostly within the Po basin. In 1898, the Paderno d'Adda power plant (owned by Società generale di elettricità sistema Edison) started supplying the electric network of Milan. In 1901, an even larger plant on the Ticino River, (owned by the Società Lombarda per la distribuzione di energia elettrica) began supplying the industrial district north-west of the city. This was the beginning of a great hydroelectric "rush", resulting in the construction of dozens of large plants across the Po basin within just a few years[21].

Knowledge of flow rates became vital for the economics and politics of hydroelectric power generation. Hydroelectric power plants required substantial capital investments, backed by a rapidly evolving banking sector. The assessment of foreseeable flow rates conditioned plant size, with immediate implications for investment prospects. The turbines needed to be scaled according to the available flow and any assessment errors could compromise the profitability of an infrastructure over the long term. From the outset, hydroelectric energy also raised hopes of geopolitical independence from imported British coal. In order to fulfill such expectations, the national government needed to assess the potential hydroelectric resources of the country. This required a knowledge of the mean discharge rates of all the country's rivers. Such information was also useful to the authorities for arbitrating between competing developers and managing the hydroelectric rush. This became especially important after World War I, when hydroelectricity was classed a matter of national security, and the development of all available water resources was an imperative written into the new water law[22].

As a result, the mean discharge estimation methods elaborated in the nineteenth century became even more important, as did their limitations. The main problem with the nineteenth-century approach was the spatial scale of observations. Localized intermittent observations and measurements were not reliable enough and did not adequately assess all available water resources. Hydrologists and engineers believed that two interrelated measures were necessary to resolve this problem. First, expand monitoring to cover entire watersheds, rather than

21 M. Semenza, *Les installations hydro-électriques de la Haute-Italie,* in "La Houille Blanche", 5, 1906, 4, pp. 49–54.

22 I. Bonomi, *Decreto luogotenenziale concernente le derivazioni delle acque pubbliche,* Pub. L. No. 1664, in "Gazzetta Ufficiale del Regno d'Italia", 1916; Regio Decreto-Legge n. 2161 che reca disposizioni sulle derivazioni ed utilizzazioni d'acque pubbliche, stabilendo altresì le norme di giurisdizione e di procedura del contenzioso sulle acque pubbliche, Pub. L. No. 2161, 1919.

just single rivers. The notion of the river basin as the relevant scale for understanding river hydrology was already widely established in the nineteenth century. However, hydrologists like Elia Lombardini did not consider it possible to perform measurements and observations on that scale[23]. This changed in the twentieth century. Second, it was necessary to combine flow measurements with precipitation monitoring. The inclusion of precipitation data would offer an improved understanding of the general regime of a river and its tributaries, as well as their spatial and temporal interconnections[24].

This scaling up was an institutional process, with an essential moment being the creation of the Po Hydrographic Service within the Ministry of Public Works. This service was first established in 1912 as an experimental service under the aegis of a royal commission on the hydraulic regime of the Po[25]. During World War I it became a permanent institution and part of a national hydrographic service established within the Ministry of Public Works. The service embodied the new approach: it combined a network of pluviometry observations distributed across the entire river basin, and flow measurement stations. The results of these continuous observations were published monthly in bulletins. The hope was that in time this monitoring would lead to better understanding of the mean discharge of rivers and their seasonal variations[26].

The scaling up was not just horizontal, across the breadth of the watershed, but also vertical. In 1915 the bureau established a special monitoring station on the Lys glacier in the Piedmont Alps[27]. Then in 1925, in partnership with the Italian Glaciological Committee, the bureau produced the first inventory of Italian glaciers, and later the first systematic cartography[28]. Understanding glaciers was

23 E. Lombardini, *Importanza Degli Studi Sulla Statistica Dei Fiumi*, p. 33.

24 L. Romanin-Jacur, *Relazione del Presidente Della Commissione per gli studi Sul Regime Idrografico Del Po a Sua Eccellenza Il Comm. Avv. Ettore Sacchi Ministro Dei Lavori Pubblici*, Reale Commissione per Gli Studi Sul Regime Idrografico Del Po, Prima Pubblicazione dall'ottobre 1910 al dicembre 1913, Ministero dei Lavori Pubblici, Parma 1914.

25 I discuss the creation of this bureau in G. Parrinello, *Charting the Flow*.

26 G. Fantoli, *Relazione Sul Servizio Idrografico in Italia e Sulla Necessità Di Un Rinnovato Ordinamento Di Esso* (Roma, 10 Maggio 1917), in *Istituzione e Funzionamento Del Servizio. Norme, Disposizioni e Notizie Sull'andamento Del Servizio Dal Suo Impianto al 31 Dicembre 1919*, ed. by Ministero dei Lavori Pubblici, Consiglio Superiore delle Acque Pubbliche, Servizio Idrografico, Roma 1920, pp. 7–22.

27 M. Giandotti, *Studi Sul Bacino Glaciale Del Torrente Lys*, in *Seconda Pubblicazione (Dal Dicembre 1913 al Giugno 1917)*, ed. by Ministero dei Lavori Pubblici, Reale Commissione per gli studi sul regime idraulico del Po, Ufficio Idrografico del Po, Parma 1917, pp. 195–210.

28 C. Porro, *Elenco dei Ghiacciai Italiani: monografia statistica del generale Carlo Porro redatta secondo il programma e sotto gli auspici del Comitato Glaciologico Italiano*, Parma 1925; C. Porro, *Atlante Dei Ghiacciai Italiani: Carta Corografica: Scala 1:500.000*, Parma 1927.

essential for understanding and effectively predicting fluctuations in discharge rates of glacier-fed tributaries, and ultimately of the entire Po River system. The bureau, moreover, initiated parallel investigations of underground aquifers. This also involved systematic monitoring and analysis of the relationships between precipitation, surface water, and aquifers[29].

Mario Giandotti, a state engineer and Director of the Po River Hydrographic Bureau from 1914, explicitly presented this work as aiming to convert water into infrastructure. Hydrography to him provided "the technical and scientific basis" for the most complete "utilization of the hydraulic forces" of the nation, as Giandotti himself put it in an important national congress on water power in 1916. Later, Giandotti would also define the work of the Bureau as aiming to determine the "yield" (*rendimento*) of river catchments for hydroelectricity. This quantitative assessment, which was no more than a prediction based on past averages, was essential to avoid inaccurate matching between rivers and hydroelectric power plants, with consequent "disappointments" when flow and profit expectations could not be achieved by actual river hydrology[30].

This new knowledge supported new infrastructural decisions, new scalar matches. Starting in World War I and especially during the Fascist regime, the watershed was subjected to a series of very ambitious infrastructural interventions aimed at coordinating water use to increase availability for economic applications. This involved construction of reservoirs connected to the power plants they supplied, as well as the construction of dams on the outlets of the major Italian lakes, to regulate their outflow and distribute it to interconnected infrastructures. At the outlet of Lake Maggiore, for example, the water of the Ticino River was divided between several pipes and canals in specific volumes, calculated by the public works administration on the basis of mean flow rates during the winter and summer months[31].

This new hydraulic infrastructure was conceived with the aim of scaling up the coordination and regulation of water resources for agriculture and energy generation. As I have written elsewhere, it entailed scaling up "envirotechnical" system building, or in other terms infrastructural interconnection[32]. This scaling up was based upon the new understanding of the scale of water flows right across the watershed: mean precipitation, mean discharge rates, and the relationships between them.

---

29 M. Giandotti, *Ricerche e Studi Sulle Acque Freatiche Della Pianura Padana*, in *Seconda Pubblicazione (Dal Dicembre 1913 al Giugno 1917)*, pp. 165–174.

30 M. Giandotti, *Rendimento dei bacini imbriferi*, in "L'Elettrotecnica", 9, 1922, 25, pp. 553–555.

31 Consorzio del Ticino (Milano), *Regolazione del Lago Maggiore*, Milano 1930.

32 G. Parrinello, *Systems of Power*.

4 Scalar mismatches

The scaling up of the twentieth century was a major success, at least in the medium-term. It provided enhanced predictability and enabled infrastructural consolidation, while also avoiding the repetition of major debacles like the Cavour Canal. There was improved scalar matching between hydrological processes and hydraulic infrastructures, making it possible to achieve large-scale infrastructural integration. Large-scale interconnected hydraulic infrastructures, in turn, powered the massive economic growth of the region during the twentieth century, in both the agricultural and industrial sectors. Some scales, however, remained out of the picture.

One of these was the spatial scale of pollutant circulation. While state hydrologists devoted much time and attention to enhancing their understanding of water availability for hydraulic infrastructure, they ignored issues of water quality. Water quality was obviously an issue already in the nineteenth century, when public policy aimed to limit or completely prevent contamination. Nevertheless, water quality regulations focused almost exclusively on drinking water, with public health officers performing water quality measurements only on a local scale (typically urban) to check suitability for human consumption. Conflicts over water pollution abounded, but remained mostly local, and the approach of industrialists and overseeing authorities relied largely on the long-standing belief in the universal diluting power of watercourses[33].

In the 1960s the alarms became more frequent for the unforeseen (or perhaps disregarded) circulation of toxicants and pollution across the drainage basin. New research initiatives by hydrobiologists at newly established water monitoring institutions began documenting this circulation and its consequences. Research at the Istituto di Idrobiologia on Lake Maggiore by a team that included the Swiss researcher Richard Vollenweider (later one of the architects of the trans-boundary agreement on pollution in the Great Lakes), started to reveal the consequences of excess nutrients like phosphates and nitrogen, the phenomenon known as "eutrophication"[34]. In parallel, hydrobiologist and ecotoxicology pioneer Roberto Marchetti and his team, at a new water research center based in Brugherio, started systematically

---

33 S. Neri Serneri, *Acque per le industrie, acque per le città*, in *Incorporare la natura: storie ambientali del Novecento*, Roma 2005, pp. 163–186.

34 R. Mosello / R. de Bernadi / O. Ravera, *Richard A. Vollenweider: Contribution to Our Knowledge of Italian Lakes*, in "Aquatic Ecosystem Health & Management", 14, 2011, 2, pp. 174–178.

measuring pollution from urban and industrial sources across the river basin, including phenols, surfactants, heavy metals, and radioactivity[35].

The basin-wide circulation of pollutants had a direct impact on hydraulic infrastructures. Water quality was obviously a factor for establishing the usability of irrigation canals, and extremely polluted water would be unsafe for downstream irrigation. One example was the Emiliano Romagnolo Canal, the last major diversion from the Po River before the delta. The construction of the canal started in 1955 with the purpose of supplying irrigation water from the Po to farmers in Emilia-Romagna. The infrastructure was managed by a consortium, a compulsory public association of the landowners who used the canal water. In 1977, the Consorzio per il Canale Emiliano Romagnolo partnered with the newly established Ministry of the Environment to launch a major multidisciplinary study of the entire river basin, which included an investigation of the widespread circulation of pollutants[36].

In 1976, a new national law (known as the "legge Merli") inaugurated an era of tighter water pollution control, imposing stricter limitations and establishing new forms of monitoring for river systems that explicitly included water *quality* and not just quantity[37]. These late twentieth-century regulations have not eliminated pollution altogether, but they have reduced the circulation of pollutants and at least partially cleaned some of the most polluted tributaries of the Po, like the River Lambro[38]. This made an important contribution to maintaining the usability of agricultural hydraulic infrastructures like the Canale Emiliano Romagnolo.

As pollution levels became a policy concern, the planetary processes responsible for local climate remained outside the scope of interest. As hydrologists expanded the spatial scale of their observations regarding the drainage basin, they never questioned one fundamental premise: the stability of the system they were monitoring. The assumption of water system stability was the underlying basis of the quantification methods for annual, seasonal, and monthly discharge. In this approach, hydrologists integrated extreme variations such as floods and droughts by assigning them specific recurrence intervals (for example, a centennial flood), but within a fundamentally stable hydrological regime. They assumed that local observations, even over a short time scale, could provide an accurate picture of

---

35 Consiglio Nazionale delle Ricerche / Istituto di Ricerca sulle Acque, *Indagine sulla qualità delle acque del fiume Po*, Roma 1977.

36 Consorzio per il Canale Emiliano-Romagnolo (ed.), *Po: AcquAgricolturAmbiente. Inquinamento e zone protette*, 12 vols., Bologna 1990, vol. 3.

37 *Norme per La Tutela Delle Acque Dall'inquinamento*, Pub. L. No. 319, 1976.

38 P. Redondi et al., *Milan, sa nappe et le Lambro. La quantité au détriment de la qualité*, in C. Carré / L. Lestel, *Les rivières urbaines et leur pollution* (eds.), Versailles 2017, pp. 123–172.

the *permanent* state of a river's hydrology, and thus provide a reliable basis for future predictions. At the turn of the 1980s this approach was still central in official institutional analyses, like the one authored by Lino Cati, then director of the Po River Hydrographic Bureau[39].

Links between the river system and large-scale climatic processes were well known to researchers during much of the twentieth century. Extreme droughts, like the one that affected energy production in 1921–22, provided early opportunities to reflect on the role of planetary processes in the Po River system's hydrology and discharge rate. Writing in the journal of hydroelectric producers in 1922, meteorologist and member of the National Hydrographic Service, Filippo Eredia, hypothesized that droughts were "intimately linked to atmospheric circulation" and that only global observations could "improve [. . .] drought forecasting" in the Po basin[40].

Historical variations in climate were also known to some scientists. Glaciological studies during much of the twentieth century documented significant variations in Alpine glaciers and investigated correlations with climatic variations[41]. In the 1980s this sometimes included historical variations associated with the Little Ice Age. Until the mid-1980s, however, Italian glaciologists interpreted contemporary variations in terms of oscillations between periods of advance and periods of retreat, not as signs of structural change. Only at the turn of the 1990s did glaciologists start to interpret contemporary variations as distinct indicators of larger structural processes of climatic change worldwide, and to explicitly consider the implications for water availability for energy and agriculture[42].

The exclusion of planetary processes and long-term climatic variations from twentieth-century hydrological research generated two scalar mismatches. A spatial mismatch between water as infrastructure on river basin scale, and global climate. And a temporal mismatch resulting from the exclusion of the longer time scale in calculations of mean discharge and hydrological cycles. The understanding of the hydrology of the basin was conditioned by these spatial and temporal mismatches. They underlay the faulty belief of a stable system.

These mismatches have major political and economic consequences for the present and future of the region. At the turn of the twenty-first century, it has become clear that changing global climate is modifying water availability in the Po

39 L. Cati, *Idrografia e Idrologia Del Po*, Roma 1981.

40 F. Eredia, *La siccità del 1921 (Milano, 1–8 Ottobre 1922)*, in "L'Elettrotecnica", 9, 1922, 32, p. 748.

41 S. Belloni, *Oscillazioni Frontali Dei Ghiacciai Italiani e Clima: Un Sessantennio Di Ricerche*, in "Geografia Fisica e Dinamica Quaternaria", 15, 1992, 1/2, pp. 43–57.

42 A. Biancotti, *Introduzione al Convegno – Introductive Remarks*, in "Geografia Fisica e Dinamica Quaternaria", 15, 1992, 1/2, pp. 7–10.

water basin, rendering the notion itself of "mean discharge" increasingly problematic[43]. However, the hydraulic infrastructures of the basin, and the dependent economic and social configurations, were sized according to such notion, which in turn was based on the wrong scale. The result is an inability to fulfill its promises in the new century. Fast-changing and increasingly unpredictable hydrological processes cannot satisfy the needs and expectations of water as infrastructure. The entire infrastructural coordination system needs to be rethought and adjusted to the new reality, reappraising water as infrastructure in a context of increased uncertainty.

5 Conclusions

Twenty-first-century droughts are emblematic of the contradictions outlined above. These issues are not unique to the Po watershed, or even to water as infrastructure. Much of the environmental history of infrastructure can be interpreted as a "history of scaling"[44]. Environmental processes are multi-scalar, and so are infrastructures, regardless of whether we understand the latter as just physical hardware, or also include organizational networks. Matching these scales requires considerable effort and is an essential part of the work required in order for "nature [to] *become* infrastructure"[45]. Scale is sometimes implicit in envirotechnical scholarship, but is rarely addressed explicitly. Scale facilitates analysis of the way environmental systems and infrastructures can be coupled (made to match), which has been a fundamental challenge for environmental management and infrastructures through history. As demonstrated with the example of the Po water basin, to a large extent this is achieved through production of knowledge. This again demonstrates the importance of environmental knowledge for environmental technology, and underlines its functional role in the calibration of scalar matches.

In the case of the Po watershed, producing knowledge is essential for establishing predictability, which is the basis for modern hydraulic infrastructure. Predictability is what transforms water into infrastructure, and is essential for the existence and operation of any water-based envirotechnical systems. Predicting discharge rates was necessary for the functioning of irrigation canals in the nineteenth century and hydroelectric power plants in the twentieth century. Early attempts at predicting

43 S. Pecora (Arpa Emilia-Romagna, Servizio IdroMeteoClima), *L'andamento stagionale climatico del bacino del fiume Po. L'allarme siccità 2012 a confronto con le siccità del 2003 e 2006–07*, Fondazione EnI Enrico Mattei, Venezia, 26 Settembre 2012.
44 D.R. Coen, *Climate in Motion*, p. 16.
45 A. Carse, *Nature as Infrastructure*, p. 540.

discharge based on historic values were performed on the scale of individual watercourses for the purpose of developing new irrigation canals. In the twentieth century, hydrologists and engineers were faced with new demands from hydropower producers, and they came to the conclusion that occasional observations on individual watercourses were inadequate for reliable predictions. They called for scaled up observations on entire water basins, including rain, snow, glaciers, and underground aquifers. Scaling up to entire water basins improved the predictive capacity of water knowledge, enhancing the performance of water as infrastructure in both agriculture and energy production. Knowledge production, in other words, was a technology of scaling.

Scale also teaches something about the historical limits of this project. The technology of scaling that hydrologists and engineers developed to turn water into infrastructure excluded pollution, with direct consequences for the operability of the infrastructure itself. Perhaps even more critically, predictability was based on the assumption of a stable nature and the temporal scale of climatic and hydrological variations was excluded. This assumption has been overturned by climate change and there is growing evidence that the regularities mapped out in hydrological research are disappearing. The issue today is whether the water infrastructure inherited from previous centuries can deal with the structural mismatch generated by the climate breakdown, and at what economic and political cost. More broadly, the issue for historians of environment and infrastructure is not only to consider how the scales of natural processes and infrastructures can be made to match each other. It is also (and perhaps above all) to grapple with the reality that they can never really be perfectly matched, and confront the historical implications of this fact.

Frédéric Graber

The Ideal Public for Infrastructures

Towards a Long-Term History of the Environment-Infrastructure-Participation Nexus

1 Introduction

Infrastructure is a recent and rather blurry concept[1]. It is possible to distinguish at very least between a broad and a narrow definition. In the broad sense, infrastructures include all material and social prerequisites for human action, which embraces almost everything. However, the editors of this publication were clearly referring to infrastructures in a more restricted sense, as technological systems. Dirk van Laak, one of the major historians studying infrastructures, defines them as networks offering the material basis for circulations of all kinds, which typically means transport, communication, supply, and sanitation[2].

As an actor's category, infrastructure is obviously recent, becoming particularly relevant only in the second half of the twentieth century. Nevertheless, this does not exclude it as a useful component for analysis of earlier periods. Applying the concept of infrastructure to earlier periods is interesting because it leads into larger issues like state building, mass society, and liberalism. Dirk van Laak, for instance, notes that while there are some notable "forerunners", like the Romans with their aqueducts and roads, they nevertheless lacked a certain typically modern aspect of infrastructures, which is the systematic ambition to network space and society together. Van Laak sees this as characteristic of modern societies, starting somewhere in the eighteenth century and crucially linked to state building, territorial ambitions, and development, as well as mass society and liberalism[3].

If circulation is central to infrastructures, then the question arises, circulation of whom? Van Laak argues quite convincingly that circulation was never intended for everybody, since infrastructures always embody restrictions and inequalities, typically fares to be paid beyond the means of some citizens. In principle however, circulation is open to all, without a defined category of users. "Users" might not

1 D. van Laak, *Der Begriff 'Infrastruktur' und was er vor seiner Erfindung besagte*, in "Archiv für Begriffsgeschichte", 41, 1999, pp. 280–299.

2 D. van Laak, *Alles im Fluss. Die Lebensadern unserer Gesellschaft. Geschichte und Zukunft der Infrastruktur*, Frankfurt a.M. 2018. D. van Laak, *Infrastrukturen*, in "Docupedia-Zeitgeschichte", http://docupedia.de/zg/Laak_infrastrukturen_v1_de_2020, last accessed August 20, 2021.

3 *Ibid.*

https://doi.org/10.1515/9783111112756-007

always be the most appropriate term, and sometimes they could be better defined as “consumers” or “citizens”. In any case, it can be generally agreed that infrastructures usually have a collective dimension, directed towards the public for the use and benefit of all, even if in practice they are typically unequally distributed[4]. This collective dimension clearly emerges in the terminology used to describe infrastructures in the eighteenth and nineteenth centuries as “public works”, “public utilities”, etc. These are the areas of interest that will be addressed here.

The public is important for infrastructures, at least in symbolic and rhetorical terms. Historians have considered the issue of the public of infrastructures by conceiving of them as either decision-makers or users[5]. Both these dimensions are important, but this paper will demonstrate an alternative approach to the issue. Every infrastructure-project has to address a public, which is an abstraction, an indefinite number of unknown people, which at the same time could become a very concrete number of people concerned about the project. This includes not only users and decision-makers, but also owners, taxpayers, competitors, and ordinary citizens, with a wide variety of interests[6]. The public is a source of great uncertainty because people can emerge at various stages of a project, raising concerns and significantly disturbing its development. The present study aims to investigate the domestication of the public in the context of infrastructure projects, which has a long history in France. Participatory procedures have been developed there, especially since the eighteenth century, with the specific purpose of delineating, aligning, controlling, and instrumentalizing the public. First, a research project is presented. This has been ongoing for a number of years and regards public participation in projects in France since the eighteenth century. This is followed by an attempt to establish what is specific to a more recent period, starting in the late 1960s and 1970s, with the emergence of environmental issues as a new perspective and object of concern.

4 *Ibid.*

5 Users especially have got important attention in the history of technology since the publication of N. Oudshoorn / T. Pinch, *How Users Matter. The Co-Construction of Users and Technologies*, Cambridge MA / London 2003.

6 For a recent and refreshing approach to publics, see especially M. Warner, *Publics and Counterpublics*, in “Public Culture”, 14, 2002, 1, pp. 49–90.

2 Participation as a legal and technocratic justification for infrastructures

The author's research is centered on administrative inquiries that in the early nineteenth century came to be known as *enquête publique*, which is the French translation of the English term "public inquiry", although there are important differences between the two[7]. These administrative procedures went under various names, or none at all, but they all functioned in the same way. They appealed to an indefinite public to react to a project, opening a register in the city halls or in the prefectures, in which everybody could express their opinion, of whatever nature. After a specified time, a commissioner was appointed to assess the importance of the various opinions, which in most cases he declared to be irrelevant. Then the inquiry was closed, the project was authorized, and no further form of opposition was considered admissible[8]. Right from the start, *enquêtes publiques* were a very disappointing form of public participation, but nevertheless survived up to the present, because they were and remain an essential mechanism for authorizing infrastructural developments.

Enquêtes publiques came to be very important because they provided the legal justification for project implementation: each *enquête* proved the *utilité publique* of a project, literally its "public usefulness". The notion of *utilité publique* conveys a general sense of common good, common welfare, but also a more restrictive legal sense of superior right, justifying the infringement of lesser rights. The notion goes back to the ancien régime, when it was widely applied[9]. In ancien régime France, when a person or a group had any form of project, they first had to seek authorization. This usually took the form of a private law assigning them specific rights and privileges. Since these rights could contradict general laws and other private rights, private

---

7 The expression *enquête publique* directly refers to its English counterpart "public inquiry", though this reference is largely a misinterpretation. The notion was introduced in France in the 1820s by liberal activists, who promoted the British model as an alternative to the French procedures. But what they actually had in mind were not British public inquiries but private bill inquiries, which were held in parliamentary committees before large projects were authorized. Though these French promoters definitely referred to a parliamentary model, *enquête publique* quickly became associated with French administrative preliminary inquiries. On private bill inquiries in Britain, see O.C. Williams, *The Historical Development of the Private Bill Procedure and Standing Orders in the House of Commons*, London 1948.

8 F. Graber, *Enquêtes publiques, 1820–1830. Définir l'utilité publique pour justifier le sacrifice dans un monde de projets*, in "Revue d'histoire moderne et contemporaine", 63, 2016, 3, pp. 31–63.

9 F. Graber, *Entre commodité et consentement. Des enquêtes publiques au 18e siècle*, in "Participations. Revue de sciences sociales sur la démocratie et la citoyenneté", 2, 2012, 3, pp. 93–117.

laws were subjected to a series of inquiries, conducted by the public prosecutor in the higher courts, typically the Parlement de Paris[10].

The initial inquiry was judicial and called the *de commodo et incommodo* procedure. It aimed to establish whether the project was of public usefulness, a necessary condition before the promoters could be assigned new rights, which usually involved limiting the rights of others. The logic behind *utilité publique* was clearly monarchical: the monarchy could override some rights and assign specific rights to others because it professed perfect knowledge of the project and its possible consequences, standing above all interests and actors. Thanks to this abstract higher position it was able to assess the balance of advantages and disadvantages, take all factors into account, and decide whether the public advantage outweighed the sacrifice it would require from others. The *utilité publique* was established within a legal framework and according to the procedures of traditional legal inquiries: a number of witnesses were summoned to court to relate what they knew about the project, in order to establish its true legal status. The striking observation about these witnesses is that, although they were heard separately and spoke directly without being questioned by the judge, they usually presented a unanimous position regarding the project[11]. In the legal order of the ancien régime, the number of witnesses did not really matter, but their unanimity was central for establishing legal truth, and this was obviously achieved by carefully selecting the witnesses. There is evidence that in some cases the promoters suggested the names of potential witnesses[12]. However, witnesses were not always in favor of projects. In some cases, the public prosecutor selected witnesses who all declared a project to be of no public usefulness[13]. The public prosecutor thus played a central role in this procedure and his personal opinion on a project could easily determine the outcome of an inquiry.

---

10 In the case of the Parlement de Paris the attorney general in the eighteenth century was Guillaume François Joly de Fleury (1705 to 1746), followed by his son Guillaume François Louis (1746 to 1787). Their *Conclusions* are a central historical source for investigating these early inquiries. Bibliothèque Nationale de France (BNF), Paris, *Collection Joly de Fleury*.

11 There are very few exceptions, which usually reveal an incorrect appraisal of the position of witnesses by the prosecutor. Witnesses were usually chosen with no direct connection to the project, but this was not always easy to establish. Not reaching unanimity was considered a legal problem and usually resulted in the inquiry being held again.

12 See, for instance, a sale by a religious institution. BNF, Paris, *Collection Joly de Fleury*, vol. 610, fol. 269, "Liste des témoins que les curé et marguilliers de Saint-Nicolas du Chardonnet proposent de faire entendre dans l'information sur l'acquisition d'une maison pour servir de presbytère", 1763.

13 See, for instance, a land reclamation project in Laon. BNF, Paris, *Collection Joly de Fleury*, vol. 719, fol. 26, "Information de commodo et incommodo pour le dessèchement des marais de Laon", 1724. All witnesses disapproved the project.

While the number of participants was not important for these *de commodo* inquiries, in the higher courts public prosecutors made a concerted effort to comprehend the reactions of potentially interested citizens, especially since the promoters tended to embellish their plans without considering the full range of consequences that others might have to bear. They thus completed their examination with two further inquiries. The first was usually called *avis,* and involved asking various experts to evaluate the economic, legal, and technical impacts of the project. The second inquiry directly investigated the reactions of potentially impacted citizens. This inquiry was significantly termed *consentement,* or "consent", even though the consulted citizens often rejected projects[14]. The prosecutor limited the inquiry to selected groups and individuals considered at particular risk of impact from the project. Unlike the *de commodo* inquiries, the purpose was not to establish legal truth, but to ensure no important matters had been overlooked, while also surveying potential opponents as regards their intentions and legal means.

The ancien régime procedure therefore distinguished between a judicial formality, proving the *utilité publique* of a project, relying on a limited number of selected and obliging witnesses, and a larger consulting procedure, not open to all, but allowing many potential opponents to voice their opposition. These procedures ceased to exist with the French Revolution, for two main reasons. Firstly, privileges and private laws disappeared or became marginal; and secondly, legal courts could no longer rule on future matters to authorize or prohibit projects. This instead became the prerogative of the new sphere of administrative law, much of which was created by the administration itself in the nineteenth century.

The need for a mechanism for controlling and authorizing projects persisted, especially for the contested economic ventures that postrevolutionary regimes were actively encouraging[15]. In effect, authorization embraces both regulation and promotion, and after the Revolution new administrative procedures were introduced on a piecemeal basis in order to authorize projects, while also providing some participatory mechanisms. A few examples include: the act of 1791 for mining projects; that of 1796 for mills, dams, factories, and any form of fluvial transformation; that of 1801 for municipal projects of various kinds; that of 1807 for land reclamation projects; that of 1810 for potentially polluting industrial plants;

---

14 See, for instance, the case of the Givors canal. Archives départementales du Rhône, BP 3604, "Arrêt du conseil du roi et lettres patentes sur icelui, qui permettent au sieur Zacharie de faire construire un canal et lui en accordent la jouissance pendant 40 années", 28 October 1760 and 6 September 1762. Along the 12-kilometer route of the canal, 10 village communities were asked to give their consent. Only two actually consented, the other 10 refused.

15 T. Le Roux, *Le Laboratoire des pollutions industrielles. Paris, 1770–1830,* Paris 2011. J.-B. Fressoz, *L'Apocalypse joyeuse. Une histoire du risque technologique,* Paris 2012.

that of 1829 for public works projects; and that of 1833 for all projects involving expropriations.

Initially, some of these procedures operated in a manner similar to ancien régime inquiries. They did not extend a general summons but selected a few witnesses, usually neighbors or owners, sometimes inviting them to visit the site where the project was supposed to be implemented. However, after the 1820s all these procedures started to converge towards a common model, which began to be referred to as *enquête publique*. The convergence was a response to numerous problems within the early inquiries, especially as regards the selection of witnesses. Local administrations were always suspected of choosing compliant individuals to establish apparent consent while muting opponents. In the increasingly liberal context after 1815, the selection of witnesses to produce explicit consent was declining in legitimacy. A solution to the problem was provided in the form of administrative posters, which gradually became central tools for these inquiries. These made it possible to summon everyone affected by a project to speak out, without defining in advance who they were. The use of posters to announce inquiries also enabled the administrations to claim that all those who did not participate and remained silent were effectively consenting. In most cases this meant nearly everybody, compared to the small number who dared or bothered to participate[16].

The nineteenth-century *enquêtes publiques* therefore differed significantly from ancien régime inquiries. *Enquêtes publiques* no longer distinguished between a wider consulting procedure and a narrow legal procedure proving the *utilité publique* of a project. *Enquêtes publiques* still aimed at proving the *utilité publique*, with exactly the same logic, an abstract point of view standing above all interests and rights, and justifying a redistribution of rights and interests in the name of public benefit. However, nineteenth-century *enquêtes publiques* established *utilité publique* in a new way, by asking for the consent of everyone, and claiming that silence implied implicit consent.

The widening of participation also changed its significance. Participation was no longer simply a legal issue, and was not limited to assessing the rights and potential damage to those impacted by the project. By calling everybody, the administration increasingly emphasized that directly impacted citizens where not necessarily the best participants, because they were often blinded by their private interests. The administration also suggested that widening participation might generate productive

16 On this convergence of the various inquiry procedures and the rise of the poster as a central tool, see F. Graber, *Une histoire de l'affichage administratif au 19e siècle*, Habilitation à diriger les recherches, SciencesPo, Paris 2020, chapter 10: "Les projets et les voisins. Manifester l'intérêt général par l'enquête publique".

feedback, allowing people with no direct interests to contribute towards projects, providing a form of control and even a counterbalance to the administration itself if the latter had failed to identify a project's defects. Participation thus extended beyond legal implications, increasingly assuming a more liberal-technocratic significance, with the ideal participants being experts who would compare arguments to improve projects, even though in reality such experts seldom appeared spontaneously in the *enquêtes publiques*[17]. Through the *enquêtes publiques* the French administration invented a radically new form of widespread participation open to everybody, even foreigners and women, regardless of social and economic status. The administration could legitimately profess to have called everybody, which was central to its claim of allowing the public to speak, to express the will of an abstract totality of "everyone", even if this totality was somewhat incongruous since in most cases the public remained completely silent.

However, this radical opening towards participation bore a potential political weight, identifying this totality of everybody as "the people". In the early decades of the nineteenth century the administration remained very cautious about countering this interpretation, and *enquêtes publiques* were interpreted as purely administrative with no political significance whatsoever. This was coherent with the dominant political theories of the early nineteenth century. The doctrinaire movement, for example, sustained that while only very few people should have political rights, no form of government could persist in the long term if it did not find some connections with the masses and establish a sense of what is desirable or acceptable in society. *Enquêtes publiques* were typically seen as one of various administrative devices that allowed decision-makers to maintain contact with citizens[18].

3 Participation as democratic justification for infrastructures

Enquêtes publiques did not significantly change from the 1830s onwards, remaining one of the main tools for justifying and authorizing industrial and infrastructural projects through the nineteenth and twentieth centuries. *Enquêtes publiques* proliferated increasingly as development progressed, with unchanging legal and technocratic implications[19]. On the one hand, an inquiry secured the rights of project

---

17 F. Graber, *Enquêtes publiques, 1820–1830.*
18 *Ibid*, p. 39.
19 F. Graber, *Inutilité publique. Histoire d'une culture politique française,* Paris 2022.

promoters against claims from injured parties, establishing the *utilité publique* of a project as a superior right. In the case of infrastructure projects, the assignation of *utilité publique* was almost tautological. On the other hand, an inquiry supposedly proved the quality of the project, since all potential arguments against it had been heard and resolved. During the nineteenth and most of the twentieth century this participatory procedure never carried significant political weight.

Enquêtes publiques were nearly always disappointing, which largely explains why many of the inquiries were unattended. However, from the 1960s onwards they were increasingly criticized, especially by emerging movements concerned with protecting nature and cultural heritage. These movements called for a more active role of civil society in decision-making in substantial projects. They rejected *enquêtes publiques* as a pure formality, in which arguments and opinions were simply collected in order to liquidate them[20]. They called for reforms so that projects could be openly discussed at an early stage, taking environmental concerns into account and enabling adequate adjustments to reduce impact. These claims progressively entered the political agenda in the 1970s and even gained supporters within the state administration[21].

This rapid development was a response to changing expectations within French society as well as international pressure. In 1970 the United States adopted the NEPA, the *National Environmental Policy Act*, which introduced the principle of environmental impact assessments as a preliminary obligation before large scale projects potentially affecting the environment could be authorized[22]. The NEPA procedure included forms of public participation, especially regarding the issues that needed to be considered in the assessment. Similar procedures rapidly spread all over the world as a result of active promotion by international organizations. The OECD was among the main protagonists of this international movement in the 1970s and 1980s, promoting impact assessment as a model linking participation and the environment[23]. The issue was discussed on a European level after 1973 with environmental regulations perceived as both inevitable and potentially compromising

20 See for instance SEPANSO, *Une parodie de démocratie*, in “La Gueule Ouverte. Le journal qui annonce la fin du monde”, 5, 1973, p. 27. Founded in 1969 in the south-west of France, SEPANSO is one of many NGOs emerging in this period that denounced *enquêtes publiques* as a parody of democracy.

21 One typical figure was René Bourny, a French state engineer who promoted several reforms in the late 1970s and 1980s, and later founded the *Compagnie nationale des commissaires enquêteurs*, a major professional organization for *enquêtes publiques* commissioners.

22 L.G. Llewellyn / C. Peiser, *NEPA and the Environmental Movement. A Brief History*, US National Bureau of Standards, Final Report, Washington 1973, https://nvlpubs.nist.gov/nistpubs/Legacy/IR/nbsir73-218.pdf, last accessed September 28, 2021.

23 N. Baya-Laffite, *Études d’impact environnemental (global, fin 20e siècle)*, in F. Graber / M. Giraudeau (eds.), *Les projets. Une histoire politique (16e–21e siècles)*, Paris 2018, pp. 223–234.

economic competitiveness, since assessment and public participation might be more expensive and time consuming in some countries rather than in others. It was thought that member states needed to try and harmonize their environmental legislation in line with preliminary procedures. The European commission ran several studies investigating how impact assessments could be introduced across Europe without disrupting existing national participation procedures[24]. However, the fear of raising costs hindered adoption of European-wide measures until 1985[25]. Several countries therefore decided to introduce environmental impact assessments on their own. France, for example, introduced a very mild version of impact assessments in its 1976 nature protection law[26].

Enquêtes publiques posed a question in the 1970s for politicians and administrators alike: could this very old procedure, almost unchanged since the nineteenth century and cherished by planners and investors, still count as participation in relation to growing demands by environmental movements and emerging international standards? The answer was essentially negative, leading to various attempts to reform the procedure from the late 1970s to the 1990s. Despite these reforms, the procedure hardly changed, and observing how the inquiries were conducted in practice suggests that *enquêtes publiques* were instead considered perfectly adequate!

A major attempt at reforming the *enquêtes publiques* occurred in 1983 with the so-called "Bouchardeau Law", officially titled *Loi sur la démocratisation des enquêtes publiques*, announcing a democratization of these inquiries[27]. An examination of the text of the law, the implementing decrees later adopted by the government, and the practice of these inquiries in the 1980s, reveal no major changes. The only novelty was the possibility of organizing a meeting with the public, but such meetings had to be authorized by the prefect and seldom took place. Meetings also had no binding outcomes, and did not significantly affect an inquiry, calling into question the reference to democratization in the title.

---

24 Historical Archives of the European Commission, Brussels, ENV/785/78-EN; C.W.A. Timmermans, *Citizen Participation in Decisions of Public Authorities within the Member States of the European Community*, 1979.

25 *Council Directive 85/337/EEC of 27 June 1985 on the Assessment of the effects of certain public and private projects on the environment*: https://eur-lex.europa.eu/legal-content/EN/TXT/?uri=CELEX%3A31985L0337, last accessed September 29, 2021.

26 Most environmental movements were very disappointed by the 1976 law. See for instance, C. Garnier, *Etudes d'impact: la grande illusion?*, in "Aménagement et Nature", 1979, 55, pp. 12–15. Christian Garnier was one of the leaders of the *Fédération Française des Sociétés de Protection de la Nature* at the time.

27 See the 1983 issue of the "Amenagement et nature", 71, entirely devoted to this law.

The problem emerges clearly in the parliamentary debates of 1983, when the proponents of the law obviously had great ambitions for democratization. Huguette Bouchardeau, the secretary for the environment, declared that "the environment is a privileged ground for democracy, and democracy itself a condition for the preservation of the environment"[28]. This was a typical 1980s assertion that people should be allowed to participate in decision-making in order to avoid them deviating towards either resignation or revolt. However, participation could not be allowed to impede infrastructural projects, which were still considered central to the economic development of the country. Public participation did not imply allowing them to decide. They could offer constructive contributions, monitor the process, and suggest improvements, but democracy still required that democratically elected authorities made the final decision themselves so that they could be held responsible for their choices[29].

In 1983 participation was not yet linked to the idea of a crisis of representative democracy, as would be the case later in the 1990s[30], but it had obviously become necessary to redefine the *enquêtes publiques* with political and democratic significance. What was new after 1983 was not the inquiry itself, but instead that it could be presented as democratic. This did not affect the other aspects: *enquêtes publiques* were still held firstly for legal reasons, and secondly, in a liberal-technocratic spirit, in order to improve projects by incorporating constructive criticism, as was the case since the early nineteenth century. The difference was that it could now be presented as a democratic tool.

4 Conclusion

This paper includes two narratives. One is about industrial and infrastructural projects and how participation was used to justify them from the early nineteenth century onwards. The other deals with the global rise in participatory procedures from the 1970s onwards, directly linked to the emergence of environmental issues as political and social concerns. The environment and public participation became

28 Assemblée nationale, *Comptes-rendus des débats de la 7e législature*, 20 avril 1983, Paris 1983, pp. 420–432, here p. 423.
29 Robert de Caumont, the reporter of the text, made this point quite clearly. *Ibid.*, p. 424.
30 On the emergence of a "participatory imperative" in the 1990s, linked to a discourse on the crisis of representation, see L. Blondiaux, *Le nouvel esprit de la démocratie. Actualité de la démocratie participative*, Paris 2008 and M.-H. Bacqué / Y. Sintomer, *La démocratie participative. Histoire et généalogie*, Paris 2011.

so closely intertwined after the 1970s that addressing one inevitably implied the other. By the 1990s every important actor on a global scale had become green and participatory, usually at the same time[31]. The link between the two terms often involved infrastructures, or rather infrastructural projects. A significant part of environmental regulations after the 1970s did not directly regard the environment, but instead how to regulate economic projects to render them less harmful to the environment, without hindering the projects themselves, since economic development remained a central priority.

There has been a close relationship between environment and infrastructure in the last fifty years or so, when these terms have had relatively clear and consistent definitions. However, this relationship actually involves three terms, with infrastructures acting as an operator: there is environment and participation because there are infrastructures. Infrastructures are the time and place where participation and environment meet, and to some extent, where they come into existence.

What this paper aims to establish is that these three terms, though previously less crucial than in more recent times, have nevertheless been intertwined for as long as what might be called the Industrial Revolution. Forms of participation have long been exploited to justify industrial and infrastructural projects impacting the environment.

Most of the nineteenth-century administrative procedures mentioned in this paper were linked with what today would be called environmental issues. Many of the significant projects involved the exploitation of natural resources, like mining, land reclamation, fluvial engineering, etc. Though these activities were treated separately under specific legislation, in terms of participation they were conceived similarly and addressed shared problems: projects affecting the rights and interests of injured parties, projects which might have unintended consequences and thus needed to be checked and improved. The continuity with recent decades is striking with very similar issues arising today. The emergence of the environment as a concept in the 1960s and 1970s is not just a consequence of a change in perception, of seeing development, greater resource consumption, and increased transport as coming at the price of sacrifice and degradation, which, albeit not new, was becoming more and more unacceptable[32]. Environment as a term may also have been coined to identify an old and familiar problem with industrial and infrastructural projects: how to authorize them?

---

31 D. Pestre, *Les entreprises globales face à l'environnement, 1988–1992. Engagements volontaires, management vert et labels*, in "Le Mouvement Social", 2, 2020, 271, pp. 83–104.

32 On the long-term history of opposition to development see, J.-B. Fressoz, *L'Apocalypse joyeuse*, and C. Pessis / S. Topçu / C. Bonneuil (eds.), *Une autre histoire des "Trentes glorieuses". Modernisation, contestation et pollution dans la France d'après-guerre*, Paris 2013.

Simone M. Müller

Dirty New Natures

Infrastructures and the Global Waste Economy

1 Introduction

The ash would no doubt bring progress to the village of Puerto Castilla, or so thought Edgardo A. Pascall, proprietor of Almacenadora Amodami, a one-size-fits-all construction and import company from San Pedro Sula, Honduras' commercial capital and second largest city. It would revive the small Honduran port city on the Caribbean Sea, where Christopher Columbus allegedly first set foot on the Central American mainland, and which had been a key port for the US American United Fruit Company until early in the twentieth century. In a letter to the Honduran National Port Authority, Pascall detailed the many benefits of importing up to 200,000 tons of incinerator ash from Philadelphia for this coastal region, which had been disconnected from larger national and international trade and travel networks for much of the twentieth century. By using the ash as landfill for the swamp and mangrove area around the port of Puerto Castilla, they could reclaim wetlands for road construction, eventually reaching isolated communities further inland. According to Pascall, the project would create jobs, revenues, and eradicate malaria. Although he did mention the potential contamination of the incinerator ash with heavy metals and trace chemicals, the Honduran businessman from San Pedro Sula almost entirely disregarded the potential environmental and health implications that might derive from using such materials for land reclamation in a wetland area. Instead, he expressed his sincere belief that his country would greatly "benefit from this project because [the] material afford[ed them] a good opportunity for stabilizing areas that currently present hostile environments"[1].

Using potentially hazardous waste to transform "hostile environments" into what would implicitly become "civilized" and manufactured landscapes, according to a Western model of progress, was a defining feature of the global waste economy and the unequal international trade of hazardous waste materials that had developed

1 Translation of a letter from Edgardo A. Pascall to Jorge E. Cramiotis, General Manager, National Port Authority (Honduras), March 1987, Jim Vallette Private Archive.

Note: Research for this essay has been made possible through funding from the Germany Research Foundation (DFG).

https://doi.org/10.1515/9783111112756-008

since the 1970s. The 1987 Honduran waste import scheme for incinerator ash from Philadelphia exemplifies hundreds of similar cases, when potentially hazardous waste from industrial countries like the United States was sent to what was then framed as "the developing world". The story of US waste in Honduras as described in this chapter, illustrates how the creation of infrastructures, and the conception of nature as being hostile to progress, became oddly intertwined with the globalization of hazardous waste, to create what the author calls "dirty new natures".

"Dirty new natures" are emblematic both of the widening gap since the advent of modern environmentalism between greening industrial countries in the Global North and economically struggling countries of the Global South, and of the asynchronous nature of global environmental protection processes. They became fundamental components of an unequal trading system that allowed people in the Global North to safeguard their own health and environment at the expense of others far away. The same system forced people in the Global South to decide whether they would rather suffer from hunger and unemployment, or accept the detrimental effects of living alongside a hazardous-waste dump[2]. In that sense, "dirty new natures" equally embodied a promise and a threat.

Infrastructures, here represented by roads and port facilities, together with human-made commercial lands that could be used to erect further transport and business facilities, played a key role in the production of "dirty new natures" all across the Global South. As the case of Puerto Castilla illustrates, infrastructures made those (hazardous) import schemes attractive for actors in Honduras despite their known trade-offs. The building, repair, or improvement of roads, railways, or port facilities became almost inseparably connected to trajectories of an American model of economic growth and prosperity in which 'unused' and even 'dangerous' wastelands, like the mosquito-prone mangrove wetlands surrounding Puerto Castilla, could be transformed into productive sites for commerce[3]. The wetlands, in turn, were reduced to a mere (re)source for local development to achieve (re)connection into global networks. This particular narrative of infrastructure and nature

2 S. Lessenich, *Living Well at Others' Expense: The Hidden Costs of Western Prosperity*, Cambridge 2019; J.W. Moore, *Capitalism in the Web of Life: Ecology and the Accumulation of Capital*, London / New York 2015.

3 They thus bought into a narrative of infrastructures, such as communication (telegraphy) and transport (railways, steam- and containerships) as gateways to globalization, which first appeared in the nineteenth century, see S. Müller, *Wiring the World. The Social and Cultural Creation of Global Telegraph Networks*, New York 2016; S.M. Müller / H.J.S. Tworek, *The Telegraphy and the Bank. On the Interdependence of Global Communications and Capitalism, 1866–1914*, in "Journal of Global History", 10, 2015, 2, pp. 259–283. W. Schievelbusch, *The Railway Journey. The Industrialization of Space and Time in the 19th Century*, Leamington Spa 1986; M. Levinson, *The Box. How the Shipping Container Made the World Smaller and the World Economy Bigger*, Oxford 2008.

being mutually exclusive along Honduras' path to progress appeared to overwrite any concerns for potential damage to the local environment and ultimately human health at remote and often disconnected places like Puerto Castilla. However, it happened at a time when the American model for this form of progress had come under scrutiny in the United States and in other parts of the industrialized world, creating an asynchronous relationship between importing and exporting nations.

The observations in *Dirty New Natures: Infrastructures and the Global Waste Economy* draw inspiration from the work of cultural anthropologists Ashley Carse and Kegg Hetherington (and others), as set out in *Infrastructure, Environment, and Life in the Anthropocene*[4]. Both scholars emphasize how boundaries and gaps, like those between environment and infrastructure, are conceptual spaces and cultural artifacts that are highly charged with meaning and value. Focusing on the proposed import of up to 200,000 tons of incinerator ash from Philadelphia arriving in Puerto Castilla, the chapter teases out the competing narratives that populate this conceptual space between mangrove forests, incinerator ash, and construction space. This includes negotiations of environmental protection vs. economic development, or the value and meaning of mangrove forests as such.

The title of this chapter, *Dirty New Natures*, is an acknowledgement of the work of scholars in the fields of environmental history and the history of science and technology, that seek to build bridges between their respective fields in their analysis of "new natures" created at the crossing of technology and the environment[5]. While this chapter interprets infrastructures on wetlands as envirotechnical systems, its focus is primarily on the socio-cultural spaces emerging within such a system. This perspective highlights the power dynamics in play between Global North and South, but also between the Honduran center and periphery. It observes how asynchronous narratives and approaches to environmental protection and economic progress, combined with legacies of colonial exploitation, determined the waste transfer deal[6].

The chapter covers the time period from the 1920s and the presence of the US company United Fruit Inc. at Puerto Castilla, until the 1980s and the emergence of the US waste traders. It begins with a short introduction to the mechanisms of the

---

4 K. Hetherington, *Infrastructure, Environment, and Life in the Anthropocene*, Durham NC 2019; A. Carse, *Dirty Landscapes: How Weediness Indexes State Disinvestment and Global Disconnection*, in K. Hetherington (ed.), *Infrastructure, Environment, and Life in the Anthropocene*, pp 97–114.

5 D. Jørgensen / F.A. Jørgensen / S.B. Pritchard, *New Natures. Joining Environmental History with Science and Technology Studies*, Pittsburg PA 2013.

6 This makes it also a study of (global) environmental justice based on the works of S. Lessenich, *Living Well at Others' Expense* and D. Pellow, *Resisting Global Toxics: Transnational Movements for Environmental Justice*, Cambridge MA / London 2007.

global waste trade and then teases out the asynchronous nature of the proposed deal, before ending with a discussion of wetlands and wastelands from a Honduran perspective. Overall, the chapter explains how actors in the global waste economy, both buyers and sellers, packaged their waste deals as essential to an American model of progress, built on the transformation of 'wastelands' by way of infrastructures, despite known ecological side-effects. It also underlines how this was done at a time when the very same model was already being questioned in some parts of the world, and it extrapolates how the hazardous waste deal was still attractive from an import perspective[7].

2 Growing pressure on the US waste system

Edgardo A. Pascall's letter to the Honduran National Port Authority in March 1987 was written during the heyday of unequal export/import schemes of hazardous waste materials globally. Modern environmentalism in the richer parts of the world had started in the 1970s and intensified over the 1980s giving birth to an ever stricter system of waste classification and disposal regulations. The combination of rising waste levels, increasing disposal costs, and conflicts about location of waste in industrial countries led waste traders to look South[8]. In the Greater Caribbean, Western Africa, or Southeastern Europe (and other places in the developing global South) hazardous waste regulations were less stringent or even non-existing. Meanwhile, the same areas were hungry for infrastructural development and foreign currency, with a perceived need to participate in global networks of trade and commerce in order to boost the local economy. All this made waste transfer a cheap and attractive trading scheme for both sides, albeit especially for the industrial countries[9]. The resulting global waste economy was often an amoral, but legal trading system based on a global patchwork of regulations regarding what constituted (hazardous) waste and its disposal, allowing traders to move waste down the most economic path for disposal.

7 On envirotechnical systems see S.B. Pritchard, *An Envirotechnical Disaster. Nature, Technology, and the Politics at Fukushima*, in "Environmental History", 17, 2012, 2, pp. 219–243.
8 S.M. Müller, *Hidden Externalities. The Globalization of Hazardous Waste*, in "Business History Review", 93, 2019, 1, pp. 51–74.
9 For a list of unequal trading schemes, see J. Vallette / H. Spalding (eds.), *The International Trade in Wastes. A Greenpeace Inventory*, Washington DC 1990. For a historical perspective on global inequality in the postwar era see C.O. Christiansen / S. Jensen, *Histories of Global Inequalities. New Perspectives*, Cham 2019.

This chapter singles out the United States, both as the largest producer of (hazardous) waste materials and most prolific trader of (hazardous) waste in the 1980s. Over the course of the twentieth century, the United States became the global leader in mass consumption and associated waste production[10]. According to estimates from the US Environmental Protection Agency (EPA) and the US General Accounting Office (GAO), the country's production of municipal solid waste (MSW) rose from 88.1 million tons in 1960 to 267.8 million tons in 2017. The hazardous waste output was between 264 million and 400 million tons annually in the 1980s alone. Today the country remains at the top of global per-capita waste charts, where it has been for almost six decades[11].

In the face of massively growing trash heaps, waste emerged as an environmental and regulatory problem in the United States, and with the rise of modern environmentalism in the 1960s and 1970s, scientists, politicians, and citizen activist groups increasingly turned their attention to the issue[12]. The potential health and environmental threats from leaking sanitary landfills or waste incinerators became a focus of attention and there was increasing public opposition to existing or potential waste disposal facilities near human settlements[13]. All across the United States people took to the streets to protest for better environmental and ultimately health protection from waste[14].

The growing volumes of waste and public concern about disposal sites led to a major regulatory shift in the United States. This is crucial for understanding the dynamics of waste exports heading South and the asynchronous nature of the global waste economy. The 1976 Resource Conservation and Recovery Act (RCRA) was

---

10 On the nexus between waste and consumption see S. Strasser, *Waste and Want. A Social History of Trash*, New York 2013.

11 J. Karliner, "Backyard Dumping: Toxic Waste Export to the Third World" undated, *Delaware Valley Toxic Coalition Records*, Urban Archives, Temple University, Philadelphia PA; J. Goldstein, "Waste", in F. Trentmann (ed.), *The Oxford Handbook of the History of Consumption*, Oxford 2012, p. 336; United States Environmental Protection Agency, *National Overview: Facts and Figures on Materials, Wastes and Recycling*, https://www.epa.gov/facts-and-figures-about-materials-waste-and-recycling/national-overview-facts-and-figures-materials#Trends1960-Today, last accessed July 16, 2020.

12 See for example M.V. Melosi, *Down in the Dumps: Is there a Garbage Crisis in America?*, in M.V. Melosi (eds), *Urban Public Policy: Historical Modes and Methods*, University Park PA 2010; L. Blumberg / R. Gottlieb, *War on Waste: Can America Win Its Battle With Garbage?*, Washington DC 1989, or D. Sicotte, *From Workshop to Waste Magnet: Environmental Inequality in the Philadelphia Region*, New Brunswick 2016.

13 On waste siting: C.O. Uzo / A. Armour, *Post-Landfill Siting Perceptions of Nearby Residents. A Case Study of Halton Landfill*, in "Applied Geography", 20, 2000, 2, pp. 137–154, or B.G. Rabe, *Beyond Nimby. Hazardous Waste Siting in Canada and the United States*, Washington DC 1994.

14 For waste protests see J. Sze, *Noxious New York. The Racial Politics of Urban Health and Environmental Justice*, Cambridge MA / London 2007.

implemented in the United States in 1980, and combined with the HSWA Amendments of 1984, this greatly increased the number of waste export notifications[15]. Standards for the safe treatment, storage, and disposal of hazardous waste, together with an elaborate tracking system, came into force on November 19, 1980. The amended RCRA mandated state or regional waste management plans and established standards for sanitary landfills, as well as guidelines for upgrading existing open dumps[16]. Prior to RCRA, corporations producing hazardous waste had usually hired external haulers or chemical brokers to take the waste off their hands and free them of liability for the materials, for a small fee. Many states did not require permits for waste haulers to operate, and so anyone who owned or rented a truck could enter the business, and hazardous materials ended up wherever these freelance haulers dumped them[17]. After RCRA, waste producers had to differentiate between hazardous and non-hazardous waste and follow a strict protocol for the disposal of the new hazardous waste category[18].

The new process was complicated and expensive for landfill operators and waste producers alike. Across the United States, the number of landfills fell by almost 50 percent compared to 1976 due to their failure to satisfy the new environmental standards. Between 1982 and 1987 around 2,700 landfills closed across the country[19]. As a consequence, problems of trash disposal became so severe that prices exploded and producers faced the prospect of paying double or even higher disposal costs[20]. In 1978, landfill disposal of one ton of toxic material cost US $ 2.50, but by 1987 this had risen to US $ 200[21]. Costs for the landfill disposal of hazardous waste materials according to legal requirements soared to US $ 2,500 per ton[22]. It soon became cheaper to consider international options for waste disposal.

---

15 P.E. Rosenfeld / L.G.H. Feng, *Risks of Hazardous Wastes*, Oxford 2011, p. 1.

16 Environmental Protection Agency, *EPA's Program to Control Exports of Hazardous Wastes Report of Audit*, Washington DC 1988, 8; G.E. Louis, *A Historical Context of Municipal Solid Waste Management in the United States*, in "Waste Management & Research: The Journal for a Sustainable Circular Economy", 22, 2004, 4, p. 317; H.L. Hickman, *American Alchemy: The History of Solid Waste Management in the United States*, Santa Barbara CA 2003, pp. 70–73.

17 R. Nordland, *Poison at Our Doorsteps*, in "Philadelphia Inquirer", September 23, 1979.

18 C.E. Davis / J.P. Lester, *Hazardous Waste Politics and the Policy Process*, in C.E. Davis / J.P. Lester (eds.), *Dimensions of Hazardous Waste Politics and Policy*, New York 1988, pp. 2–3.

19 G.E. Louis, *A Historical Context of Municipal Solid Waste Management in the United States*, p. 317; C. Hilz / J.R. Ehrenfeld, *Transboundary Movements of Hazardous Wastes*, in "International Environmental Affairs", 3, 1991, 1, pp. 26–63, here p. 31.

20 R. Nordland, *In New Jersey the Trash Piles Runneth*, in "Philadelphia Inquirer", August 19, 1973.

21 B.D. Moyers / L. Bergman, *Global Dumping Ground*, with the assistance of Center for Investigative Reporting, October 2, 1990, p. 7.

22 P. Shabecoff, *Irate and Afraid, Poor Nations Fight Effort to Use Them as Toxic Dumps*, "New York Times", July 5, 1988.

3 US waste in the Greater Caribbean

As a result of soaring prices and public protests, US hazardous waste materials started going South as early as 1970, but this increased massively after RCRA came into effect in 1980. In 1979, for instance, Nedlog Technology Group of Colorado negotiated a deal with Sierra Leone worth US $ 25 million if the country agreed to accept the company's hazardous waste for disposal and recycling[23]. In 1980, the US company Arbuckle Machinery successfully shipped PCB waste to the Dominican Republic. In 1982, Stewards Environmental Systems attempted to sell hazardous waste from a nuclear plant to Haiti. Starting in 1986, thousands of tons of toxic furnace dust crossed the US-Mexico border on a regular basis for recycling. In 1987, Allied Technology negotiated the consignment of dioxin waste from Love Canal to Morocco. From 1986 onwards, Thor Chemicals and American Cyanamid exported around 120 drums of mercury-contaminated waste annually to South Africa[24]. There was a direct correlation between the increasing resistance to local waste disposal in the United States, and the number of waste export notifications, rising from 12 in 1980 to 570 in 1988[25]. The scheme to export up to 200,000 tons of incinerator ash from Philadelphia to Puerto Castilla, Honduras was only one among hundreds.

In the case of Puerto Castilla, Edgardo A. Pascall's potential trading partners were the Bahamas based Amalgamated Shipping Corporation, which served as an extension of the US American company Coastal Carriers Corporation, based in Annapolis. Coastal Carriers was in turn a subcontractor for a local Philadelphian firm that had acquired a contract for the disposal of 200,000 tons of municipal incinerator ash from Philadelphia. Originally, Coastal Carriers and Amalgamated Shipping Corporation had secured a deal with Panama for the disposal of the material. However, increasing anti-Americanism in Panama had caused the Panamanian government of General Noriega to cancel the deal[26]. Coastal Carriers were therefore looking for alternatives and they initiated negotiations with agents in the Bahamas, Cost Rica, Jamaica, the Cayman Islands, the Dominican Republic, Chile, and Honduras.

23 L. Dash, *Sierra Leone Bristles with Economic Discontent*, in "Washington Post", July 14, 1980.
24 J. Vallette / H. Spalding, *The International Trade in Wastes: A Greenpeace Inventory*, Washington DC 1990, pp. 17–40.
25 C. Hilz, / J.R. Ehrenfeld, *Transboundary Movements of Hazardous Wastes*, p. 29.
26 T.A. Meade, *A History of Modern Latin America. 1800 to the Present*, Chichester UK / Malden MA 2009, p. 301.

At the time, the Greater Caribbean was the primary destination for US waste traders aiming to find a bargain under the unequal trade relations. Waste destinations all shared a number of key characteristics, including unstable political systems as states transitioned from (military) dictatorships to civilian rule, weak or failing domestic economies still trying to overcome the Latin American debt crisis, and less strict or even nonexistent environmental, health, and labor protection regulations, all of which made the disposal of US hazardous waste materials economically attractive. Honduras in the 1980s was a typical case. It was generally perceived as the most moderate example in Central America's history of brutal repression, when class and political struggles were accompanied by extreme violence, but the country was nevertheless still struggling severely on several fronts in the 1980s. Civil wars in all of Honduras' bordering nations (Nicaragua, El Salvador, and Guatemala) challenged the state politically and militarily at a time when Honduras was transitioning from a military dictatorship to civilian rule over the course of the decade. By the mid-1980s, Honduras was stuck in an economic depression that made the country increasingly dependent on foreign currency, primarily in the form of US investments or foreign aid. Per capita income massively declined over the decade and only one in ten Hondurans had what could be described as a stable job. In response to the generally unstable political climate in Central America at the time, the United States increased its presence in Honduras, both in terms of financial support and military presence[27]. In the face of these economic, political, and military challenges, environmental issues were largely ignored in Honduras. A general environmental law was only adopted in 1993, creating the Ministry of the Environment and other environmental institutions to encourage environmental protection in the country[28].

Alongside these socio-political aspects, there was also an ecological and an infrastructural perspective that drew waste traders to Greater Caribbean countries like Honduras: their coastal wetlands. These were seen as ideal locations for transforming unused, disease-prone wastelands into commercial land. As Coastal Carriers' representatives explained to Edgardo A. Pascall, the Americans were looking for "countries where there [were] disposal sites near a dock which must

27 T.L. Pearcy, *The History of Central America*, Westport, Conn. 2006, pp. 13–14; B. Sewell, *Intervention in Honduras*, in A. McPherson (ed.), *Encyclopedia of U.S. Military Interventions in Latin America*, Santa Barbara CA 2013, p. 293; T. Barry, *Central America Inside Out. The Essential Guide to Its Societies, Politics, and Economies*, New York 1991, p. 288.

28 Pan American Health Organization, *Health in the Americas 1998. Honduras*, last updated in 2001, https://www.paho.org/english/sha/prflhon.htm, last accessed November 23, 2021.

be filled in in order to improve humid health conditions"[29]. Mangrove wetlands and swamps were characteristic of the coastlines from Honduras to Panama and from the Cayman Islands to Puerto Rico. There were also extensive and industrially undeveloped shorelines dotted with small ports that theoretically could enable access to global networks of trade, tourism, and migration. The remote Honduran village of Puerto Castilla with its port surrounded by mangroves and wetlands, a historically important landing point for the United Fruit Company, was a perfect fit for what the US traders were looking for.

By the mid-1980s, deals to reuse US dirt or waste to create new land and space for more people, businesses, and port facilities were widespread. Waste traders like Coastal Carriers had learned that their projects sold more easily if packaged together with an American model for modernization that included land-filling and ultimately infrastructures as a means to economic and social development in the importing region. Their sales packages drew on an old and pervasive practice that had been central to the industrial development of the US and other countries centuries earlier. All around the globe from medieval times onwards, people had felt the need to "drain wetlands and to fill them in so that they could build on them, grow crops on them, and build roads across them"[30]. Filling marshes and swamps served "to convert a problematic or useless site into solid ground", and extending landfill into oceans and rivers "replaced what appeared to be an inexhaustible aquatic space with a more serviceable terrestrial one"[31].

The benefits appeared obvious. The soil under wetlands is very rich in plant nutrients, making these human-made lands especially attractive for agriculture. Many coastal and riparian cities had successfully expanded by building on human-made land reclaimed with landfills. In the United States, the Swamp Land Acts of 1849, 1850, and 1860 turned federal land over to states that agreed to drain the land and so serve the massive US population expansion of the nineteenth century. About 1/3 of present day Manhattan and as much as 1/6 of Boston is reclaimed marshland filled with rubble, dirt, and waste. Around the world, parts of Amsterdam, Brussels, Dublin, Saint Petersburg, Helsinki, Beirut, Mumbai, Rio de Janeiro, Manila, and Singapore were constructed on human-made land. These policies led to a vast reduction in wetlands across the United States and by the late twentieth

29 Translation of a letter from Edgardo A. Pascall to Jorge E. Cramiotis, General Manager, National Port Authority (Honduras), March 1987, Jim Vallette Private Archive.

30 Berkshire Environmental Action Team, *A History of Wetlands Protection in the United States*, 2021, https://www.thebeatnews.org/BeatTeam/history-federal-wetland-protection/, last accessed November 25, 2021.

31 M.V. Melosi, *Fresh Kills. A History of Consuming and Discarding in New York City*, New York 2020, p. 35.

century the country had lost more than 50 percent of its wetlands overall, since the arrival of European settlers[32].

4 An asynchronous system

Promoting the practice of land reclamation together with the export of hazardous waste US waste traders attempted to reproduce an American practice under entirely different conditions, both in time and materials. Coastal Carriers were promoting the ecological destruction of wetlands in Honduras and other countries in the Greater Caribbean, at a time when a variety of social actors in their own country no longer viewed them as wastelands, instead emphasizing their ecological importance as natural habitats, flood protection, shoreline erosion control, or natural water quality improvement zones. For centuries, people all around the world had treated wetlands as wastelands, useless impediments to human expansion and progress. Commencing in the 1960s, and underlined in 1971 with the UN Convention on *Wetlands of International Importance Especially as Waterfowl Habitats*, this perspective had started to shift fundamentally, at least in the industrial countries[33]. In the United States, hunters and biologists had been arguing for the protection of wetlands as wildlife habitats since the 1900s, but they had remained outliers to the general discourse which continued to view wetlands as wastelands. This changed with modern environmentalism and 1970s legislation. The 1973 US Flood Disaster Protection Act, the 1976 Toxic Substances Control Act, and the 1977 Clean Water Act all supported the protection of wetlands in the United States against development, toxic substances, and other forms of water pollution. Also in 1977, US President Jimmy Carter ended federal support for wetland conversion (i.e. draining and filling). The first report on the nation's wetlands as habitats was published in 1982. In 1986, the Emergency Wetlands Resources Act required the Secretary of the Interior to produce updated reports on wetlands on a ten-year cycle[34].

32 *Ibid.*; N.S. Seasholes, *Gaining Ground. A History of Landmaking in Boston*, Cambridge MA 2003; P.G. van den Ven (ed.), *Man-Made Lowlands. History of Water Management and Land Reclamation in the Netherlands. International Commission on Irrigation and Drainage*, Utrecht 1993. Berkshire Environmental Action Team, *A History of Wetlands Protection in the United States*.

33 R. Rattan et al., *Structure, Operations, and Relevance* in P. Singh / S. Sharma (eds.), *Wetlands Conservation. An Up-To-Date Overview of Approaches for Addressing Wetlands Degradation and its Effects on Ecosystem Services, Human Health, and Other Ecosystems*, Hoboken NJ 2021, pp. 17–39.

34 Berkshire Environmental Action Team, *A History of Wetlands Protection in the United States*, 2021; T.E. Dahl et al., *Wetlands, Status and Trends in the Coterminous United States, Mid-1970s to Mid-1980s*, US Department of the Interior, 1991.

The asynchronicity was exacerbated by the fact that US waste traders were promoting the filling of wetlands with potentially hazardous US waste materials, a radical change from the traditional rubble and dirt. This made it hard to compare earlier land reclamation projects in the United States with those planned for the Greater Caribbean. Up until the nineteenth century, US waste had been mostly organic, in the form of ash, food waste, animal carcasses, and sewage[35]. The emergence of mass consumption at the turn of the twentieth century, with packaging, plasticization, the pervasiveness of oil based energy, and the electrification of the home radically altered consumption practices and waste production. By the late 1960s, United States waste had largely assumed the form we know today. On average, people produce about 1 kg of garbage each day, including paper products, packaging, bottles, cans, and food scraps, alongside increasing quantities of plastic[36].

A key development was the introduction of the new *hazardous* waste category. Particularly after World War II, the United States underwent a massive increase in the quantity and types of waste that posed a substantial threat to both human health and the environment[37]. Petroleum-based organic chemistry enabled the manufacture of a host of new materials, including synthetic fibers, pesticides, wood preservatives, plastics, drugs, new paints, and solvents. Synthetic chemicals were used in a variety of new applications ranging from cyclic intermediates, to dyes, plasticizers, flavors, perfumes, and surface-active agents. Each of these new products and processes left behind diverse by-products, waste materials, and intermediate chemicals used for processing, all of which had to be disposed of and resulting in a massive new source of hazardous waste materials[38]. Hazardous waste was also produced at the end of the commodity chain, for example in the process of waste incineration. Originally intended to greatly reduce the volume of waste, the incineration process potentially created even more highly toxic trace chemicals, dioxins and furans[39]. Although at the time, US regulators did not yet classify incinerator ash as hazardous waste, the US Environmental Protection Agency were aware of the environmental and health risks associated with incinerator ash, especially if

---

35 J. Goldstein, "Waste", p. 329; S. Strasser, *Waste and Want: A Social History of Trash*, New York 2013.

36 T. McCarthy, *Auto Mania: Cars, Consumers, and the Environment*, New Haven CT 2007, pp. 66–72; J. Goldstein, "Waste", p. 335.

37 US EPA definition cited in P.E. Rosenfeld / L.G.H Feng, *Risks of Hazardous Wastes*, p. 1.

38 S.S Epstein / L.O. Brown / C. Pope, *Hazardous Waste in America*, San Francisco 1982, pp. 9–11; N. Langston, *New Chemical Bodies: Synthetic Chemicals, Regulation, and Human Health*, in A.C. Isenberg (ed.), *The Oxford Handbook of Environmental History*, Oxford 2014, p. 260.

39 Barry Commoner cited in Committee on Environment and Public Works, *Resource Conservation and Recovery Act Oversight*, 1987, p. 12.

this material was used for landfilling in wetland areas, where it would easily disperse in the aquatic environment and enter the human food chain. National protests against waste incineration induced EPA administrators to investigate the topic in depth, also analyzing the ash produced by US cities[40]. In relation to the ash from Philadelphia, they explicitly stated that using such materials for landfill in wetland areas could pose a "significant long-term health threat," presenting a "reasonable potential for environmental damage and an increased risk of human cancer"[41].

5 Waking Sleeping Beauty

The situation was framed differently in Honduras. Despite a potential environmental and health hazard looming on the horizon, Edgardo A. Pascall and his supporters, including Puerto Castilla's port superintendent, Fredo A. Lopez, still found the American waste import proposal an attractive deal. Importantly, the Hondurans did not try to hide the toxicological information on US incinerator ash, and they were not unaware that incinerator ash could potentially contain toxicants beyond a critical threshold. This information was included in Pascall's letter to the Honduran National Port Authority. The Honduran supporters of the deal chose to emphasize a different narrative, that the ash was "excellent material for landfill in low lying zones and swampy areas". Philadelphia incinerator ash would "stabilize areas [. . .], eliminating swamps and watery areas which constitute breeding grounds for mosquitos [. . .] and in this way improve the health of the port farmers. [. . .] The port facilities [. . .] would be utilized thus bringing unforeseen revenues for the national port authority, creating new jobs in the process". Finally, as part of the landfill project "an access road to Caserio Barranco Blanco would be improved". Coastal Carriers would build this road and "create any other infrastructure necessary for the management of the landfill"[42].

Anthropologist Ashley Carse has pointed out how people treat infrastructures as indices for a variety of other social, economic, and political phenomena[43]. For Pascall in Honduras and many others in countries of the Greater Caribbean who

40 On protest against waste incineration see J. Sze, *Noxious New York. The Racial Politics of Urban Health and Environmental Justice*, Cambridge MA 2007.

41 Environmental Protection Agency, "EPA Flash Report", Radio Haiti Papers, 1968–2003, Duke University Library, October 5, 1987.

42 Translation of a letter from Edgardo A. Pascall to Jorge E. Cramiotis, General Manager, National Port Authority (Honduras), March 1987, Jim Vallette Private Archive.

43 A. Carse, *Dirty Landscapes: How Weediness Indexes State Disinvestment and Global Disconnection*, in K. Hetherington (ed.) *Infrastructure, Environment, and Life in the Anthropocene*, pp. 97–114.

supported similar waste import schemes, the use of incinerator ash as landfill material was interwoven with their understanding of progress, and exhibited a desire to integrate their respective locations with the wider world. It was also significant that Edgardo A. Pascall was not from Puerto Castilla, but from San Pedro Sula, Honduras' commercial center.

The dream of development caught on easily in Puerto Castilla. In 1987, the community of Puerto Castilla resembled the Brothers Grimm story of Sleeping Beauty, it had fallen asleep decades ago and was waiting to be kissed back to life. Like the other communities approached by the waste traders during this decade, Puerto Castilla was a remote port village of only a couple of hundred people, offering some basic shipping infrastructure. In the 1980s it was practically disconnected from the world at large and was remote even by Honduran terms. Puerto Castilla is located about 20 kilometers north of Trujillo, the capital of the Colón Department of Honduras in the North of the country, and about 400 kilometers from San Pedro Sula, Honduras' commercial center where Pascall was from. The village sits on the inland side of a peninsula that forms the Bay of Trujillo and shelters the small shrimp fishing community from the heavy Atlantic waves and winds. The peninsula also forms a deep-water port, which distinguishes this settlement from other Honduran coastal villages. At Puerto Castilla, the water drops abruptly to a depth of 20 feet, making the port suitable for relatively large ships. Strategically located on the northern Atlantic shore of Honduras, almost facing Havana, Puerto Castilla appeared to be a place that could be quickly and inexpensively re-connected into larger, global networks of commerce and travel, once again becoming an important port of entrance for foreign goods and investments coming into Honduras[44].

Imagining Puerto Castilla as a major Honduran port connected with international trade networks was not unrealistic considering the history of the settlement. Originally famous as the place where Christopher Columbus allegedly first set foot on the Central American mainland, it was fortified by the Spanish during the colonial period[45]. Later, the village enjoyed a short economic boom as an outpost of the trade empire of the United Fruit Company in the early part of the

44 M. Holleman, US Peace Corps, *The Americas. Puerto Castilla*, in "Peace Corps Times. Focus Honduras", July August 1988, 9.

45 L. Lemus, *Castilla, historico pueblo hondureno sumido en el abandono*, in "Laprensa", May 24, 2014, https://www.laprensa.hn/honduras/regionales/712393-98/castilla-hist%C3%B3rico-pueblo-hondure%C3%B1o-sumido-en-el-abandono, last accessed November 27, 2021; *Encyclopedia Britannica*: "Puerto Castilla", https://www.britannica.com/place/Puerto-Castilla, last Accessed November 27, 2021.

twentieth century. United Fruit, a US based producer and trader of tropical fruits for export to the United States, opened its facilities in Puerto Castilla in 1919[46]. The company was originally founded in Boston in 1899 and had become the largest employer in Central America by the early 1930s. It owned or leased properties in Honduras, Costa Rica, Guatemala, Panama, Colombia, Cuba, Jamaica, and other countries in Central and South America, and the West Indies. In many of these countries United Fruit was more than simply an employer, often taking on the traditional responsibilities of states, such as building infrastructures. The company cleared and planted undeveloped tracts of land, created extensive railroad and port facilities, and operated a large steamship service known as "The Great White Fleet"[47]. When United Fruit expanded in Honduras in the early twentieth century, incorporating lands around the ports of Tela and Puerto Castilla, it brought one of its engineers over from Guatemala to build a railroad, improve the ports, and clear the land for plantations[48]. The United Fruit Company set up the Truxillo Railroad Company as a subsidiary to exploit the contracts and concessions it had recently received from the Honduran government. The American company began the construction of the railroad in 1913, reaching Puerto Castilla, the final destination of the 96-kilometer line starting in Olanchito in August 1921. Olanchito is the capital of the Honduran department of Yoro and its wealthy citizens viewed the railroad connection to Puerto Castilla and its port as symbolizing a quick and easy route to the United States of America. Puerto Castilla was transformed once again into a nodal point of global networks, as it had once been under Spanish rule[49].

Little remained of these prospects for Puerto Castilla after United Fruit left the area in the late 1930s. The company closed down its facilities as a result of Panama disease, a blight on the roots of banana trees. Along with its port facilities in Puerto Castilla, United Fruit also abandoned the railroad it had built two decades earlier, leaving Hondurans to deal with an increasingly deteriorating infrastructure, which they eventually dismantled. By 1952, the once busy port stood almost entirely abandoned[50]. In the 1940s, the Honduran government moved the

46 J. Colby, *The Business of Empire*, Ithaca NY 2019.

47 Harvard Business School Archives, United Fruit Company, https://www.library.hbs.edu/hc/pc/large/united-fruit.html, last accessed November 27, 2021.

48 J. Colby, *The Business of Empire*, p. 124.

49 Mario Posas Industrias, *Monografia de Olanchito*, 1993, cited in "Olanchito: La Era del Ferrocarril", http://ferrocarrilhonduras.synthasite.com/truxillo-railroad-company.php, last accessed July 1, 2022.

50 La Era de la Ferrocarill, http://ferrocarrilhonduras.synthasite.com/truxillo-railroad-company.php, last accessed November 26, 2021; US Hydrographic Office, *Sailing Directions for the East Coasts of Central America and Mexico*, US Government Printing Office, 1957.

village east along the peninsula to allow American forces to establish a small naval base beside the port of Puerto Castilla to support the Allies in their fight against Nazi Germany. At the time, the Allies believed Nazi Germany was planning an attack on the Panama Canal and so Puerto Castilla was incorporated into a defensive ring around the Caribbean and Central America[51]. However, for the local community, the obligatory move only produced a significant deterioration in their lives. The Honduran National Port Authority, which took over the port from the villagers, had promised that it would build 250 decent houses and give villagers work. Four decades later, none of this had happened and the people were still waiting for a modern sewage system[52]. Edgardo Pascall travelled from San Pedro Sula to visit Puerto Castilla in February 1987, the same year that the US Peace Corps started community based projects there. He described a poor and underdeveloped region suffering from massive unemployment, poverty, ill-health, and a general lack of infrastructure[53]. When the American company Coastal Carriers Inc. approached Pascall and the Honduran National Port Authority with a project that included the infrastructural development of Puerto Castilla, it seemed like a perfect opportunity.

However, it was an opportunity that perpetuated the relationships between Honduras and various western countries established during three-hundred years of colonialism. In this relationship, the foreign powers, starting with Spain and culminating with the United States, assumed the role of developing land by constructing infrastructures like fortifications, roads, ports, and railroads, in the place of the Hondurans and their local government. The relationship also required that these infrastructures be paid for through the exploitation of Honduran nature and resources. During the colonial period, the Spanish had extracted vast riches from the country and traditionally the Caribbean coastal lowlands around Puerto Castilla had been Honduras' most exploited region because of its wealth of tropical fruits, forests, and seafood[54]. Under the regional control of the United Fruit Company, Puerto Castilla was the largest port for tropical fruit exports from Honduras to the United States. After World War II there was a relatively quiet period for Puerto Castilla, during which US exploitative relations with the Greater Caribbean were redefined. Loans from Washington were used to plan and finance a shift towards extensive monocultures of rubber, rice, bananas, coffee, cacao, and abaca, as the

---

51 https://en.wikipedia.org/wiki/Puerto_Castilla,_Honduras.

52 M. Holleman, US Peace Corps, *The Americas*; Lemus, *Castilla*.

53 Translation of a letter from Edgardo A. Pascall to Jorge E. Cramiotis, General Manager, National Port Authority (Honduras), March 1987, Jim Vallette Private Archive.

54 E. Echeverri-Gent, *Geography*, in T. Merrill (ed.), *Honduras: A Country Study*, Washington DC 1995, pp.66–74.

United States recolonized almost the entire Greater Caribbean. Under titles like "Development Aid", "Green Revolution", or "Technical Cooperation", countries in the region witnessed the modernization of their agriculture and infrastructure according to a US model, which aimed at an important, mandatory step towards modernity, but not always to the real benefit of the host countries[55]. The potential importation of Philadelphia incinerator ash in 1987 marked the return of the Americans to Puerto Castilla, exploiting Honduras' environment for the disposal of their hazardous waste.

6 Wetlands as wastelands and hostile nature

The neocolonial interpretation falls short of capturing all the dimensions of the waste import story. The land around the port of Puerto Castilla, which the Hondurans were considering allowing the US waste traders to use for waste disposal, was land they themselves regarded as useless. Throughout the country wetlands and mangrove forests came under threat in the 1980s. People used them for waste disposal or filled them to create agricultural or commercial land. One of the key stressors on Honduras' mangroves and wetlands was the mass expansion of aquaculture and large-scale shrimp farms, producing for export. This development was strongly supported by the Honduran government in an effort to boost exports and improve the economy. By 1987, income from the export of shrimps cultivated in aquaculture ranked third, after coffee and bananas, in total export earnings for Honduras. As a consequence of this policy, the Gulf of Fonseca in southern Honduras became the second largest producer of farmed shrimps in the Western Hemisphere, with enormous large-scale shrimp cultivation sites that attracted many Hondurans into the area. The expansion of shrimp farms into Honduras' wetlands had serious consequences for the environment, although this was mostly disregarded at the time. The shrimp farms resulted in destruction of habitats, blocking of estuaries, and rechanneling of rivers. This generated ecological imbalances and the consequent destruction of flora and fauna. Shrimp farmers were reported to be using the pesticide Rotenone to eliminate unwanted species in ponds, leading to a massive loss of fish stocks. Other factors contributing to the widespread loss of mangrove forests and wetland areas in Honduras over the course of the 1980s included increased sedimentation caused by erosion at higher elevations, a

55 N. Cuvi, *Big Science and the Enchantment of Growth in Latin America*, in "Global Environment", 10, 2012, pp. 16–41, here pp. 17–18.

decade of drought, El Nino conditions, and pollutants from uncontrolled use of pesticides[56]. Since 1980, Honduras has lost about 85,000 ha of mangrove forests[57].

At Puerto Castilla, the situation differed since there was no large-scale shrimp aquaculture, but it was similar in the sense that people shared the general disregard for wetlands and mangrove forests. Writing about communities on Paraguay's rural frontier, Anthropologist Kregg Hetherington observed that infrastructural investments can materialize the promise of development by "slotting the landscape along a narrative of progress". In such narratives, according to Hetherington, infrastructures often symbolize "that which holds nature and culture apart, marking a temporal break between chaos and order"[58]. As if demonstrating Hetherington's point, Edgardo A. Pascall perceived Puerto Castilla in terms of just two things: the port and the swamp[59].

Puerto Castillo stands on the northern side of the Bay of Trujillo, with Trujillo itself on the southern side. A shallow channel in the eastern side of the bay leads to a large sheltered lagoon. The coastline is low, wooded, and swampy and the environment around Puerto Castilla includes mangroves and lagoons, periodically flooded grasslands, and lowland savannas. The coastal climate is tropical with a rainy season from June to December[60]. Most Hondurans refer to the region simply as "the coast", in contrast to the more mountainous area just south of Trujillo. Thanks to its mangroves, Puerto Castilla is ideal for fishing, and shrimps provide the primary livelihood for the villagers. Coastal mangrove swamps are critical nursery grounds and refugia from predation for penaeid shrimps, spiny lobsters, and more than 200 species of fish[61]. However, good fishing was only one aspect of Puerto Castilla's mangroves.

---

56 S. Stonich, *Development, Rural Impoverishment and Environmental Destruction in Honduras*, in M. Painter / W.H. Durham (eds.), *The Social Causes of Environmental Destruction in Latin America*, Ann Arbor 2001, pp. 63–92, here pp. 80–85.

57 Food and Agriculture Organization of the United Nations, *The World's Mangroves, 1980–2005*, FAO 2007, 32.

58 K. Hetherington, *Waiting for the Surveyor. Development Promises and Temporality of Infrastructure*, in "Journal of Latin American and Caribbean Anthropology", 19, 2014, 2, pp. 195–211, here pp. 197–198.

59 Translation of a letter from Edgardo A. Pascall to Jorge E. Cramiotis, General Manager, National Port Authority (Honduras), March 1987, Jim Vallette Private Archive.

60 Ecoregional Workshop: A Conservation Assessment of Mangrove Ecoregions of Latin America and the Caribbean. 1994. Washington DC, World Wildlife Fund. https://www.worldwildlife.org/ecoregions/nt1426, last accessed November 26, 2021; US Hydrographic Office, *Sailing Directions for the East Coasts of Central America and Mexico*, US Government Printing Office, 1957.

61 A.M. Ellison / E.J. Farnsworth, *Anthropogenic Disturbances of Caribbean Mangrove Ecosystems: Past Impacts, Present Trends, and Future Predictions*, in "Biotropica", 28, 1996, 4/A, pp. 549–565, here p. 551.

With the region's wet climate and months-long rainy season, the mangroves around Puerto Castilla were also ideal breeding grounds for mosquitos and sand flies, both vectors for a number of serious diseases, including pappataci fever and malaria. Already in the 1920s, the United Fruit's Medical Department identified the region as disease-ridden. In their annual reports to headquarters, medics pointed out how the area around the United Fruit facilities at Puerto Castilla, which they had established on a low sandy point originally covered with a tidal mangrove swamp, provided ideal breading grounds for sandflies and mosquitos. During the wet season, the rain formed numerous shallow puddles of stagnant water throughout the town, where sandflies in particular could live and breed. Moving through the mangrove swamps or in the dense and humid patches of forest surrounding the town, one would be "frequently attacked by so-called 'wild mosquitos'"[62]. The United Fruit medics reported that the sand flies caused "intolerable itching" and a feverish condition that could "seriously interfere with health", but they were particularly worried about the mosquitos and malaria. Despite taking various measures that included working in screened quarters, chemical repellants, and a mosquito-free bar, 43.2 percent of United Fruit's workers contracted malaria[63]. Five years later, Edgardo A. Pascall agreed with the American waste traders about trying to "improve health conditions", and emphasized health concerns when talking about the wetlands of Puerto Castilla and the Greater Caribbean in general. The area around Puerto Castilla supposedly had one of the highest malaria levels in the world at the time. This severely impacted the health of local fishermen and the economic progress and well-being of the region as a whole[64].

The focus on mangroves as a refuge for mosquito-borne disease, rather than as the habitat providing the primary livelihood for the fishermen, transformed Puerto Castilla's ecosystem into a "hostile environment" that was severely harming the local community. Following this logic, the area's coastal wetlands and breeding ground for sand-flies and mosquitos needed to be eliminated. Already in 1924, United Fruit's medics had concluded that, "to eliminate such possible breeding grounds [like that of stagnant water], there appears to be no other method than to cover the loose sand as much as possible"[65]. Edgardo A. Pascall

62 United Fruit Company, Medical Department. *Annual Report*, 1924, pp. 200–202.
63 *Ibid.*, p. 50.
64 Translation of a letter from Edgardo A. Pascall to Jorge E. Cramiotis, General Manager, National Port Authority (Honduras), March 1987, Jim Vallette Private Archive.
65 United Fruit Company, Medical Department, *Annual Report*, 1924, p. 200.

echoed these words when he argued that Puerto Castilla's swamps needed to be "filled" with incinerator ash, "in order to improve humid health conditions"[66].

7 Conclusion

In the spring of 1987, the US American waste trader Coastal Carriers approached the remote and impoverished community of Puerto Castilla, in Honduras, with a proposal packaging waste disposal with land reclamation and ultimately infrastructural development, economic growth, and improved health. Up to 200,000 tons of Philadelphia incinerator ash would be used to drain and fill the 'hostile' disease-prone wetlands surrounding Puerto Castilla, creating human-made land for the expansion of the derelict village port and the construction of roads going inland from the coast, while helping to eradicate malaria in the region by drying out the ideal mosquito breeding grounds. The waste import-land reclamation project would ultimately reconnect Puerto Castilla with the world at large, after being largely abandoned and forgotten during much of the twentieth century.

This waste import proposal is a representative example for the many other similar waste deals offered to places like Puerto Castilla in the Greater Caribbean or West Africa, exemplifying both the dynamics of the global waste economy as a system founded on inequalities and asynchronicities, and the allure of an American model of progress that portrayed development as incompatible with nature and environmental protection. With their ash deal, the US American waste traders not only attempted to export incinerator ash from Philadelphia to Honduras, but also an associated western practice of land reclamation based on an understanding of wetlands as wastelands in need of improvement. For centuries, urban and agricultural growth in much of the Western world and its colonies had depended on conversion of wetlands into cultivated and commercial land by draining and landfilling. It is nevertheless noteworthy that the Americans attempted to sell this particular product for achieving American style modernity, after the same process had already begun to be criticized at home. In the 1980s waste materials and wetlands were viewed differently in the United States than in Honduras. In the United States, waste was strictly regulated and controlled, while wetlands were increasingly protected from environmental pollution, land degradation, and commercial exploitation. As exporters, the Americans were continuing the colonial relationship of exploitation of Honduras' natural resources, in this case seeking land for waste disposal.

---

66 Translation of a letter from Edgardo A. Pascall to Jorge E. Cramiotis, General Manager, National Port Authority (Honduras), March 1987, Jim Vallette Private Archive.

From the Honduran perspective the story was more complicated. The main actors there remained attracted to the waste import deal because it embodied the American model of progress, and notwithstanding more recent contemporary concerns expressed in the United States about the nature of waste incinerator ash and the importance of wetlands. As this chapter reveals, they did so not through lack of knowledge of potential detrimental environmental effects of using incinerator ash to landfill a wetland area, but because they gave precedence to a different narrative. In this narrative, development was at odds with the environment, seeing nature as something that needed to be overcome for the sake of economic growth, and wetlands solely as dangerous landscapes harboring mosquitoes and sandflies, the vectors of serious diseases that needed to be eliminated. A national policy that generally targeted the nation's wetlands and mangrove forests in order to promote large-scale aquaculture, provided an overall framework for this narrative.

Ultimately, Philadelphia's incinerator ash did not end up in Honduras, but in Gonaives, Haiti, a place that shared many of the structural features of Puerto Castilla. Why exactly the deal with Puerto Castilla was not concluded remains unclear. The community's aspiration to develop their port was nevertheless achieved, and today Puerto Castilla is the largest container port in Honduras in terms of total tonnage transferred[67].

67 Avalon Travel, *Moon Central America*, Emeryville CA 2016.

IV. Hybrid Landscape: Infrastructures of Water Control

Matteo Di Tullio

Coping with Water

Managing a Living Infrastructure in Early Modern Lombardy between Economy, Ecology, and Conflicts

1 Introduction

The study of the history of water management has a long tradition[1], but certainly it has become an increasingly popular research subject over recent decades, in line with the environmental shift involving hard science as well as the humanities[2]. This was also true for early modern Lombardy, where the relationship between people and water was (and remains) so crucial that it would be easy to get lost investigating the thousands of different aspects in a detailed analysis. Generally speaking, it is reasonable to define the preindustrial European economy as a "wood age", due to the relevance of lumber in these societies, especially for energy[3], but

1 It is impossible to summarize the vast and extended timespan of historiographic production on this subject. Readers are simply reminded that the study of the relationship between mankind and environment goes back at least to the *Annales* school, passing through English local history, and more generally, through European and international rural history. A recent summary of individual national historiographic experiences is provided, for example, in the essays edited by F. Graber / F. Locher, *Posséder la nature. Environnement et propriété dans l'histoire*, Paris 2018.
2 Within the scope of water management in the early modern period, among the different approaches and just limiting to the last few years for brevity reasons see T. Soens, *Flood Security in the Medieval and Early Modern North Sea Area: A Question of Entitlement?*, in "Environment and History", 19, 2013, 2, pp. 209–232; A. Ingold, *Writing on Nature: From Social History to the Environmental question?*, in "Annales HSS", 1, 2011, 1, pp. 11–29; R. Morera, *L'assèchement des marais en France au XVIIe siècle*, Rennes 2011; P. Van Cruyningen, *Dealing with Drainage: State Regulation of Drainage Projects in the Dutch Republic, France, and England during the Sixteenth and Seventeenth Centuries*, in "Economic History Review", 68, 2014, 2, pp. 420–440; P. Van Dam, *An Amphibious Culture. Coping with Floods in the Netherlands*, in P. Coates / D. Moon / P. Warde (eds.), *Local Places, Global Processes*, Oxford 2016, pp. 78–93; L.J. Skelton, *Tyne After Tyne: An Environmental History of a River's Battle for Protection, 1529–2015*, Winwick 2017; J. Morgan, *The Micro-Politics of Water Management in Early Modern England: Regulation and Representation in Commissions of Sewers*, in "Environment and History", 23, 2017, 3, pp. 409–430; G. Nigro (ed.), *Water Management in Europe (12th–18th Centuries)*, Firenze 2018; A. Duarte Rodrigues / C. Toribio Marín, *The History of Water Management in the Iberian Peninsula*, Cham 2020; F. Cazzola, *Uomini e fiumi. Per una storia idraulica ed agraria della bassa pianura del Po (1450–1620)*, Roma 2021.
3 This assumption was raised again some years ago by Paul Warde in his wonderful book on the early Modern Würtenberg, taking up the assumptions of Werner Sombart: P. Warde, *Economy, Ecology and State Formation in Early Modern Germany*, Cambridge 2006.

https://doi.org/10.1515/9783111112756-009

looking more specifically at Lombardy and the Po Valley, the same period could equally be defined as essentially a "water age". It was primarily the human-water relationship that induced and guided cooperation between societies and interaction with the environment in that part of the world over these centuries[4].

The centrality of this natural resource and its intricate relationship with local societies and economies, led the present author to abandon any idea of focusing on any specific case studies or individual aspects, and instead the current essay presents some more general ideas developed by the author while studying this subject. The following pages are based on diverse research ideas developed on water management during the long early modern period (namely, from the mid-fourteen hundreds to the eighteen hundreds) in Lombardy, which includes mainly the low plains of the State of Milan, and part of the western provinces of the Republic of Venice[5]. The focus is on waterworks and water networks as infrastructure in the abovementioned period and territory, presenting and discussing four main points.

Firstly, in early modern Lombardy, coping with water was primarily an ecological issue. For the sake of clarity, in this essay "ecology" is defined as all human actions directed towards the local environment and implemented in order to integrate the human need to live (and work) in a given place with independent natural

4 Entire libraries have been written regarding the value of water in determining human settlements, landscape formation and economic choices. As foundation references, see at least, L. Febvre, *La terre et l'évolution humaine. Introduction géographique à l'histoire*, Paris 1922; E. Sereni, *Storia del paesaggio agrario italiano*, Roma / Bari 1961; R. Furon, *Le problème de l'eau dans le monde*, Paris 1963; J. Bethemont, *De l'eau et des hommes. Essai géographique sur l'utilisation des eaux continentales*, Paris 1977; L. Gambi, *Una geografia per la storia*, Torino 1973 and by the same author *Acqua ed ecologia*, in A. Guarducci (ed.), *Agricoltura e trasformazioni dell'ambiente (secoli XIII–XVIII)*, Firenze 1984, pp. 662–664; P. Bevilacqua, *Tra natura e storia. Ambiente economie e risorse in Italia*, Roma 1996; L. Pagani / A. Tosi (eds.), *Acqua e Paesaggio*, Bergamo 2005; G. Alfani / M. Di Tullio / L. Mocarelli (eds.), *Storia economica e ambiente italiano (ca. 1400–1850)*, Milano 2012.

5 See by M. Di Tullio, *Tra ecologia ed economia: uomo e acqua nella pianura lombarda d'età moderna*, in G. Alfani / M. Di Tullio / L. Mocarelli (eds.), *Storia economica e ambiente italiano*, pp. 283–299; *The Wealth of Communities. War, Resources and Cooperation in Renaissance Lombardy*, Farnham 2014; *Cooperating in Times of Crisis. War, Commons, and Inequality in Renaissance Lombardy*, in "Economic History Review", 71, 2018, 1, pp. 82–105; *Croce e delizia. La risicoltura in Lombardia e nella Pianura padana d'età moderna*, in M. Cavallera / S. Conca Messina / B.A. Raviola (eds.), *Le vie del cibo. Italia settentrionale (secc. XVI–XX)*, Roma 2018, pp. 135–151; M. Di Tullio / C. Lorenzini, *La ricerca della sostenibilità. Economia, acqua, risorse e conflitti nell'Italia settentrionale (secc. XV–XVIII)*, in *Gestione dell'acqua in Europa (XII–XVIII secc.)*, Selezione di ricerche, Firenze 2018, pp. 165–185; by the same authors, *Natural Resources, Conflict and Sustainability in Northern Italy in the Early Modern Period*, in D. Canzian / E. Novello (eds.), *Ecosystem Services in Floodplains*, Padova 2019, pp. 73–96.

processes. From this perspective, the search for an ecological balance represents the attempt to satisfy human needs by exploiting and shaping the independent "production" of nature as far as possible, while also partially adapting to the environment. Likewise, the term "economy" refers to all activities designed to exploit local resources, primarily to ensure local needs rather than the production goals typical of a market economy[6].

Secondly, water management was a collective goal that encouraged cooperation. The abovementioned ecological and economic aspects of water, made water management such an important issue that it could not be left to the initiative of a few individuals, instead emphasizing the importance of local institutions and generally promoting cooperation[7].

The consequence of this leads to the third point, which is that water management involved the development of an infrastructure that could be considered 'alive' from several points of view. Lastly, and as a consequence of the previous three points, water management led implicitly towards disputes, and these were not necessarily a direct consequence of increasing exploitation of the resource. These four main points are argued and explained below.

2 The lands are never at rest

Philippe de Commynes was returning from Naples together with the army of the King of France between the spring and summer of 1495. As a good chronicler and expert diplomat, he spent his days carefully recording everything that happened or surprised him on the Peninsula in his notebooks. A few years later he used these notes to draft his *Memoires,* which included numerous political, diplomatic, and military observations, as well as his amazement at seeing the "Lombardy plain, which is one of the most beautiful and richest lands in the world and the most populated [. . .] fertile as much for good crops as for good wines and fruit [. . .]

6 M. Di Tullio, *Tra ecologia ed economia*, p. 283.

7 M. Granovetter, *The Strength of Weak Ties*, in "American Journal of Sociology", 78, 1973, 6, pp. 1360–1380 (here pp. 1373–1376); G. Hanlon, *Human Nature in Rural Tuscany. An Early Modern History*, Basingstoke 2007, pp. 39–68; T. De Moor, *The Silent Revolution: A New Perspective on the Emergence of Commons, Guilds, and Other Forms of Corporate Collective Actions in Western Europe*, in "The International Review of Social History", 53, supplement, pp. 179–212 (here pp. 183–184); T. De Moor, *The Dilemma of the Commoners: Understanding the Use of Common Pool Resources in Long-Term Perspective*, Cambridge 2015; M. Di Tullio, *The Wealth of Communities* and, by the same author, *Cooperating in Time of Crisis.*

[and where, surprisingly,] the lands are never at rest"[8]. Like many other travellers visiting Italy on a personal grand tour or for institutional purposes, De Commynes was clearly impressed by the already quite widespread use of the 'four-field' or 'continuous rotation' system in use. Unlike conventional agricultural practice elsewhere, plots of land were not left cyclically to lie fallow, and transhumant and stable livestock were integrated into the farming cycle. The landscape praised by the French diplomat, "full of ditches like the [native] Flanders and more"[9], was the result of a centuries-long process of domestication of the environment[10], the result of cooperation between the reproductive forces of Nature[11] and constant human husbandry and care.

To fully understand the implications of the French chronicler's notes, it is necessary to be aware of some geopedological and hydrographic peculiarities of northern Italy. As the Po Valley descends from the Alps it can be divided into an upper dry plain, characterized by permeable soils, and a lower impermeable plain, characterized by an abundance of water.

This water is supplied by numerous rivers constantly fed by the perennial Alpine snows, and by springs generated when the water beneath the dry upper plain meets the impermeable soils of the lower plain causing it to emerge. As the watercourses descended from the higher land at the foot of the Alps towards the lower Po plain, they became poorly defined (later they were constructed artificially) with low banks, increasingly wider beds, and interweaving confluences, making entire regions almost permanently swampy and unsuitable for human settlement. The abundance of springs mentioned above greatly augmented the extensive system of swamps already created by the dispersed river water. As a consequence, it is obvious why water management has always been the *conditio sine qua non* to settling and working on the lower Po Valley plain, even during the early modern period[12].

8 P. De Commynes, *Memorie*, ed. by M.C. Daviso di Charvensod, Torino 1960, Book VIII, chap. VII, p. 473.

9 *Ibid.*

10 C. Cattaneo, *Notizie naturali e civili sulla Lombardia*, Milano 1844; G. Bigatti, *La provincia delle acque. Ambiente, istituzioni e tecnici in Lombardia tra Sette e Ottocento*, Milano 1995, p. 35; S. Jacini, *La proprietà fondiaria e le popolazioni agricole in Lombardia*, ed. by F. Della Peruta, Milano 1996, pp. 9–10.

11 P. Bevilacqua, *Ecologia del tempo. Note di storia ambientale*, in "Contemporanea", 2005, 3, pp. 409–421.

12 For some examples referring to Lombardy, see the drawing by M. Bellabarba, *Seriolanti e arzenisti. Governo delle acque e agricoltura a Cremona fra cinque e seicento*, Cremona 1986, and the essays collected in L. Faccini et al. (eds.), *I tempi della terra. Campi, acque e case nel pavese rurale dalla fine del '500 ai nostri giorni*, Pavia 1983.

The latter point is the first to be specifically emphasized in this essay: coping with water on the lower Lombardy plain was most of all an ecological issue, because part of this plain was unsuitable for human settlement without prior hydraulic stabilization, with land reclamation being one of the primary actions required. This does not imply that no economic activities or forms of temporary settlement were possible in the lower Lombardy plains before hydraulic remediation measures, but rather that the establishment of stable rural settlements and associated systematic adaptation of natural resources to human needs was only possible after the domestication of the environment. In other words, the development of an agrarian economy on the lower Po Valley plain was only possible after achieving a degree of hydraulic equilibrium (from the human perspective, obviously), with the contingent advantage of having abundant availability of a primary resource for the agricultural exploitation of the land. The details of issues already analyzed in previous essays will not be addressed here[13], but it is worthwhile at least summarizing the main aspects of the intricate relationship between humans and water on the lower Lombardy plain.

The first systematic reclamation of the lower plains was favoured by so-called *centuriazione* during the Roman period. Then starting from the thirteenth century a "new water culture" stimulated a generalized process of hydraulic works[14]. The Navigli and Muzza canals (excavations commissioned by the Duke and municipality of Milan) immediately became the main axes of an increasingly dense network, thanks also to the practice of establishing consortia and companies of landowners for the excavation of new channels, in order to share construction and management costs[15]. Controlling the water was an important aspect of social and political power, as well as a great economic advantage. For example, the income statement for the Cavallera Crivella ditch, owned by the Trivulzio family, showed an enormous net income for 1569, representing more than 70% net revenue (Tab. 1).

---

13 See note 5.

14 G. Bigatti, *La provincia delle acque*, pp. 31–40. During the Middle Ages, a particularly important reclamation project was conducted by the Cistercians on their *grange*. See R. Comba, *I cistercensi fra città e campagna nei secoli XII e XIII. Una sintesi mutevole di orientamenti economici e culturali nell'Italia nord-occidentale*, in "Studi storici", 26, 1985, 2, pp. 237–261; L. Chiappa Mauri, *Paesaggi rurali di Lombardia (secoli XII–XV)*, Roma / Bari 1990; P. Grillo, *Cistercensi e società cittadina in età comunale: il monastero di Chiaravalle milanese (1180–1276)*, in "Studi Storici", 40, 1999, 2, pp. 357–394.

15 E. Roveda, *Il beneficio delle acque. Problemi di storia dell'irrigazione in Lombardia tra XV e XVII secolo*, in "Società e Storia", 7, 1984, 24, pp. 269–287.

Tab. 1: Summary of the economic statement of the Cavallera Crivella ditch (1569, value in Lire. Soldi. Denari)

Revenue		Expenses	
Rent of water	5879.00.00	Fiscal burden	654.10.00
		Maintenance	1082.03.02
		Total expenses	1736.13.02
		Net income	4142.06.10
Total	5879.00.00	Total	5879.00.00

Source: Archivio di Stato of Milan, *Triviulzio, Archivio Novarese*, folder 5, p. 24.

However, participation in irrigation networks was not a prerogative of the richest class of society. Construction of large canals and extraction of water from rivers required a Ducal license (since rivers were considered state property) and these permissions were mostly granted to urban and rural communities, major religious or 'social' institutions, and noble families. The development of secondary networks was instead favoured by the so-called *servitù d'acquedotto*, a legal institution based on customary law, recognized in the municipal statutes and by the state. This enabled anyone to build a canal on another person's land against payment of the price of the land occupied increased by a quarter of its market value[16]. As a result, once the right to dig and supply a main canal had been acquired, or a spring was domesticated to create a fountain, the water network could spread rapidly and extensively over a vast area, thanks to the construction of dividers and a dense network of canals overlapping each other by way of "bridges" and "underpasses". In some cases, the interweaving of canals was so dense that it was difficult to immediately identify the origin of each one.

Land reclamation and excavation of canals in themselves became cause and effect for other developments, each fundamental to the process of creating this artificial landscape. They created concentrations of peasants in new rural buildings (so-called *cassine*) scattered across the countryside, along with other structures in order to organize workers and promote an embryonic working class. There was a gradual transition from partial to fixed leases paid in cash, and there was aggregation of plots of land to establish large farms along with integration of

16 G.D. Romagnosi, *Della ragion civile delle acque nella rurale economia*, Milano 1829–1835. More in general, for the legal framework of water management see L. Moscati, *In materia di acque: tra diritto comune e codificazione albertina*, Roma 1993.

agriculture and livestock[17]. These characteristics began to spread on the lower Lombardy plains in the fifteenth-sixteenth centuries and were rather unusual in Italian and European agricultural practice at the time. The phenomenon was stimulated by a high rate of urbanization in central-northern Italy with consequent rapidly growing demands for foodstuffs in cities[18]. The large noble and ecclesiastical landholdings became the focus for these innovations, thanks to the spread of long-term lease contracts (usually nine-year contracts paid in cash rather than in kind).

Huge unified farmlands were assigned to wealthy intermediaries, so-called *fittabili*, who became leaders of the agricultural avant-garde of Lombardy and of the spread of capitalist agriculture across the territory[19]. Through rational exploitation of funds and producing for a market rather than for family growth and sustenance[20], the *fittabili* implemented the structural and agronomic changes described above, guaranteed by *ad meliorandum* contracts that allowed them to discount any improvements from the rent, as certified by engineers engaged to compile "delivery" and "redelivery" reports for the farm. The spread of this capitalist agriculture accelerated the process of transformation of the agricultural landscape, with an expansion of crops at the expense of pastures and woods, and the spread of artificial meadows and irrigated crops. Thus, the local socio-economic organization changed

---

17 C.M. Cipolla, *Per la storia delle terre della "bassa" lombarda*, in *Studi in onore di Armano Sapori*, Milano 1957, vol. 1, pp. 665–672; A. De Maddalena, *Contributo sulla storia dell'agricoltura della bassa lombarda. Appunti sulla possessione di Belgioioso (sec. XVI–XVIII)*, in "Archivio Storico Lombardo", 8, 1958, 8, pp. 165–183; G. Chittolini, *Alle origini delle "grandi aziende" della bassa lombarda*, in "Quaderni Storici", 13, 1978, 39, pp. 828–844.

18 L. Chiappa Mauri, *Riflessioni sulle campagne lombarde del Quattro-Cinquecento*, in "Nuova Rivista Storica", 69, 1985, 1/2, pp. 123–130; *Terra e uomini nella Lombardia medievale: alle origini di uno sviluppo*, Roma / Bari 1997.

19 The renting of large farms with nine-year contracts was typical of the lower Lombardy plain, on the land-holdings of noble families, ecclesiastical institutions, and "non-profit" organizations. On this subject, in addition to the studies mentioned above, see the example of the Ospedale Maggiore of Milan analyzed by S. Zaninelli, *Una grande azienda agricola della pianura irrigua lombarda nei secoli XVIII e XIX*, Milano 1964, in particular pp. 57–81. This kind of contract was already widespread in the fifteenth and sixteenth centuries, although during the economic reconversion of the early seventeenth century (D. Sella, *Crisis and Continuity. The Economy of Spanish Lombardy in the Seventeenth Century*, Harvard 1979; A. De Maddalena, *Dalla città al borgo. Avvio di una metamorfosi economica e sociale nella Lombardia spagnola*, Milano 1982) there was a return to more traditional forms of management, particularly on the middle and upper plains. See L. Faccini, *La Lombardia fra '600 e '700*, Milano 1988, pp. 177–182.

20 M. Cattini, *L'economia rurale in epoca preindustriale. Proposta di un modello interpretativo*, in G.L. Basini (ed.), *Dall'età preindustriale all'età del capitalismo*, Studi e ricerche della Facoltà di Economia e Commercio, 13, Parma 1977, pp. 121–150.

profoundly, with an increasingly few wealthy tenants organizing the work of numerous poor peasants[21]. These changes did not always follow linear trajectories, leading in the long term to the so-called "agrarian revolution" of the eighteenth-nineteenth centuries[22], which at the dawn of the early modern period was limited to some specific areas (the countryside between Milan, Pavia and Lodi) and a few innovative farms[23].

3 Water rights

In late medieval and early modern Lombardy, the water of rivers and large canals was the property of the state and its use was subject to sovereign concession[24]. The development of the irrigation network following the long-term changes described above accelerated in the second half of the fifteenth century. The State of Milan experienced a period of political stabilization with the affirmation of the Sforza seigniory and considerable economic and demographic developments, including an important growth in agriculture. As a consequence, the number of ducal concessions for water extraction increased. Water rights were assigned to important institutions (of the local community, charitable-welfare, or religious), as well as eminent families close to the ducal power. The lists of beneficiaries for these concessions include the wealthiest institutions and members of the most prominent Lombard families, who were granted this privilege both for economic motives (like colonization of new areas, and exploiting hydraulic energy for mills), and for the social function that the control of water resources provided[25]. The main canals were based on these basic concessions, and from these the small to medium sized land owners obtained rights to use water for their own operations. In this way, access to water defined (and maintained) social hierarchies, favoring the development of a network of loyalty towards local elites and state power. These institutions and noble families had multiple interests in the territories over which

---

21 M. Di Tullio, *Rese agricole, scorte alimentari, strutture famigliari. Le campagne dello stato di Milano a metà Cinquecento*, in G. Alfani / M. Barbot (eds.), *Ricchezza, Valore e Proprietà in età preindustriale*, Venezia 2009, pp. 293–318. For a recent discussion of the concept of proletarianization and its relationship with economic inequality dynamics see G. Alfani / M. Di Tullio, *The Lion's Share. Inequality and the Rise of the Fiscal State in Preindustrial Europe*, Cambridge 2019.

22 L. Cafagna, *La "rivoluzione agraria" in Lombardia*, in "Annali Feltrinelli", 2, 1959, pp. 363–428.

23 G. Chittolini, *La pianura irrigua lombarda fra Quattro e Cinquecento*, in "Annali dell'Istituto Alcide Cervi", 10, 1988, pp. 207–221.

24 G. Bigatti, *La provincia delle acque*, pp. 28–40.

25 E. Roveda, *Il beneficio delle acque*.

they obtained water derivation, since they often had large landholdings and enjoyed various feudal rights. As already noted however, while assignment of water rights was not equal, it was a collective process that included larger and smaller landowners, "private" owners, "public" institutions, religious and welfare organizations, and so on.

It was an unwritten rule that those obtaining water extraction rights from canals (the users) would form consortiums to which they delegated the authority to coordinate the management of each canal and resolve disputes between users in the preliminary stages. Normally, each of the users could draw water for a certain number of hours, depending on the shifts established by the so-called "wheel", even though episodes of irregular appropriation beyond the permitted amounts were commonplace, often involving the fraudulent opening of a new intake.

The central importance of water for these territories made it the object of continuous disputes between different users and different forms of use, involving institutions, landowners, state magistrates, local bodies, and in particular the municipal authorities. The disputes were often long and complex, testified by veritable "rivers of ink" consumed in appeals to courts and for writing detailed records[26].

The issue of litigation associated with the spread of the waterworks will be discussed further below, but now the focus will be on the second main point. The observations immediately above demonstrate that water management was a collective goal involving public and private institutions, local and central government, rich and poor. In addition to the primary ecological value of waterworks already noted, they offered many other general advantages, like protection, disinfection, nutrition, commerce, and so on. In many cases, this public utility was guaranteed by the common ownership of part of the water system under local communities or the state. In many others, as already noted, collective ownership or management was possible thanks to the creation of consortia or other institutions that implemented collective actions among those entitled to benefit from a specific canal or irrigation ditch. The importance of irrigation consortia for maintaining profitable management of waterworks is confirmed not only by the extended persistence of this institution, but also in the

---

26 E. Roveda, *I beni comuni nella Bassa fra Ticino e Sesia (secoli XV e XVI)*, in G. Andenna (ed.), *Insediamenti medievali tra Sesia e Ticino. Problemi istituzionali e sociali*, Novara 1999, pp. 47–63; S. Tomiato, *Dalla foresta alla risaia. Litigare per l'acqua: le comunità lomelline e le ragioni d'acqua di fronte all'evoluzione dell'agricoltura e all'ascesa della risicoltura*, Varzi 2012; M. Barbot, *Non tutti i conflitti vengono per nuocere. Usi, diritti e litigi sui canali lombardi fra XV e XX secolo (prime indagini)*, in L. Mocarelli (ed.), *Quando manca il pane. Origini e cause della scarsità delle risorse alimentari in età moderna e contemporanea*, Bologna 2013, pp. 35–56; M. Di Tullio / C. Lorenzini, *La ricerca della sostenibilità. Economia, acqua, risorse e conflitti nell'Italia Settentrionale (secc. XV–XVIII)*, in *Gestione dell'acqua in Europa (XII–XVIII Secc.)*, Firenze 2018, pp. 165–185.

analyses produced by numerous agronomists and engineers even into the eighteenth and nineteenth centuries. The best known of these included John Symons, Arthur Young, and Richard Baird Smith, who visited Lombardy to study the sophisticated irrigation networks, and who were favourably impressed by the extension and excellent operation of these irrigation consortia[27].

Some decades later the commission set up to create the Villoresi canal north of Milan noted, among other technical issues, that the realization and future management of this infrastructure would have been almost impossible if the landowners of the area had not formed a consortium[28]. In brief, the collective status of the waterworks was justified by the specific geopedological condition of the territory, the plurality of uses for this natural resource, the multiplicity of actors and institutions interested and involved in its use, and finally the need to implement a collective management system in order to guarantee "sustainable" use of this important resource.

However, this is not the end of the story, because there is a further element that can help explain the deeper ecological and collective nature of the water network in early modern Lombardy, and probably elsewhere. This is the third main point, and regards the fact that the water supply network is a peculiar infrastructure, in that it could be considered to be alive. It is alive from an ecological point of view, not only because of the hydraulic equilibrium required for human settlement already mentioned. While water infrastructures certainly alter the local ecosystem, at the same time they become an integral part of it. They have an immediate effect, for example, on the local flora and fauna (and the collateral economic interests that might derive from this). Changing the flow and course of rivers affects the landscape, perhaps making new land available, offers the possibility of developing new transport networks, makes new energy sources available, and so on. This class of infrastructure certainly impacted the local climate, influenced humidity levels, and could even help to ameliorate the consequences of the climate cycles that affected the Po Valley in the early modern period. At the same time, climate change also influenced the waterworks, with changes in temperature,

27 M. Ambrosoli, *John Symonds. Agricoltura e politica in Corsica e in Italia*, Torino 1974; L. Cafagna, *La "rivoluzione agraria"*, pp. 31–112; C. Marini, *Lodi e la pianura padana alla fine del Settecento negli interessi di Arthur Young, Thomas Jefferson e Maria Cosway*, in "Archivio Storico Lodigiano", 2001, 120, pp. 183–235; M. Di Tullio, *Il mito delle campagne lombarde nella cultura inglese sette-ottocentesca*, in G. Bigatti (ed.), *Quando l'Europa ci ammirava. Viaggiatori, artisti, tecnici e agronomi stranieri nell'Italia del '700 e '800*, Truccazzano 2016, pp. 67–120.

28 M. Di Tullio, *Interessi privati e rappresentanza degli utenti nella storia del canale*, in G. Bigatti (ed.), *Il canale Villoresi, un capolavoro d'ingegneria idraulica*, Milano 2010, pp. 33–43; G. Bigatti (ed.), *Il Villoresi. L'ultimo naviglio*, Truccazzano 2010.

and rainfall intensity and distribution during the year. Certain adverse conditions could even induce depopulation and abandonment of the infrastructures themselves.

The water network could also be considered a living infrastructure because its impact might change in both time and space. A single canal or ditch could encounter different soil consistencies, even over short distances, providing benefits or otherwise to the various plots of land on the basis of their consistency and economic vocation. Examples include disputes over the spread of irrigated crops, or the cultivation of mulberry trees in which Lombardy invested during the eighteenth century, or regarding the growth of rice paddies from the sixteenth century onwards because they were thought to encourage the spread of malaria[29].

The water supply network is also a living infrastructure because it creates and feeds a new water cycle that influences not only the flow of rivers and the dynamics of springs, but also the levels of underground aquifers. All the water flowing in the water supply network is returned to rivers and underground aquifers thanks to the ability of farmers and other workers involved in water management, and through the implementation of a specific system of canals for recycling water. In other words, the water supply network is influenced by, and at the same time influences, the natural water cycle.

Finally, the network of waterworks could be considered alive because it continuously expanded almost "naturally", inducing the emergence of other activities. As already noted, over time the creation of the main canals encouraged the development of secondary and tertiary networks, while also stimulating the exploitation of this resource for novel purposes. So, the growth of the water system stimulated new economic activities, and this established a feedback loop that fostered further development of the waterworks. All this strongly influenced the transformation of the local ecosystem, causing these cycles to be repeated over and over again (Fig. 1).

---

29 L. Faccini, *L'economia risicola lombarda dagli inizi del XVIII secolo all'Unità*, Milano 1976; by the same author, *La Lombardia fra '600 e '700*; M. Di Tullio, *Croce e delizia. La risicoltura in Lombardia*.

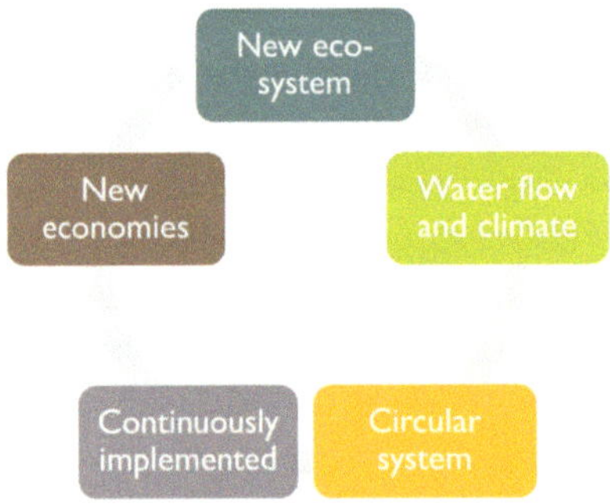

Fig. 1: The water network as a living infrastructure.

4 Conclusion: water networks and conflicts

Drawing towards a conclusion, it is necessary to redefine the stylized bucolic picture painted up to this point and note that the development of the irrigation network did not always follow a smooth linear trajectory or even chronology. As our fourth and final point, the spread of the irrigation system was not always a triumphal process, nor a neutral one.

As already mentioned, there were alterations to ecosystems caused by reclamation activities associated with the development of the irrigation network, along with new settlements and economic opportunities based on the irrigation system. It comes as no surprise that the spread of this living infrastructure, fundamental from the ecological and collective perspectives, immediately led to disputes.

This final point can be underlined by summarizing the main results of some research conducted by the present author on water management in Lombardy[30]. The goal of the study was to try to reconstruct the emergence of sustainability issues starting from a systematic analysis of conflicts over water use. It focused on an analysis of water management on the lower Lombardy plain close to Milan and Brescia and therefore embracing both the State of Milan and the Republic of Venice. It involved a systematic reading of primary sources produced by various institutions and major landowners in this area. In the case of Milan, some important 'welfare' institutions were considered, like the Misericordia consortium and the Quattro Marie *schola*, while for Brescia the focus was on the local Ospedale Maggiore[31].

30 M. Di Tullio / C. Lorenzini, *La ricerca della sostenibilità*; by the same authors, *Natural resources, Conflict and Sustainability*.

31 M. Barbot, *Non tutti i conflitti vengono per nuocere*; M. Di Tullio, *La gestione del patrimonio fondiario della Misericordia e delle Quattro Marie in età Moderna. Un'analisi di lungo periodo*, in

Both cases enabled a long-term analysis from the early fifteenth to the end of the eighteenth century. These examples were particularly suited to the aims of the study due to the abundance and seriality of documents still preserved in local archives[32], particularly regarding the financial management of the institutions and conflicts related to management of assets, including their extended waterworks systems[33]. The documents produced to resolve controversies over use (and possession) of natural resources provided extensive information about management practices and trigger issues influencing the emergence of sustainability problems.

A detailed description of sources and other data collection technicalities are provided in the author's essays already published on the subject. Here the aggregated data on the conflicts involving the abovementioned 'welfare' institutions are set out in the following figure (Fig. 2).

The incidence rates plotted in the figure show how the number of conflicts fluctuated during the fifteenth century, with a progressive increase during the sixteenth century, peaking in the seventeenth century.

The trend then inverted and declined throughout the eighteenth century, before increasing again at the end of the ancien régime. Moving beyond observation of general trends, a deeper analysis revealed that these dynamics had both external causes (mainly climate[34], but also demographic dynamics, and economic

---

L. Aiello / M. Bascapè / S. Rebora (eds.), *Il paese dell'acqua. I luoghi pii elemosinieri di Milano e le loro terre: un itinerario nel paesaggio dal medioevo ai giorni nostri*, Como 2013, pp. 47–63.

32 Archivio di Stato, Brescia, *Ospedale Maggiore*, folders 1148–1177. This project was funded by the Carlo F. Dondena Centre for the Study of Social Dynamics and Public Policy of Bocconi University in Milan, and by the University of Pavia under the "INROAd" funding program. For the history of the Ospedale Maggiore of Brescia see G. Bonelli, *L'archivio dell'Ospedale di Brescia. Notizia e inventario*, Brescia 1916; A. Marinella, *Le origini degli ospedali bresciani*, Brescia 1963; D. Montanari / S. Onger (eds.), *I ricoveri della città. Storia delle istituzioni di assistenza e beneficenza a Brescia. Secoli XVI–XX*, Brescia 2002; D. Montanari, *I poveri della città. Carità e assistenza nella Brescia moderna*, Brescia 2014.

33 On this subject see, for example, P. Fournier / S. Lavaud (eds.), *Eaux et conflits dans l'Europe médiévale et moderne*, Toulouse 2012, specifically the *Introduction* (pp. 7–31).

34 The reference is to the so-called "Little Ice Age" and its various consequences for the economy, society, and culture on a global level. Among the vast historiographic productions, see at least, E. Le Roy-Ladurie, *Histoire du climat depuis l'an mil*, Paris 1967; J.F. Richards, *The Unending Frontier. An Environmental History of the Early Modern World*, Berkeley 2003; W. Behringer, *Kulturgeschichte des Klimas. Von der Eiszeit zur globalen Erwärmung*, München 2010; G. Parker, *Global Crisis. War, Climate Change and Catastrophe in the Seventeenth Century*, London / New York 2013; P. Blom, *Die Welt aus den Angeln. Eine Geschichte der Kleinen Eiszeit von 1570 bis 1700 sowie der Entstehung der modernen Welt, verbunden mit einen Überlegungen zum Klima der Gegenwart*, München 2017.

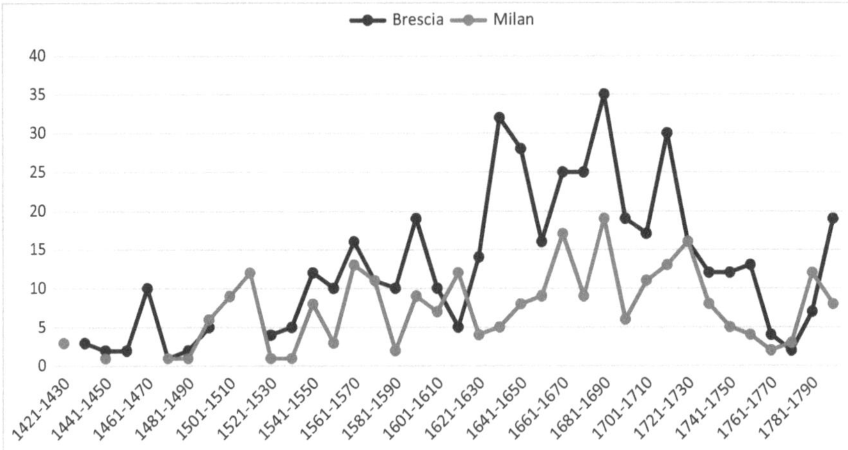

Fig. 2: Conflicts related to water use on the lower Milan / Brescia plain (1421–1800).

trends[35]), and internal causes (human intervention in water management)[36]. This dual causality (endogenous and exogenous) was seemingly confirmed in qualitative examinations of the conflicts themselves.

Among the many aspects considered in this study, it is worth noting one of the main conclusions which appears to be pertinent to the issues under discussion here. What was revealed from the quantification and, more strikingly, qualification of these water conflicts was that increased water disputes were not only correlated to increased efforts to control this resource, or a growth in conflicts of interest, or recurrent illicit extraction of water, etc. While these were certainly important reasons for disputes, they were not the only ones, and perhaps not the most relevant. The most persistent and difficult litigations to manage were those involving alterations to the local ecological balance (i.e. the spread of rice cultivation), the threat of losing the collective basis of the water supply system, and more importantly the abandonment of the infrastructure and lack of maintenance following periods of population decline or after flooding. Examining in detail within the general trend it can be observed that the number and duration of conflicts increased precisely

35 G. Alfani, *Calamities and the Economy in Renaissance Italy. The Grand Tour of the Horsemen of the Apocalypse*, Basingstoke / New York 2013; G. Alfani, *La popolazione dell'Italia settentrionale nel XV e XVI secolo: scenari regionali e macro-regionali*, in G. Alfani et al. (eds.), *La popolazione italiana del Quattrocento e Cinquecento*, Udine 2016, pp. 19–40.

36 See E. Guidoboni, *Human Factors. Extreme Events and Floods in the Lower Po Plain (Northern Italy) in the 16th Century*, in "Environment and History", 4, 1998, 3, pp. 279–308.

when these conditions (population decline and climate instability) became more marked, for example during the seventeenth century.

Clearly there were many other factors that influenced the dynamics of these conflicts, but this aspect clearly shows how the water network was a living infrastructure that required continuous care. It altered and became part of a new domesticated ecosystem, a new environment, in which the role of human activity was fundamental. While humans had altered the environment in order to live and work in this territory, at the same time they became a determining factor for maintaining the new equilibrium. If the infrastructure is to be kept working, each element needs to cooperate towards its operation. That is why demographic, economic, and climate shocks put the "traditional" operation of this infrastructure at risk, and it also explains why the conflicts connected with its management were so frequent and difficult to resolve.

Tim Soens

Slow Infrastructures, Flood Protection and Extreme Weather Events

A Historical Perspective

> *Our world is full of – mostly untold – stories of slow hope. They are inspired by anticipation and driven by the idea that things can be different. They are "slow" in their unfolding, and they are slow because they come with setbacks. In a world where developments are evolving ever more rapidly, slowness can be frustrating but also inspiring* (C. Mauch, *Slow Hopes*)[1].

The Great Acceleration is a well-known label used to characterize the rapid pace of global transformations of society and ecology starting after the Second World War. Whether discussing the use of natural resources or energy, the loss of biodiversity, population and income growth, global connectivity, global warming and so on, the pace of human transformation of planet Earth has been rapidly accelerating, and the enormous scale and speed of the transformation is now threatening our very survival as a species[2]. One of the possible answers to the Great Acceleration is 'slowing down', popular in the Degrowth movement, which argues that the relentless striving for growth and 'more' cannot continue forever, and that scientific and technological improvements alone will be insufficient to counteract the destructive impact of the Great Acceleration. Slowing down is applied to economic development, preferring a broadening of welfare and wellbeing over a quest for income growth per capita. Slowing down is applied to our mobility, no longer crisscrossing the planet on highly polluting airplanes, but rediscovering our own environment by walking and biking. Slowing down might also be applied to our food cycle: the slow food movement argues for a more conscious consumption, based on local food resources, a short chain between producer and consumer, as well as a move away from industrial processing of food.

Quite paradoxically, the urgent call to act on global climate change might be answered by a reappreciation of slowness. In the opening quotation of this contribution, Christoph Mauch argues for the importance of 'slow change': the awareness that a myriad of actors, by *decelerating* their interaction with the natural environment, can make a difference, although this difference will only become visible

1 C. Mauch, *Slow Hope: Rethinking Ecologies of Crisis and Fear*, in "RCC Perspectives: Transformations in Environment and Society", 2019, 1, p. 21.

2 The idea of the Great Acceleration became popular thanks to W. Steffen et al., *The Trajectory of the Anthropocene: The Great Acceleration*, in "The Anthropocene Review", 2, 2015, 1, pp. 81–98.

https://doi.org/10.1515/9783111112756-010

over a longer period of time. He illustrates his argument with both historical and present-day examples ranging from sustainable forestry, which involves actions only taking effect after decades or generations, to the way environmentalism itself has become a major concern for an ever larger part of the global population.

This essay investigates the potential of slowness and 'deceleration' when discussing the history of infrastructure[3]. It does so by exploring the history of flood protection infrastructures. Present-day examples are overwhelmingly 'hard' concrete, capital and technology-intensive infrastructures, although all over the world efforts are being made to 'soften' them by adding natural-based solutions (restoring wetlands, fostering the growth of dune and coral barriers etc.). But present-day flood protection is not only 'hard', it is also 'fast' – introduced as a 'project' or 'improvement' at a given moment in time, often producing a complete transformation of the natural and man-made environment. In the history of flood protection we can see not only an increased rigidity of the infrastructures, but also a transition from 'slow' to 'fast' infrastructures. Exploring the historical significance of 'slow' flood protection, the reasons for its demise, as well as its potential as a source of inspiration for coastal and riverine environments today, are the main goals of this paper.

1 The problem with hard infrastructures: the July 2021 river floods in north-west Europe

On 14 and 15 July 2021 extreme rainfall hit north-western Germany and adjacent parts of Belgium, the Netherlands, and France. The torrential rainfall of over 200 liters of rain caused river floods and landslides, taking the lives of more than 220 people, 184 in Germany and 38 in Belgium. Such a catastrophic flood was unusual for at least two reasons. Firstly, the intensity of the rainfall exceeded any historical measurements, suggesting a link with climate change. Current modeling suggests that climate change has made such an event between 1.2 and 9 times more likely, compared to preindustrial times[4]. Secondly, in this part of Europe river

3 Conceiving pre-1800 flood protection as 'slow infrastructures' was directly inspired by the keynote of Helmuth Trischler at the start of the conference that instigated the present volume. In the concluding remarks of the keynote, as well as in the discussion that followed, the idea of 'slow infrastructures' was suggested as a useful analytical category when discussing present-day and historical infrastructural challenges. Of course, any misinterpretation remains my own.

4 F. Kreienkamp et al., *Rapid Attribution of Heavy Rainfall Events Leading to the Severe Flooding in Western Europe during July 2021*, in "World Weather Attribution", 2021, p. 54, https://www.

floods have seldom caused so many fatalities. In the twentieth century, only the flood disasters of 1962 along the Elbe estuary, and 1953 in Zeeland and adjacent regions caused more deaths, but these were coastal floods caused by storm surges across the North Sea[5]. The 2021 river floods can be seen as a typical failure of modern hard infrastructure to cope with the consequences of climate change. Walls of earth and concrete have been constructed to contain water along both rivers and coastlines. Since the nineteenth century, dams have been added to regulate and stabilize the water levels[6]. The hard water infrastructure replaced the previous systems, which combined accommodation (i.e. avoiding flood-prone areas) with 'softer' infrastructures (such as the deliberate maintenance of large areas of riverine wetlands). The older systems usually allowed for highly variable water levels, distinguishing between a smaller 'summer' bed and a much larger 'winter' bed consisting of wetlands that were flooded in times of high water. With levees and dams, and rectification of river courses, they were transformed into canals, optimized for navigation and stable water supplies. Riverine (and coastal) wetlands were no longer needed to accommodate flood water, and could be developed for residential or industrial purposes. Since the 1990s, river engineering has moved away from the 'hard' model, returning towards 'softer' or more 'nature-based' technologies. In the Netherlands, the river floods of 1993 and 1995 initiated a paradigmatic shift towards providing 'room for rivers' and buffer spaces to accommodate flood waters were created where possible. Neighboring countries followed, although the prime focus remained on the major rivers like the Meuse, Rhine or Scheldt, with the tributaries being somewhat neglected[7]. It may not be a coincidence that the floods of July 2021 caused most problems along minor tributaries, the Vesdre in Belgium, the Erft and the Ahr in Germany, and the Geul in the Netherlands, while the flood protection systems along the Meuse and Rhine worked relatively well.

An exemplary case is the story of the Vesdre-river in the east of Belgium, a 70 kilometer long tributary of the Meuse running through a deep and narrow valley, and the epicenter for the 2021 flood disaster, at least in Belgium. The water level on the Vesdre is regulated by the Gileppe and Eupen dams, respectively inaugurated in 1878 and 1950. As is often the case with river dams, the Vesdre dams are

---

worldweatherattribution.org/wp-content/uploads/Scientific-report-Western-Europe-floods-2021-attribution.pdf, last accessed January 3, 2022.

5 T. Soens, *Resilient Societies, Vulnerable People: Coping with North Sea Floods Before 1800*, in "Past & Present", 241, 2018, 1, pp. 143–177.

6 See G. Parrinello's contribution to this volume.

7 W. Cornwall, *Europe's Deadly Floods Leave Scientists Stunned*, in "Scienceinsider", July 20, 2021, on-line via https://www.science.org/content/article/europe-s-deadly-floods-leave-scientists-stunned, last accessed January 25, 2022.

multifunctional infrastructures, providing both drinking water and hydropower, as well as buffering variations in water levels during times of both flood and drought. During the July 2021 floods the dams did not break, but in the night of 14 to 15 July some of the water in the Eupen dam had to be released because the reservoir had reached maximum capacity. Interestingly, in a 2015 risk assessment, drought rather than floods was considered the major challenge threatening the operation of the Vesdre reservoir system[8]. Equally important are the river banks along the Vesdre. The Vesdre valley is the true heartland of the first industrial revolution in Belgium. Already before 1800, arms manufacturers and textile plants were exploiting the water of the river Vesdre to power water mills. In the early nineteenth century, the city of Verviers became the center of the national cloth industry, following the early adoption of steam power and the mechanization of spinning (already in 1818) and weaving[9]. By the middle of the nineteenth century, hundreds of textile mills – some of which employed more than 1,000 laborers – had been established in the Vesdre region. Metalworking also continued to expand in the Vesdre valley, from the production of firearms and steam engines to a giant zinc plant. To supply the factories and market with their products, a railroad was built already in the 1840s. The laborers were housed in rapidly constructed residential developments, with a reputation for poverty and bad hygiene. Like many other European rivers in the industrial hotbeds of the nineteenth century, the Vesdre rapidly turned into a real organic machine, to quote Richard White[10] (Fig. 1).

The mills, the railroad and the workers' houses all competed for space in the small river valley. The only relatively 'flat' areas available for construction were the floodplains adjacent to the river. Before 1800, these floodplains accommodated excess capacity in periods of high water, which occurred every year in early spring when the snow on the Ardennes hills was melting, and periodically when heavy precipitation made the river swell. From the sixteenth to the twentieth century at least two major river floods per century occurred in the Meuse basin – in Liège this was the case in 1571, 1643, 1658, 1740, 1850, 1880, 1925–26, 1993, and 1995[11]. It is

8 M. Bruwier et al., *Assessing the Operation Rules of a Reservoir System Based on a Detailed Modeling Chain*, in "Nat. Hazards Earth Syst. Sci.", 15, 2015, 3, pp. 365–379.

9 C. Desama / C. Bauwens, *Een kleine stad in het hart van de industriële revolutie: Verviers en de bewerking van wol*, in B. Van der Herten / M. Oris / J. Roegiers (eds.), *Nijver België. Het industriële landschap omstreeks 1850*, Brussel 1995, pp. 87–128.

10 R. White, *The Organic Machine: the Remaking of the Columbia River*, New York 1995.

11 For the pre-1926 floods, see M. Suttor, *Etude historique d'hydrologie fluviale. L'exemple de la Meuse*, in "Bulletin de la Société Géographique de Liège", 1989, 25, p. 169.

Fig. 1: The industrial Vesdre near Brouck-Cité (Trooz), early 20th century postcard, (author's collection).

important to stress that even these exceptional floods – *crues* in French – cost few lives. In 1740 for instance, two men – a father and his son – were killed in Namur, while they were trying to salvage floating wood from the water[12]. This is in line with the overall history of river floods in Europe, which potentially caused a lot of material damage, but only minor loss of life[13]. Apparently the existing 'buffer capacity' could cope with most of the excess water while the riverine population knew that floods returned every winter, with exceptional floods once or twice in a lifetime, and they had the skills and knowledge to save their lives in time.

These material and landscape measures along with the warning and communication networks in place, were labeled "amphibious strategies" by the Dutch

12 N. Ruffini-Ronzani / C. Ledent, *Namur, XVe–XXe siècle: Une ville de confluent face aux inondations*, in "Cahiers de Sambre et Meuse: le Guetteur wallon", 94, 2017, p. 74.

13 C. Rohr, *Extreme Naturereignisse im Ostalpenraum. Naturerfahrung im Spätmittelalter un dam Beginn der Neuzeit*, Köln / Weimar / Wien 2007, p. 398: "Eine Klassifizierung der Hochwasser nach den Auswirkungen zeigt, dass die grossen, aber langsam anwachsenden Überschwemmungen zwar grossen Sachschaden anrichteten, allerdings kaum Todesopfer forderten [. . .] Dies gilt auch für die extremen Überschwemmungen wie 1316, 1501, 1508, 1567, 1572 und 1598". Only sudden flash floods in the mountains might sometimes have killed more people, and also there reliable sources on casualties remain scarce.

water historian Petra Van Dam[14], and they were essential for survival in flood-prone areas. Very obviously, these amphibious strategies are no longer in place along the Vesdre or any of the other rivers affected by the July 2021 floods. Very few river wetlands had been restored on the Vesdre, and while the heavy industries of the nineteenth and twentieth centuries have left the area, the workers' houses are still there, right in the middle of the floodplains. The former textile mills and metalworks left behind contaminated soils that are extremely difficult to transform into natural wetlands. The first analyses of the flood disaster indicated widespread disbelief in predicted flood levels, as well as huge problems of organizing and communicating for timely evacuation of the areas threatened by the flood.

This is known as the "vulnerability paradox": as people expect well-functioning infrastructure and institutions to protect them from harm, they are more likely to be taken by surprise by an extreme event such as a flood[15].

2 Flood protection before 1800: not only 'softer' but also 'slower'

Up to this point it was assumed that floods, like those that affected north-western Europe in the summer of 2021, were the result of 'hard' infrastructures unable to cope with extreme weather events, greatly intensified by climate change. It would, however, be a mistake to suggest that river and coastal flood protection infrastructures before 1800 were always 'softer', and hence better able to cope with fluctuations in water level. First of all, it is necessary to clarify the differences between soft and hard infrastructures. Generally speaking, hard infrastructures are any kind of material infrastructure – roads, waterways, electricity or cable networks – installed to organize urban and rural landscapes, whereas soft infrastructures are mostly immaterial resources – the financial system, insurance, public services – supporting everyday life. In literature on (coastal) flood protection, the distinction between 'hard' and 'soft' is different, primarily based on the type of materials used as well as the rigidity of the infrastructure, with

14 P.J.E.M. van Dam, *An Amphibious Culture. Coping with Floods in the Netherlands*, in P. Coates / D. Moon / P. Warde (eds.), *Local Places, Global Processes. Histories of Environmental Change in Britain and Beyond*, Oxford 2017, pp. 78–93.

15 A. Fekete / S. Sandholz, *Here Comes the Flood, but Not Failure? Lessons to Learn after the Heavy Rain and Pluvial Floods in Germany 2021*, in "Water", 13, 2021, 3016.

concrete dams and levees celebrated as the champions of hard protective infrastructures. In contrast, soft protective measures actively promote or replicate natural dynamics: dune formation, beach replenishment, fostering the growth of sea grasses, coral reefs, etc. Simply accommodating flood water and retreating from areas at risk of flooding can be considered a third approach to coastal flood protection[16].

Before 1800, the flood protection infrastructure along the Vesdre river can still be conceived as largely based on 'soft' flood protection measures (given the importance of carefully managed floodplains). This was not always the case however. Some European rivers had been equipped with massive earth levees or dikes from the medieval period onwards, especially in highly urbanized regions. Along the Po river in northern Italy, marshlands had effectively lost their capacity to absorb flood waters before the end of the thirteenth century, and in the later Middle Ages the Italian city states invested heavily in the construction and maintenance of embankments[17]. On a much larger scale, during the Sung Dynasty the Chinese imperial government tried to divert the course of the Yellow River, provoking massive repercussions with the river mouth relocating hundreds of kilometers away[18].

In the coastal areas surrounding the North Sea, the sea wall as archetypical 'hard' infrastructure was adopted around the year 1000 CE, from the East Anglian Fenlands across to the Low Countries, Northern Germany, and Denmark. Stephen Rippon speaks of a transition from infrastructure *modifying* the landscape, to infrastructure *transforming* the landscape. Earth sea walls enabled a complete transformation of the landscape, as farming became possible on low-lying lands, and settlements moved from higher ground onto the low-lying (former) floodplains[19]. However, most medieval sea walls were not as 'hard' as modern ones and they broke quite often, with the many horseshoe-shaped dike repairs along the coastal

---

16 Note that hard infrastructures can also be nature-based, for instance when a concrete reef is constructed in front of a coastline. L.T. Mamo et al., *Beyond Coastal Protection: A Robust Approach to Enhance Environmental and Social Outcomes of Coastal Adaptation*, in "Ocean and Coastal Management", 217, 2022, art. no. 106007.

17 M. Campopiano, *The Evolution of the Landscape and the Social and Political Organization of Water Management: the Po Valley in the Middle Ages (Fifth to Fourteenth Centuries)*, in E. Thoen et al. (eds.), *Landscapes or Seascapes? The History of the Coastal Environment in the North Sea Area Reconsidered*, Turnhout 2013, pp. 313–332.

18 L. Zhang, *The River, the Plain, and the State. An Environmental Drama in Northern Song China, 1048–1128*, Cambridge 2019.

19 S. Rippon, *The Transformation of Coastal Wetlands: Exploitation and Management of Marshland Landscapes in North West Europe during the Roman and Medieval Periods*, Oxford 2000.

landscape still testifying to long-forgotten dike breaches[20]. Moreover, the hard sea walls were still combined with soft protective measures, such as shielding saltmarshes in front of sea walls, which had the triple advantage of accommodating excess flood waters, attenuating the power of waves, and facilitating repair work when dikes were breached. During the Christmas flood of 1717, the inhabitants of northern Groningen could observe the difference between a sea wall protected by saltmarsh and a sea wall directly exposed to the storm tide: while the latter was almost completely annihilated, the former at least partially resisted the water[21].

Sea walls only very gradually became more rigid: they grew more massive, lost any accompanying 'soft' protection measures, and above all they were no longer expected to break, instead intending to contain the water in a more absolute sense (Fig. 2). From the sixteenth century onwards, (military) engineers and water authorities increasingly viewed water as an enemy that had to be subdued. Holding the line became the new paradigm in flood protection and time-honored adaptive measures, like relocating settlements when a territory became environmentally unsuitable for living, were no longer accepted[22].

However, the transition from 'soft' to 'hard' flood protection measures is not the complete story. Dikes and dams are "thick things" literally, but especially figuratively, as these are artifacts "thick with power relations and politics", to quote Wiebe Bijker[23]. Both the construction and maintenance of flood protection infrastructure and the decision-making process surrounding it involved a broad range of stakeholders. Adaptations and even transformations occurred, but only after lengthy discussions and intense political and legal disputes. As such it might be possible to conceive of both the 'hard' sea and river walls of the medieval and early modern period, and the soft flood protection measures surrounding them, as examples of 'slow infrastructures'. Whether this was indeed the case, and how and when these infrastructures lost their 'slow' character – which they eventually did – will be explored below.

---

20 T. Soens / G. De Block / I. Jongepier, *Seawalls at Work: Envirotech and Labor on the North Sea Coast before 1800*, in "Technology and Culture", 60, 2019, 3, pp. 688–725.

21 Z. Zhu et al., *Historic Storms and the Hidden Value of Coastal Wetlands for Nature-Based Flood Defense*, in "Nature Sustainability", 3, 2020, 10, pp. 853–862.

22 Before 1800 much of the 'amphibious disposition' of the coastal societies around the North Sea had already been lost. In contrast, along rivers, the continuity of soft flood protection measures and amphibious strategies endured longer: T. Soens, *Resilience in Historical Disaster Studies: Pitfalls and Opportunities*, in M. Endress / L. Clemens / B. Rampp, *Strategies, Dispositions and Resources of Social Resilience*, Wiesbaden 2020, pp. 262–264.

23 W.E. Bijker, *Dikes and Dams, Thick with Politics*, in "Isis", 98, 2007, 1, p. 115.

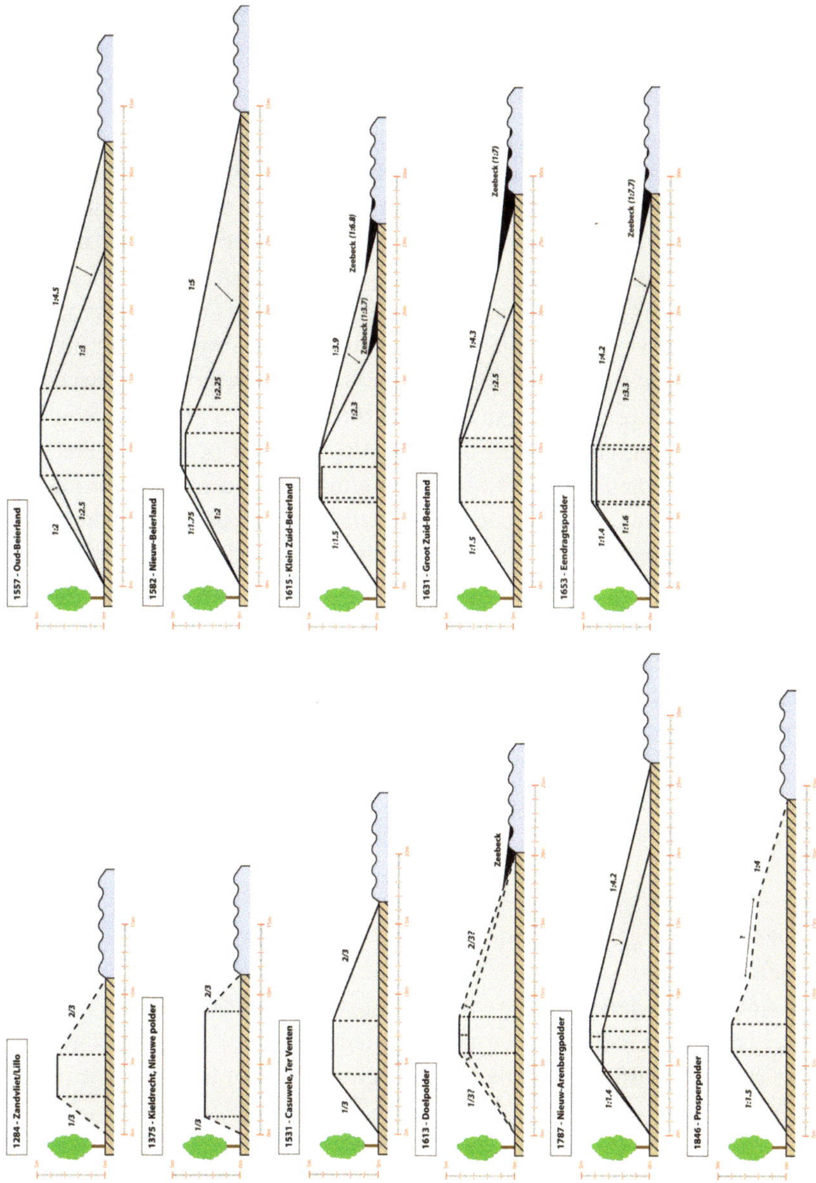

Fig. 2: Reconstructed profiles of sea walls from the 13th to the mid-19th century in the Scheldt polders near Antwerp (Flanders) (left), and the Beierland (South-Holland) (right), © I. Jongepier & T. Soens, see also T. Soens / G. De Block / I. Jongepier, *Seawalls at Work*, pp. 696–697.

3 Slow infrastructures at work: draining and ditching

Until the early modern period, the construction and maintenance of sea and river walls was mostly rooted in local farming communities, with local labor and resources both very much tied to the land and the rhythms of everyday life. Dike work was seasonal, fitted into agricultural cycles and resulted in a steady, periodic construction of sea walls, often taking several years to finish[24]. The work for the construction of a large sea wall north of Bruges in Flanders in 1288 was spread over five years. Each year, 600 rods or 2.3 kilometers of sea wall was constructed from May till August, after which the peasant workforce returned to harvesting their crops. When finished, the sea wall remained a work in progress, requiring repairs and extensions each year by the local landowners or peasants, summoned by their sheriff, *scultetus*, or dike-reeve. Sometimes a specific organization – a water board – was created to monitor these works and decide on any improvements and adaptations. These arrangements were quite similar all over the medieval North Sea area, from the South of England to the Low Countries and Northern Germany. Often an inspection committee made two or three visits to a sea wall each year, with every landowner or tenant responsible for maintenance required to attend, and risking a fine for failure to appear[25]. In Kehdingen along the Elbe Estuary, sea walls had to be raised every seven years and each peasant had to employ a well-defined quantity of earth to achieve this. The earth used to maintain sea walls could normally be drawn from the saltmarshes outside the sea wall, to which individual landowners or communities behind the sea wall had access and property rights[26].

As already mentioned, medieval sea and river walls were far from 'unbreakable', and every few years dike breaches had to be repaired. Medieval Dike Law – first codified in the Carolingian Capitulare Missorum of 802/821 – required all able-bodied men to defend the sea walls against the water in case of imminent danger, just as they had to defend against enemy invaders. From the late thirteenth century onwards, the yearly accounts of the Flemish water boards record

---

24 P. van Dam, *Digging for a Dike. Holland's Labor Market ca. 1510*, in P. Hoppenrbouwers / J.L. Van Zanden (eds.), *Peasants into Farmers? The Transformation of Rural Economy and Society in the Low Countries (Middle Ages–19th Century) in Light of the Brenner Debate*, Turnhout 2001, pp. 220–255.

25 This section is based on T. Soens / G. De Block / I. Jongepier, *Seawalls at Work*.

26 N. Fischer, *Wassersnot und Marschengesellschaft – Zur Geschichte der Deiche in Kehdingen*, Stade 2003, p. 44.

the scale of this mobilization, as water boards started to reimburse those who effectively showed up. After the 1376 flood at least 64 'men-with-spade' and a further 50 with one or two horses helped to repair the sea wall between Heist and Blankenberge. Even in 1442 dike work in the same area was still a socially inclusive, communal activity: the 109 'men-with-spade' and 90 with one or two horses included numerous commoners but also local noblemen (or at least their servants or delegates). Sometimes they were joined by friars from local monasteries, like brother Goswin of Spermalie, who in 1397 arrived with two horses[27].

Similar maintenance systems existed along rivers, although river walls were often only a minor part of flood protection mechanisms, which relied primarily on extensive wetlands able to compensate river flow rates. River wetlands were often essential components of the agricultural system, providing pasture and hay for livestock, along with a range of other 'services' such as fuel (peat or wood), construction timber, fish and birds, reeds and basketwork materials, etc. To function properly they required extensive systems of drainage ditches and sluices, which were again maintained by the local community. In manorial economies, ditch digging might be part of customary labor duties due to the lord and those unwilling to perform their maintenance duties were sued in the manor court. Both inside and outside manorial systems, village communities organized some degree of coordination. Regular maintenance of ditches and river banks provided local communities with an elaborate knowledge of the riverine environment. The finely differentiated toponomy of the wetlands demonstrates how local communities were aware of flood risks, raising flood-awareness by specific naming, as recently argued for Anglo-Saxon England by Richard Jones and Susan Kilby. Anyone encountering a field name that included *-wæsse* or *-flēot* in inland areas of England would be aware that the area was liable to periodic riverine flooding.

> For local communities, the names of minor landscape features provided [a] detailed repository of Traditional Ecological Knowledge that they could draw upon. On this base of knowledge, decisions were made regarding how particular parts of the landscape might be best settled, farmed, or otherwise managed[28].

The recurrent, cyclical nature of maintenance work, continuous albeit invisible improvements and modifications, familiarity with the local soil, vegetation and hydrology, and the collective effort of working together on an embankment or

---

27 T. Soens / G. De Block / I. Jongepier, *Seawalls at Work*, p. 712.

28 R. Jones / S. Kilby, *Mitigating Riverine Flood Risk in Medieval England*, in C.M. Gerrard / P. Forlin / P.J. Brown (eds.), *Waiting for the End of the World? New Perspectives on Natural Disasters in Medieval Europe*, Abingdon 2020, pp. 165–182.

drainage ditch, all help to explain how this category of infrastructure might be classed as 'slow'. While this type of maintenance and repair regime was most typical of small-scale, local infrastructures, they could also be deployed on larger, regional scales. Medieval flood protection sometimes included the construction of large regional infrastructures, the maintenance of which was allocated to village communities over extended regions. Communities in these territories all agreed to share a specific portion of the maintenance costs, sometimes proportional to their size, sometimes according to other criteria. Near Amsterdam in Holland, the Diemerdijk was normally maintained in the fifteenth century by local communities in the territory adjacent to the sea wall, which included about 3,164 hectares. Instead, in cases of dike breaches, communities over a much wider territory – about 18,007 hectares – were obliged to assist the former communities[29]. Along the East-Anglian Wash, the so-called "Roman" bank runs for about 241 kilometers between King's Lynn and Skegness. The sea wall was probably Anglo-Saxon in origin, and might have originated when local sea walls merged together at a given moment in time. In any case the maintenance of the sea wall required a degree of coordination over a very wide area[30]. These arrangements often lasted for centuries, and involved annual inspection of the maintenance by delegates of all the landowners or communities involved. Very unusual measures were developed to enforce the collaboration of all the landowners, such as the *teerschouw* – literally a 'consumptive inspection' during which the sea wall inspection commission would wait until all defaulted maintenance had been completed, in the meantime eating and drinking at the expense of the culprits[31].

In contrast to embankments, the maintenance of drainage sluices was more difficult to share between large groups of village communities. Nevertheless, in the twelfth and thirteenth centuries, large drainage sluices were being constructed, which sometimes served the drainage needs of very large territories. For example, the sluices of the Blankenbergse Watering in Coastal Flanders evacuated water over a territory of more than 17,000 hectares, at least since the thirteenth century. In the early sixteenth century this required the collaboration of 1,748 landowners, including 367 ecclesiastical, civic, or charitable institutions (from parishes to confraternities

29 M. Van Tielhof, *Forced Solidarity: Maintenance of Coastal Defences Along the North Sea Coast in the Early Modern Period*, in "Environment and History", 21, 2015, 3, pp. 327–328.
30 M. Chisholm, *Water Management in the Fens Before the Introduction of Pumps*, in "Landscape History", 33, 2012, 1, pp. 54–55.
31 M. Van Tielhof, *Consensus en conflict: waterbeheer in de Nederlanden 1200–1800*, Hilversum 2021, p. 85 with examples from 1284 onwards.

and abbeys)[32]. By that time land ownership in the area had already gone through a process of agglomeration. In the thirteenth century the number of landowners was at least twice as many. Maintaining outlet sluices was specialist work requiring skilled carpenters who were hired by the water authorities. This was financed with a land tax proportional to the size of land holdings in the area (or sometimes proportional to the benefit derived from the infrastructure). All individual landowners also remained responsible for the maintenance of minor drainage ditches, they could be mobilized for dike breaches, and they participated in decision-making processes. Such widespread participation in either the daily management or the organization of an infrastructure is the second essential feature for a 'slow' infrastructure, as will be discussed in the next paragraph.

4 Slow infrastructures at work: decision-making

In 1407 the drainage sluices near Blankenberge had to be renovated, and the water authorities – called "Watering" in this part of Flanders – convened the landowners to discuss the different options. Between 16 April and 22 June the landowners met at least five times in a general assembly (or *meentucht*). A commission was appointed to investigate the case, and different carpenters were invited to submit tenders. The lowest bid received was considered much too high by the general assembly, and a decision was postponed several times. Finally an agreement was reached, but when the work actually started and the old sluice was unearthed, some of the landowners who inspected the sluice argued that its deterioration was more limited than thought – "twelk eeneghe zeiden dat van gheenre nood ne was te vermakene" – and consequently the old sluice could be restored rather than completely replaced. A new meeting of the general assembly nevertheless decided that the work should continue[33].

Medieval decision-making differed from modern procedures, with the opinion of *sanior* members generally taking precedence over the *major pars*. However, this does not alter the fact that genuine discussion by a broad community of stakeholders did characterize the water management of late medieval coastal wetlands. At the general meetings landowners were invited to make comments,

---

32 T. Soens, *De spade in de dijk?: waterbeheer en rurale samenleving in de Vlaamse kustvlakte (1280–1580)*, Gent 2009, pp. 79–82.

33 T. Soens, *Polders zonder poldermodel? Een onderzoek naar de rol van inspraak en overleg in de waterstaat van de laatmiddeleeuwse Vlaamse kustvlakte (1250–1600)*, in "TSEG-The Low Countries Journal of Social and Economic History", 3, 2006, 4, pp. 14–15.

and their consent was explicitly required to ratify decisions by the board. Sometimes proceedings at the general meetings were disrupted by dissatisfied landowners, as was the case in 1406 in *Zuidover* near Bergues-Saint-Winnoc (France, Département du Nord), where some landowners shouted out loud – *overluut* – that the board had embezzled financial resources from the Watering[34]. Sometimes the participants even cast votes for counting, for instance when the election of a new board member was contested by multiple candidates. Such practices persisted into the eighteenth century, much to the displeasure of the larger landowners who complained about cottagers being able to vote on issues requiring important financial investments[35].

The 'democratic' or at least participative nature of decision-making for water management in the North Sea area has long been debated by historians. A recent synthesis by Milja Van Tielhof on water management in the Low Countries before 1800 presents a more nuanced picture, highlighting contrasting practices in different regions. Overall, direct participation was more likely to occur for local water management, whereas the decision-making process for regional water management was considerably more hierarchical[36].

Examples of 'bottom-up' decision-making are easier to find in the medieval period than in the centuries after 1500. The *polders* of the seventeenth-century Dutch Republic were home to a highly commercialized, capital-intensive farming model that hardly resembled the small-scale peasant farming of the thirteenth-century coastal wetlands[37]. In other areas, drainage and improvement projects sometimes resulted in brutal confrontations between village communities and capitalist 'adventurers' backed by royal power[38]. Nevertheless, even though the participative nature of the infrastructure gradually declined, different interests were still taken into account. Dutch investors in the early modern period developed instruments for financially compensating people whose interests were demonstrably damaged by new drainage or embankment projects, thereby eliminating some of the resistance[39].

34 *Ibid.*, p. 13.

35 M. Van Tielhof, *Consensus en Conflict*, pp. 124–126.

36 *Ibid.*, pp. 110–111.

37 T. Soens, *Flood Disasters and Agrarian Capitalism in the North Sea Area: Five Centuries of Interwoven History (1250–1800)*, in G. Nigro (ed.), *Gestione dell'acqua in Europa (XII–XVIII Secc.)*. Atti delle "Settimane di Studi" e altri Convegni, 49, Firenze 2018, pp. 369–392.

38 S. Ciriacono, *Building on Water: Venice, Holland and the Construction of the European Landscape in Early Modern Times*, New York 2006 provides an excellent overview of such 'improvement' projects. The English Fenlands are a classic example.

39 P.J. van Cruyningen, *Dealing with Drainage: State Regulation of Drainage Projects in the Dutch Republic, France, and England During the Sixteenth and Seventeenth Centuries*, in "The Economic History Review", 68, 2015, 2, pp. 420–440.

Overall, the infrastructure always remained a negotiated issue, and the negotiations often took a lot of time. In the early modern period, coastal water management became notorious for its endless debates and extended legal battles. Coastal, estuarine, and riverine environments are very dynamic landscapes and maintenance arrangements that might have worked well for centuries could suddenly become problematic if a river course was altered, or coastal erosion intensified at a certain location. In such cases the landowners responsible for the maintenance of river or sea walls would typically ask for financial assistance from a more extensive hinterland, although inland communities were generally reluctant to provide support. In Coastal Flanders, a series of storm surges in the late fourteenth and early fifteenth centuries reshaped the estuary of the Western Scheldt. Suddenly, areas that had never been exposed directly to the sea had to maintain sea walls. One such area, Gaternisse, only included about 300 hectares of land, but it had to maintain three kilometers of sea wall. From 1404 to 1551 the Gaternisse water board was in more or less constant negotiation with its neighbors for a more definitive solution. Only a century and a half later, after numerous lawsuits and interventions by the Count of Flanders, was a more or less permanent solution reached[40]. By the eighteenth century there was growing criticism for the apparent incapacity of water management authorities in the Low Countries to tackle major environmental challenges because of obstruction by certain stakeholders. A famous example involved the ever expanding inland lakes in the peat districts of Holland. From the seventeenth century onwards plans were made to drain the largest of these lakes, the Haarlemmermeer, but stubborn opposition from some of the major cities in the region, Leiden and to a lesser extent Haarlem, delayed the drainage, which in the end was only achieved in the middle of the nineteenth century[41]. The traditional narrative stressed that only a stronger central state could overcome the resistance of 'particularist' local communities, who only cared about their own short-term interests. In times of crisis, there was always a call for a strong central authority and resolute action.

However, it is important not to be misguided by contemporary narratives and the often biased interpretations of later historians, who invariably blame 'slow' decision-making for all the problems encountered in coastal and riverine water management. At least two more nuanced observations should be made. Firstly, slow decision-making, involving many stakeholders and careful consultations, did not impede innovative solutions or the elaboration of robust large-scale infrastructures[42].

---

40 T. Soens, *De spade in de dijk?*, pp. 214–215.

41 M. van Tielhof / P. van Dam, *Waterstaat in stedenland. Het hoogheemraadschap van Rijnland voor 1857*, Utrecht 2006, pp. 264–266 and 288–289.

42 Also see F. Graber's contribution in this volume.

Before 1300 impressive drainage and flood protection systems had been created. From East Anglia to Northern Germany thousands of farmers worked each year to maintain these infrastructures, gradually adapting them to changing environmental conditions. Sometimes this involved the coordination of dozens or even hundreds of villages, without requiring a central authority to impose solutions from above. Secondly, the opposite of slow-decision making, 'fast' solutions, introduced top-down and based on 'expert' knowledge, were not a guarantee for success.

5 Accelerations

Pre-1800 flood protection was far from static with both the infrastructures and decision-making processes around them in constant evolution. Sometimes, however, obvious 'accelerations' are visible, some clearly breaking with the tradition of 'slow' infrastructures. One indicator for this emerges from investments in flood control and drainage. Figure three below shows the long-term evolution of investments in an area of Western Zeeland-Flanders (the Netherlands) from the middle of the fourteenth to the end of the eighteenth centuries. At least three periods of 'acceleration' are visible, when the level of investment changed significantly and abruptly. Before 1400, yearly investments were extremely high – at a time when gross wheat yields seldom exceeded 1500 liters per hectare, a yearly investment of 200 liters of wheat per hectare was certainly a significant burden on income. Investments were also highly variable, with spikes indicating years of intensive renovation of the infrastructure, mostly after storm surges and dike breaches. Then after 1410 there was a first shift towards lower investment levels, becoming quite stable after 1450. This stability was interrupted in the 1560s, but returned – after a break during the Eighty Years War when most of the area was subject to military invasion and abandonment – in the seventeenth century. Then, after 1715 there was another very abrupt shift with investments suddenly rising to a structurally higher level. As will be discussed below, these three abrupt changes in investment levels – after 1410, in the 1560s, and after 1715 – also mark three 'accelerations' in coastal flood protection infrastructure development.

The question arises as to what extent are these major changes in investments linked to long-term changes in North Sea storm patterns? It would be tempting to link the period of high investment in the fourteenth century to environmentally unstable conditions during the onset of the Little Ice Age. However, it remains unclear whether there were actually more storms and storm surges in the fourteenth and early fifteenth centuries, compared to later periods. Storminess is much more difficult to quantify than temperature or precipitation, since there

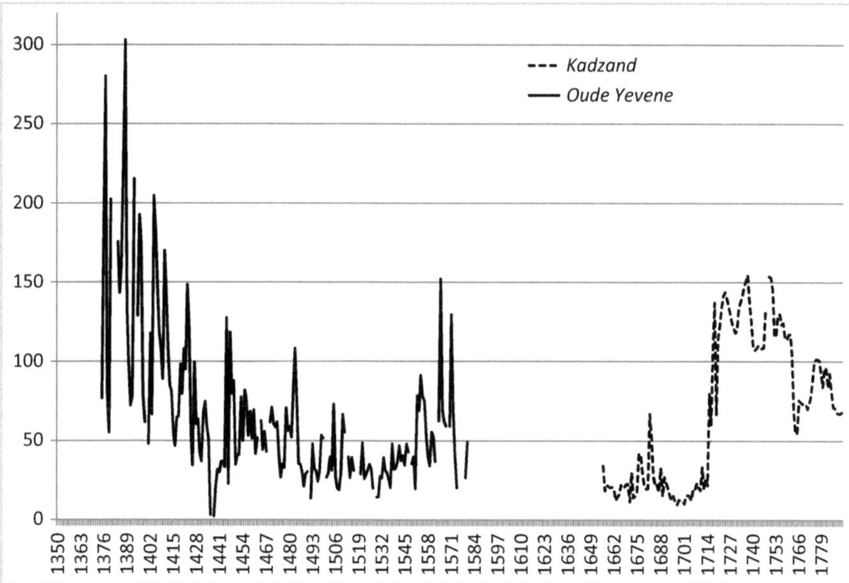

Fig. 3: Investment in flood control in two adjacent parts of Western Zeeland-Flanders (the Netherlands), Oude Yevene and Kadzand, converted to liters of wheat per hectare.
Based on T. Soens, *Floods and Money: Funding Drainage and Flood Control in Coastal Flanders from the Thirteenth to the Sixteenth Centuries*, in "Continuity and Change" 26, 2011, 3, pp. 333–365 (Oude Yevene) and P.J. van Cruyningen, *Behoudend maar buigzaam: boeren in West-Zeeuws-Vlaanderen 1650–1850*, Wageningen 2000, pp. 404–405 (for the post-1600 Kadzand series).

are few natural proxies that record wind levels[43]. From historical sources it is clear that storms caused a lot of damage in the fourteenth and early fifteenth centuries, being countered with an energetic human response and substantial investments. There was a subsequent marked shift in the early fifteenth century, with rapidly decreasing investment levels. This 'event' has been observed in both Coastal Flanders and along the English Thames estuary[44], and it indicates the emergence of a different strategy for dealing with storm flooding and a transition towards a different type of flood infrastructure. Flooded areas were increasingly abandoned and converted to wetlands, while the role of local communities in

43 A. de Kraker, *Storminess in the Low Countries, 1390–1725*, in "Environment and History", 19, 2013, 2, pp. 149–171.
44 T. Soens, *Floods and Money* and J. Galloway, *"Piteous and Grievous Sight": The Thames Marshes at the Close of the Middle Ages*, in "New Research on London and The Tidal Thames from the Middle Ages to the Twentieth Century", London 2010, pp. 15–28.

both the decision-making processes and maintenance works declined markedly. The Flemish water boards saw a decline in the frequency of general meetings in favor of closed committees of small numbers of elite stakeholders[45]. Dike labor ceased as a seasonal activity for all inhabitants or landowners in the affected areas and the water authorities began to rely on the unskilled labor market[46]. Cost efficiency became a paramount objective.

A second 'acceleration' is visible in the 1560s and might be linked to greater involvement of state control and 'experts', at a time when traditional water authorities were increasingly blamed for their uninspired management of water problems. This acceleration was also linked to a major storm flood from Flanders to Northern Germany – the 'All Saints Flood' of 1570 – although it was not triggered solely by this flood since investments were clearly rising before it occurred[47]. In the 1560s the Low Countries became the scenario for a clash between a distrustful Habsburg government desperately trying to raise money, and disgruntled local elites, which erupted into civil war. This was also the age of the first generation of self-proclaimed 'dike experts', who argued against the incompetence of 'amateur' water maintenance. Men like Andries Vierlingh and Humphrey Bradley were still profoundly rooted in practice – there was still a considerable gap in theoretical scientific literature[48] – but their plans and projects nevertheless aimed at a 'radical' transformation of coastal and wetland riverine environments, often leading to violent confrontations with the actual inhabitants of these areas. This was the time when conflicts about the drainage of the East-Anglian Fenlands gradually gained momentum, culminating in the 'Fenland Riots' of the seventeenth century[49]. When resistance was finally overcome, these major drainage or embankment schemes were typically realized by 'armies' of underpaid laborers recruited in low-cost areas far away from the coastal wetlands[50].

Finally, Fig. 3 shows a third acceleration in the early eighteenth century, which in Western Zeeland Flanders was triggered by a relatively minor storm surge in 1715. This marked the beginning of an era of increased state intervention with

45 T Soens, *Polders zonder poldermodel*, p. 23.

46 T. Soens / G. De Block / I. Jongepier, *Seawalls at Work*, pp. 700–703.

47 A reliable synthesis of the All Saints Flood of 1570, the most deadly flood before 1717, is still lacking, see M.K.E. Gottschalk, *Storm Surges and River Floods in the Netherlands*, 3 vols., Assen 1971–1977, vol. 2, pp. 622–709.

48 K. Davids, *Humanism and Water Management: Scaliger's* Discours de la jonction des mers, in "Lias", 37, 2010, 2, pp. 9–10; E.H. Ash, *Power, Knowledge and Expertise in Elizabethan England*, Baltimore / London 2004.

49 H. Falvey, *Custom, Resistance and Politics: Local Experiences of Improvement in Early Modern England*, Warwick 2007, pp. 256–365.

50 T. Soens / G. De Block / I. Jongepier, *Seawalls at Work*, pp. 703–704.

taxes used to subsidize areas structurally threatened by the sea – the so-called *Calamiteuze Polders*. As argued by Piet van Cruyingen, such a successful increase in funding for coastal flood protection systems could only be achieved when the 'entrenched' resistance against broad solidarity was overcome, and a more 'unbiased' technocratic perspective prevailed[51]. Not only the decision-making process, but also the material nature of flood protection changed considerably. State subsidies allowed reinforcement of weak points with stone facing, or more frequently with straw matting because it was cheaper, and the building of groynes. Construction and maintenance of these infrastructures were increasingly conducted by specialists, like the fascine workers who maintained the straw matting. Some of the maintenance works remained annual, recalling the old medieval collective maintenance schedules, but now without much participation of local inhabitants[52].

These infrastructural accelerations can be understood as new socio-technical regimes, implemented from outside and above, with decreasing participation of local stakeholders in the decision-making process and in the actual construction and maintenance work. This evolution had already happened in the coastal wetlands around the North Sea area before 1800, and it would become generalized in the nineteenth and twentieth centuries along coasts and rivers all over the world. This resulted in a problematic legacy of 'hard' and 'fast' infrastructures, which are consolidating an often detrimental interaction with nature. Whether it is possible and desirable to 'slow down' such infrastructures to any extent, at a time when climate adaptation is more urgent than ever, remains to be seen.

6 Conclusions: the future of slow infrastructures

The idea of 'slow infrastructures' developed in this discussion looked back to the time before the massive technological remodeling of rivers and coasts over the nineteenth and twentieth centuries. Pre-1800 river and coastal management was not by definition more 'sustainable' or in balance with nature. As David Blackbourn reminds us in a recent overview of river history in Germany, "none of the rivers [. . .] was remotely 'natural' before they were corrected, regulated or dammed"[53].

---

51 P. Van Cruyningen, *Sharing the Cost of Dike Maintenance in the South-Western Netherlands: Comparing 'Calamitous Polders' in Three 'States', 1715–1795*, in "Environment and History", 23, 2017, 3, pp. 363–383.

52 T. Soens / G. De Block / I. Jongepier, *Seawalls at Work*, pp. 701–703.

53 D. Blackbourn, *"Time is a Violent Torrent". Constructing and Reconstructing Rivers in Modern German History*, in C. Mauch / Th. Zeller (eds.), *Rivers in History. Perspectives on Waterways in Europe and North America*, Pittsburgh 2008, p. 25.

Rivers and coastlines had been socio-natural ‘hybrids’ for centuries. Since at least the year 1000 CE both hard and soft infrastructures were implemented to limit flood risks. For a long time, however, these infrastructures developed very slowly, a slowness not so much in terms of time to implement changes, but rather as a never-ending cycle of maintenance work that mobilized a substantial portion of the local population to maintain the infrastructure year after year, and involving continuous consultation with a wide number of stakeholders for decisions regarding subsequent developments.

It is also true that these slow infrastructures could not be taken for granted. Long before 1800 there were accelerations when time-honored, traditional infrastructures were erased and replaced with grand new schemes introduced abruptly from above. These accelerations were seldom the unexpected results of an external shock or crisis. Infrastructures did not simply become more rigid and prone to disruption, standing by until a crisis redefined the system. The so-called “rigidity” of an infrastructure is a discursive construction and only exists in the eye of the beholder[54]. The accelerations were the consequence of certain stakeholders remaking infrastructures to better suit their own interests.

Just as the accelerations were not inevitable and were instead the result of a political process, so too is the option of slowing down the infrastructures again today. This should not be inspired by feelings of nostalgia for the past. The agricultural populations who once inhabited the riverine and coastal wetlands and were accustomed to drainage and ditch digging work every winter, no longer exist. Over the past centuries the wetlands have been densely populated and urbanized, and to a large extent hard infrastructures will always be needed to protect these populations from flooding. The remaking of the rivers is a path-dependent process which cannot be undone. Moreover, climate change has raised the stakes and innovative technological solutions are urgently needed to avoid new flood catastrophes. However, if slowing down means broadening consultations, involving all stakeholders in the decision-making process, raising awareness of flood risks, and commitment to infrastructure maintenance, then slowing down is urgently needed. When the millions of people living along rivers and coastlines can be reconnected to their wetland environment, adaptation might be more successful (than) by implementing yet another grand scheme aiming for a degree of control that we now know cannot be sustained.

54 The idea of dynamic systems getting increasingly rigid before a shock triggers a crisis and revitalizes the system, is central to resilience theory and very prominent in historical disaster studies, see T. Soens, *Resilient Societies, Vulnerable People*, p. 144.

David Gentilcore

Decadent Infrastructure?

Representations of Water in the Kingdom of Naples in the Early Nineteenth Century

1 Introduction: Teodoro Monticelli and the "Statistica"

The Abbé Teodoro Monticelli was in no doubt: the worst problems encountered in the Kingdom of Naples were closely linked to deficiencies in the management of water courses, the fault of a "Government that never did anything"[1]. Water, Monticelli argued, merited "the most serious and constant attention by any well-ordered People", but centuries of disregard were the "physical cause of our calamities and that depression in which we wallow for many centuries"[2]. This had resulted in two devastating phenomena: on the one hand, a shortage of water, which "causes vegetation and people alike to languish", and on the other hand, after the rains, the "abundance" of waters that generates marshes which, "infecting the air with their effluvia, deprive the inhabitants of their vigor and health, wretchedly shortening their lives and laying waste to entire populations"[3].

So wrote the Brindisi native, teacher and naturalist, director of the Jesuit college in Naples, the "Gesù Vecchio", and secretary of the city's Academy of Sciences, in a short work entitled *Dell'economia delle acque da ristabilirsi nel Regno di Napoli* (On the economy of the waters to be re-established in the Kingdom of Naples)[4]. Published for the first time in 1809, Monticelli's book experienced a moderate success and was reprinted three times. More pamphlet than technical manual,

1 T. Monticelli, *Sulla economia delle acque da ristabilirsi nel Regno di Napoli*, Napoli 1820, pp. VI–VII.

2 *Ibid.*

3 *Ibid.*

4 I have made use of the third edition, the most complete and containing the most extensive apparatus of notes, published in Naples during the brief experience of constitutional government, 1820–1821. On the figure of Monticelli, see F.P. De Ceglia, sub voce, *Dizionario Biografico degli Italiani*, 2012, vol. 76, http://www.treccani.it/enciclopedia/teodoro-monticelli_(Dizionario-

Note: As part of the "The Water Cultures of Italy, 1500–1900" Advanced Grant, of which I am PI, this study has received funding from the European Research Council (ERC) under the European Union's Horizon 2020 research and innovation program (grant agreement no. 833834). All translations are my own unless stated otherwise.

https://doi.org/10.1515/9783111112756-011

it explores issues of policy and landscape study, mixing proto-environmentalism with concerns for the state and material conditions. In the words of the political and environmental historian Giuseppe Foscari, Monticelli focuses on "the most varied questions on the subject, from public works to feasibility studies, from the management of rivers and water courses to the correct forest management, to the encouragement of new forms of cultivation"[5].

Given that Monticelli was part of a group of scholars who together compiled the chapter on the province of Naples for the *Statistica* commissioned by Joachim Murat, it makes sense to ask to what extent his ideas were reproposed in the *Statistica* and to what extent they were shared by his fellow compilers. We will do this by comparing Monticelli's own ideas with what the *Statistica* has to say about water-related infrastructure in the Kingdom of Naples, in terms of both their presence in the landscape and their working condition[6].

But first a word on the *Statistica Murattiana* itself and its interest as a historical source[7]. In 1809 Joachim Murat – French military commander, brother-in-law to Napoleon and King of Naples from the previous year – ordered a detailed survey aimed at obtaining a clear picture of the situation in the kingdom, its natural, physical, demographic, social and economic conditions. A "foundational moment of the French-Neapolitan colonial project"[8], the work was begun by the Ministry of the Interior in 1811, charging the intendants of each of the kingdom's twelve provinces (Fig. 1) with appointing a provincial editor, who would be responsible for compiling the responses to a series of questions[9]. The main themes were: 1) the nature of the soil and the climate; 2) population numbers; 3) subsistence and condition of the populace; 4) agriculture and livestock rearing; 5) trades and manufactures[10].

Biografico)/, and G. Foscari, *Teodoro Monticelli e l'"Economia delle acque" nel Mezzogiorno moderno. Storiografia, scienze ambientali, ecologismo*, Salerno 2009, pp. 59–88.

5 G. Foscari, *Teodoro Monticelli*, p. 90.

6 I have discussed the *Statistica* and the quality of water in the kingdom in another study, which should be seen as complementary to the present one: *"La qualità delle acque". Le risorse idriche nel Regno di Napoli agli inizi dell'Ottocento*, in E. Bini / D. Carnevale / D. Cecere (eds.), *L'acqua: risorsa e minaccia. La gestione delle risorse idriche e delle inondazioni in Europa dal Medioevo all'età contemporanea*, forthcoming.

7 D. Demarco (ed.), *La "Statistica" del Regno di Napoli nel 1811*, 4 vols., Roma 1988.

8 S. Barca, *Enclosing Water. Nature and Political Economy in a Mediterranean Valley, 1796–1916*, Cambridge 2010, p. 41.

9 It followed on from a questionnaire sent to the provinces in 1807, also by the Interior Ministry, in response to a government request to study the kingdom's water resources, but the initiative did not go very far. A. Scirocco, *La Statistica Murattiana nel Regno di Napoli: ricerche e dibattiti*, in S. Martuscelli (ed.), *La popolazione del Mezzogiorno nella statistica di re Murat*, Napoli 1979, p. VII.

10 D. Demarco, *La "Statistica": Introduction*, I, p. LIII.

The *Statistica* provides a "real investigation into the conditions of the country and its inhabitants"[11], which allows us to "get to know its geographic spaces, including those little-studied, at a key moment in the passage from the modern period to the contemporary"[12]. And because the question of water, and in particular hydraulic infrastructure, regarded most of the above-mentioned themes, the *Statistica* is a precious resource for understanding and evaluating the reality of water resources, their use and condition in the kingdom during a precise moment in time.

The hydraulic reality was challenging enough, in a country dominated by the Apennine mountains and rivers that were torrential in winter and dry in summer[13]. And while this reality does emerge from the pages of the *Statistica*, there are several reasons why we should not consider it an objective and factual snapshot of the situation in the Kingdom of Naples.

The first limitation lies in the structure of the survey itself, consisting as it does in a series of quite specific questions, which often elicit brief answers. Secondly, not all of the provincial editors – chosen from members of the provincial agricultural societies, clerics, teachers and doctors – were possessed of the same zeal or cultural background for the task. Moreover, the editors were dependent on their local informants and correspondents, whose task it was to provide the information (for example, on the water system) and they might reply according to their own interests, too summarily, too slowly or in disagreement with the provincial editor. Having said that, from another perspective one could argue that it is precisely these limitations that make the *Statistica* more interesting for the historian: we should regard it less as a reliably, accurate and objective survey and more as a cultural construction suited to the new political reality under French rule.

One final point is worth making: the *Statistica* is not concerned with infrastructure *per se*, but rather with the geography, environment, economy and living conditions throughout the kingdom. As a result, the questionnaire contains no single query relating to what we call "hydraulic infrastructure" on which the provincial editors were called to provide local information. And yet the information is there, even if it has to be culled from a number of distinct sections (and their relative sub-sections): physical topography (hydrography; waters: town fountains, mineral springs, rivers and streams, lakes and marshes); subsistence and diet (foodstuffs: water; public health; pathology; agriculture); manufactures (clothing:

11 V. Ricchioni, *La Statistica del Reame di Napoli del 1811: relazioni sulla Puglia*, Trani 1942, p. 7.

12 E. Sarno, *Il decennio francese e la qualità della vita in una provincia del Mezzogiorno italiano: analisi geo-storica della Statistica murattiana*, in "Biblio 3W. Revista bibliográfica y ciencias sociales", 16, 2011, 908, http://www.ub.edu/geocrit/b3w-908.htm.

13 P. Bevilacqua, *Breve storia dell'Italia meridionale dall'Ottocento a oggi*, Roma 2005 [1993], pp. 32–37; L. Cafagna, *Dualismo e sviluppo nella storia d'Italia*, Venezia 1989, p. 85.

Fig. 1: Map of the Kingdom of Naples, showing its provinces around 1816. In: P. Allodi / F. Naymiller, *Atlante di geografia universale: cronologico, storico, statistico e letterario*, Milano 1865 (unpaginated).

linen and hemp; wool); hunting, fishing and rural economy (agriculture [again!]; livestock farming). Moreover, the data is not always where one would expect it. Thus, much of the information concerning the provision, condition and maintenance of aqueducts, fountains, rainwater cisterns and wells – as presented in the following pages – comes from the question relating to the condition of drinking water included in the section on the subsistence and diet of the local population. Data on irrigation practices comes partly in answer to the questions on agriculture, as one would expect, but more often in response to questions on public health and pathology – because of widespread fears that stagnant waters led to disease. The same is true of information regarding linen and hemp production, because of the need to ret them for long periods in pools of water.

2 Notions of decay in Monticelli and the "Statistica"

In his essay on the economy of the waters, Monticelli expresses a perception widely shared by the different provincial editors: the decay of water-related infrastructure when compared to those of antiquity and the neglect of waters resources more generally, with devastating effects on the entire economy. It was part of a widespread view of the kingdom's decline already voiced by key exponents of the Neapolitan Enlightenment in their late-eighteenth-century studies of the landscape, environment and economy, such as Giuseppe Maria Galanti, Giuseppe Palmieri and Francesco Longano[14]. As Monticelli would also do, they had proposed solutions: a "restoration" of ancient glories, in order to bring "nature" and "nation" back together in the life of the kingdom[15]. It was a political economy that mixed history, geography and Arcadian myth, as Stefania Barca has said of Galanti's *Descrizione*[16]. Escalating population made the decay in infrastructure all the more evident, putting increased pressure on the competition for scarce resources[17].

For Monticelli, when it came to a well-ordered and attentive management of the waters, the point of reference was the ancient Greeks. They "created" reservoirs and aqueducts, "abhorred" stagnant waters and "showed sacred respect" to

---

14 G.M. Galanti, *Della descrizione geografica e politica delle Sicilie*, ed. by F. Assante / D. Demarco, Napoli 1969; G. Palmieri, *Riflessioni sulla pubblica felicità relativamente al Regno di Napoli e altri scritti 1787–1792*, ed. by A.M. Fusco, Roma / Bari 1991; F. Longano, *Raccolta di saggi economici per gli abitanti delle Due Sicilie*, Isernia 1988, and *Viaggio per lo contado di Molise nell'ottobre dell'anno 1786*, ed. by R. Lalli, Isernia 1980.

15 S. Barca, *Enclosing Water*, pp. 16–25.

16 *Ibid.*, p. 23.

17 On this link, see A.F. Saba, *L'allocazione delle acque dolci fra teoria e storia*, in L. Mocarelli (ed.), *Quando manca il pane. Origini e cause della scarsità delle risorse alimentari in età moderna e contemporanea*, Bologna 2013, pp. 57–58.

forests[18]. But the successive conquests of Magna Graecia and Samnium by the Romans brought only ruin. (Monticelli's judgement here is strangely negative, "summary and contradictory"[19], but he is following Galanti's lead here.) From the Saracens onwards follows a litany of disasters, especially along the coasts which become marshy and unhealthy[20]. As Monticelli comments in an aside, "the limits of this essay do not allow me to list the ruins and remains of so many aqueducts, canals, wells and thermal baths, which can nevertheless be quite easily noted in our ancient cities, even if they are largely in decay"[21] (Fig. 2). Monticelli details the harm done to the kingdom's coastlines and the resulting economic decline, as with regard to his native Brindisi[22]. Curiously, he does not discuss provinces like the Abruzzi which in his own time still possessed examples of sophisticated, imposing and largely functioning hydraulic infrastructure (as remarked upon both by local historians[23], as well as the provincial editors of the *Statistica* for the Abruzzi provinces, as we shall see below). Rather, Monticelli's interest in the mountainous parts of the kingdom is limited to the problem of deforestation and the resulting floods[24].

Given this, how does the *Statistica* compare? In Nola (Terra di Lavoro), for instance, fresh water is drawn from wells and rainwater cisterns, but "in ancient times the *Nolani* were much more attentive to the provision of good water", according to the provincial editor Francesco Perrini, cathedral canon in Capua and corresponding member of the agricultural commission[25]. With regard to the towns of S. Apollinare and S. Ambrogio he remarks that "if one could revive the genius of the beautiful ancient aqueducts, it would doubtless bring the greatest of benefits"[26]. Such is the awe with which the editors tended to regard the Ancients that even natural features are attributed to their handiwork, such as the *vore* of Terra d'Otranto: "large pits, partly opened up by nature and partly the work of ancient inhabitants [. . .] which devour the waters"[27]. Monticelli likewise regarded it as

18 T. Monticelli, *Sulla economia delle acque*, p. 6.
19 G. Foscari, *Teodoro Monticelli*, p. 103.
20 T. Monticelli, *Sulla economia delle acque*, p. 10.
21 *Ibid.*, p. 79.
22 *Ibid.*, p. 18.
23 C. Ciccarelli, "Storie locali nell'Abruzzo di età moderna (1504–1806)". Unpublished PhD thesis, Università degli studi di Udine, 2010/11, pp. 38, 307.
24 T. Monticelli, *Sulla economia delle acque*, p. 25.
25 D. Demarco, *La "Statistica"*, IV, p. 151.
26 *Ibid.*, IV, p. 182.
27 *Ibid.*, II, pp. 148–149. V. Manghisi, *Leggende carsiche salentine*, Castellana Grotte 1981, http://www.salogentis.it/2009/04/30/le-vore-di-barbarano/.

Fig. 2: Taranto's ancient aqueduct as picturesque ruin. Watercolor by the Swiss artist and engraver Louis Ducros, from his album *Voyage en Italie, en Sicile et à Malte*, 1778. Rijksmuseum, Amsterdam.

"not likely" that the *vore* were natural in origin, rather providing "yet another argument in support of the concern of our betters to avoid mephitism"[28].

In the case of Basilicata it is the lack of waterworks or their state of abandon that most strikes the provincial editor, the lawyer Giulio Girolamo Corbo. This is true in Viggiano, where

> in the summer [water] is often lacking and it is necessary to search for stagnant water far away, which has none of the qualities of potable water; whereas with a small outlay the channel could be restored which would bring most abundant water, as it formerly did, from a distance of one kilometer from the town, which has all potable qualities[29].

28 T. Monticelli, *Sulla economia delle acque*, p. 45, note 26.

29 D. Demarco, *La "Statistica"*, III, p. 92. By "potable qualities", the editors have in mind the definition suggested by the *Statistica* itself, which they often repeat word for word in their reports: "perfectly limpid, without odor, of lively and fresh flavor, pleasant, easily and readily boiled without becoming cloudy, able to cook legumes well without turning them to mush, able to dissolve soap completely and consistently, of easy passage through the stomach and favorable to the digestion of other foods".

At the town of Stigliano "the ancient reservoir, which was well built, is abandoned; [the water] comes via discontinuous and poorly maintained channels, so that it arrives turbid, especially during the rains"[30]. The same at Tursi, where

> there is an abundant spring that has its origins in sandy soil and which would therefore have all potable qualities if extraneous materials were not occasionally immersed in it producing putrefaction; it should be blocked and the water allowed to flow through pipes[31].

Other provincial editors indicate examples of insufficient maintenance, such as in Venafro (Terra di Lavoro), where the fountains provide waters that are "certainly the province's most limpid and good, and yet the basins are so poorly kept that they cause disdain to look at"[32]. If the province of Abruzzo Ultra II can boast impressive water works, as we will see below, in other places, as in the district of Achillopoli, the aqueducts "are propped up and poorly kept [. . .] indeed tumbledown and decayed for a long stretch", while in Manforno "the Fontacciano aqueduct is more or less ruined"[33]. At Volturara (Capitanata) the waters "are spoilt for a long stretch by the conduit which is in bad repair"[34].

Meanwhile in the kingdom's capital, the problems are *sui generis* given the unique nature of the city's ancient underground water system[35], and occur primarily when water enters these subterranean spaces, causing "alterations" in water quality. According to the provincial editors, one of whom was Monticelli:

> The inappropriate architectural construction of the water reservoirs close to sewers and washbasins, as well as the underground aqueducts that cross one another or are adjacent, with filthy conduits, sometimes broken and these not well plastered, often results in the depositing of a slime of vegetable and animal substances at the bottoms of the said reservoirs, which steeping there give off noxious gases and provide a nesting ground for the eggs of numberless insects, with the waters becoming foul smelling, tepid, turbid and disgusting[36].

30 *Ibid.*, III, p. 161.
31 *Ibid.*, III, p. 195.
32 *Ibid.*, IV, p. 209, note 2.
33 *Ibid.*, I, pp. 54–55.
34 *Ibid.*, I, p. 393.
35 D. Gentilcore, *Cool and Tasty Waters. Managing Naples's Water Supply, c. 1500–c. 1750*, in "Water History", 11, 2019, 3, pp. 125–151.
36 D. Demarco, *La "Statistica"*, IV, pp. 26–27. Monticelli's fellow authors for the contribution on the city of Naples were Melchiorre Delfico (councillor of state), Giovanni Battista Gagliardo (agronomist), Luigi Petagna (zoologist) and Michele Ferrara (chemist). D. Demarco, *La "Statistica": Introduction*, I, pp. LXXIX–LXXX.

3 Hydraulic typologies

In fact the water resources available to local populations in the kingdom vary widely from province to province, as well as within single provinces, depending on a range of factors, from physical (geography and geology) to infrastructural. In those areas where sourcing water for human use does not present particular difficulties and the needs are fairly limited the infrastructure is correspondingly basic. "All the province makes use of spring waters, having fountains in abundance", according to the editor of Calabria Citeriore[37]. The same is true of Calabria Ulteriore, where springs are likewise abundant so that it is enough "to place gutters made from tree trunks or large leaves into the crevices in the rock to make it possible to draw water into pitchers"[38]. In Sant'Angelo le Fratte (Basilicata), "the fountain near the town, with most abundant water, gushes up out a pile of stones, is collected into a masonry container and from there flows into a basin through a covered channel"[39]. Some of the towns in Abruzzo Ultra II "make use of very pure spring waters, but which lack purpose-built fountains, and draw their water from the natural fountain where it springs forth"[40]. Elsewhere there is more artifice, as in Lauria (Basilicata), where the water "gushes out of a boulder and is channeled into a covered conduit, from which it flows through various iron pipes into a chiseled stone basin"[41]. The nature of water fountains differs from town to countryside, for instance in Calabria Citeriore. Here the fountains in town are generally built in the following manner: "through underground conduits, almost all imperfect, the water flows from the spring into a limewashed container commonly called a *botte*. The water is extracted via a small pipe of bronze or iron located at the bottom". In the countryside, by contrast, "only on rare occasions does artifice embellish the gifts bestowed by nature: a small concave piece of wood, resting on a rock, offers the water to those who go to draw it"[42].

Elsewhere in the kingdom the hydraulic infrastructure is much more sophisticated and impressive, in the views of the provincial editors themselves. The aqueduct supplying Aquila "is truly remarkable", according to the editor of Abruzzo Ultra II[43], while Leonessa's "is due to the magnificence of Marguerite of Austria,

37 *Ibid.*, II, p. 313.
38 *Ibid.*, II, p. 534.
39 *Ibid.*, III, p. 113.
40 *Ibid.*, I, p. 50.
41 *Ibid.*, III, p. 174.
42 *Ibid.*, II, p. 331.
43 *Ibid.*, I, p. 53.

duchess of Parma", he adds in historical vein[44]. The town of Faicchio (Terra di Lavoro) "has a noteworthy aqueduct, which is probably of Roman construction"[45] and the province of Terra d'Otranto possesses several remarkable aqueducts, according to the provincial editor, like Gallipoli's, which feeds "a fountain located at the entrance to bridge which unites it to the continent", the Fontana Greca[46] (Fig. 3).

On the island of Ischia (province of Naples) "there are also good flowing waters which gush out of volcanic rocks and flow via well-constructed aqueducts, covered and fully maintained, and from the distant springs reach the inhabited area"[47]. And in the capital itself what strikes the editors is the "surprising branching out of the waters of the Carmignano and Bolla", the two aqueducts which together supply Naples (the former dating from the seventeenth century and the latter ancient in origins): "surprising" because they flow underneath the urban space "by means of underground conduits, plastered internally and paved". "In most houses", the editors continue, access to these waters is via "the so-called *formali* [. . .] large basins for the flowing waters" which are "square in shape [. . .] [and] built entirely of stone"[48].

Needless to say, not all towns in the kingdom have the advantage of being able to access their water by impressive aqueducts or natural springs and so have to adopt a strategy of double or triple provision, according to available resources. Thus the town of Calvello (Basilicata) has recourse to a mixed supply system in order to eke out a meager water supply, relying on "spring water, river water and sometimes rain water"[49]. Even the capital (Italy's largest city) is forced to rely on mixed water provision. "For the most part" Naples depends on "the good flowing waters" of the two aqueducts just mentioned, but these are unable to supply the whole city. Thus "in the mountainous part of the city [. . .] rainwater and springs are used, the latter found in the depths of wells dug out of the tuff rock, and rainwater fountains [*fontane di acque di distilli*]"[50].

In this case, the comments provided by the *Statistica* can shed light on debates over the relative reliance on rainwater cisterns or groundwater wells in different regions of Europe. It has been suggested that in medieval Italy, rainwater

44 *Ibid.*
45 Other towns of the district "have channeled the waters flowing down from the mountains [. . .] but the aqueducts are poorly maintained, so that the water is polluted by animals and waste", *ibid.*, IV, p. 106.
46 *Ibid.*, II, p. 155.
47 *Ibid.*, IV, p. 25.
48 *Ibid.*, IV, p. 26.
49 *Ibid.*, III, pp. 83–84.
50 *Ibid.*, IV, p. 23.

Fig. 3: The "Fontana Greca" in Gallipoli. Watercolor by Louis Ducros, *Voyage en Italie, en Sicile et à Malte*, 1778. Rijksmuseum, Amsterdam.

cisterns were more common than dug wells[51]. Apart from the difficulty posed by terminological imprecision in the records, with words like "well" and "cistern" often used interchangeably, was this also the case during the early nineteenth century? Can we also conclude that rainwater cisterns predominated in drier southern Europe whilst wells were more common in wetter northern Europe?[52]. For instance, in Terra d'Otranto "it can be reckoned that half of the population [. . .] makes use of rainwater, and half of spring wells", the former primarily in towns, the latter mostly in the rural areas[53]. In many areas of the kingdom dug wells supplement other forms of water provision by necessity. The towns of the province of Naples are especially reliant on groundwater wells, where "they are normally cylindrical in shape, dug into the tuff bedrock or into the ground and entirely lined with cement from the opening down to the spring at the bottom"[54].

51 P. Squatriti, *Water and Society in Early Medieval Italy, AD 400–1000*, Cambridge 1998, pp. 23–32.

52 D. Alexandre-Bidon, *Archéo-iconographie du puits au Moyen Âge (XIIe–XVIe siècle)*, in "Mélanges de l'école française de Rome. Moyen-Âge", 104, 1992, 2, pp. 519–543.

53 D. Demarco, *La "Statistica"*, II, pp. 171, 154–155.

54 *Ibid.*, IV, p. 26.

Rainwater cisterns provide a vital type of hydraulic infrastructure, though this is truer in some areas of the kingdom more than in others. Thus in mountainous areas, as in the Aquino valley (Terra di Lavoro), rainwater basins are rare and serve only "for washing clothes and watering animals"[55]. Nor are they very widespread in Calabria Citeriore, where they appear to be a casual, semi-permanent feature, "consist[ing] of basins made of cement, built into the earth, covered with boards and then flat tiles, supported by two columns raised above the top of the basin"[56]. By contrast, in the low-lying, less water-rich provinces of the kingdom – namely Terra d'Otranto, Terra di Bari and much of Capitanata – rainwater cisterns are essential. Some of these cisterns are suitably ancient, like "the famous fountain of Manduria", according to the laconic remark of the provincial editor[57]. Monticelli provides the details, noting that "the fountain of Manduria, praised by none other than Pliny, is a large underground reservoir which captures rainwater and provisions that ancient and celebrated city"[58] (Fig. 4).

In fact, when it comes to the potential of rainwater capture Monticelli is unreservedly enthusiastic – not surprising, perhaps, given his own origins in Brindisi (Terra d'Otranto). For those places which "do not enjoy the benefits of spring waters or rivers", rainwater cisterns provide an ideal solution, since "there is no place without the benefit of more or less abundant rains, which if captured with diligence can meet the needs of a large population"[59]. For Monticelli, it is a question of carefully capturing it, and if the roofs of houses are not sufficient for the purpose, one captures the waters of torrential rivers and marshes, as the ancients did[60]. And as regards "that vast and arid plain" of the towns of Foggia, Cirignola and Lucera (Capitanata), he proposes the digging of large water reservoirs, which would serve "not only for the ordinary uses of men and animals, but also for irrigation"[61].

How do Monticell's suggestions for rainwater capture compare with the observations made by the provincial editors of the *Statistica*? Inhabitants in the towns of Terra di Bari are reliant on rainwater captured "from the roofs and terraces of their own houses, and conducted by means of earthenware pipes down to *wells* dug beneath the houses' foundations"[62]. Here the editor, the agronomist Vitangelo

55 *Ibid.*, IV, p. 78.

56 *Ibid.*, II, p. 331. Curiously, they are known locally as *pozzi*, wells.

57 *Ibid.*, II, p. 173.

58 T. Monticelli, *Sulla economia delle acque*, p. 76. Known today as the "Fonte Pliniano", after its description by Pliny the Elder in his *Natural History*, it is located at the entrance to the Parco Archeologico delle Mura Messapiche.

59 T. Monticelli, *Sulla economia delle acque*, p. 80, note 35.

60 *Ibid.*, pp. 81–82 n.

61 *Ibid.*, p. 88 n.

62 D. Demarco, *La "Statistica"*, II, pp. 38–39.

Fig. 4: The “Plinian Fountain” in Manduria. Watercolor by Louis Ducros, *Voyage en Italie, en Sicile et à Malte*, 1778. Rijksmuseum, Amsterdam.

Bisceglie, italicizes the word “wells” (*pozzi*), as if to highlight what he considers the inappropriate local usage (in place of “cistern”), and goes on to describe them as “large chambers or galleries deep in the rock rising up to ground level”[63]. Unfortunately, the quality of the water “is not of the purest [. . .] because the roofs and terraces are not always kept clean of rubbish and the conduits often become blocked”. To remedy this, better off families have their *conserve*, “that is, small wells which draw off water from larger ones after the water has deposited earth and other extraneous matter”. Despite these “minor limitations, the rainwater collected in these domestic reservoirs enjoys all the qualities of good potable water, after it has been ‘beaten’, which is to say shaken, to rid it of foreign matter”[64].

The same is true of Terra d’Otranto. The provincial editor – the medical student Oronzo Gabriele Costa – bemoans the loss of important sources of domestic water in Lecce, an unforeseen effect of the Napoleonic reforms under the French regime, “with the abolition and limiting of the monks and friars the population

63 *Ibid.*, II, p. 10.
64 *Ibid.*, II, p. 39.

has lost a great amount of rainwater, and of the most excellent quality"[65]. In Lecce only rainwater from rooftops is allowed into domestic cisterns, but elsewhere, such as in "Massapia [Mesagne] and in a few other towns, not only water from rooftops is allowed down into the cisterns but also the water that runs on the dirty and muddy streets of the town itself"[66]. This is obviously an undesirable practice, the editor comments, but it is in response to a precise need, given that "the rooftop of a small house can never be enough to capture a lot of water [. . .] and so the need to collect it from elsewhere"[67].

In the countryside of the southern Gargano (Capitanata) the inhabitants depend on water captured in so-called *piscine* (pools), which "receive water not from the roofs of houses but from public country roads", with the result that their water "is ordinarily turbid and muddy and barely suited to watering animals". Nor are they even effective, according to the same editor, given that "based on precise calculations, it is apparent that it requires at least five *linee* of water to saturate the country roads, such that if in a day seven *linee* of rain fall, only two remain for the benefit of the pools"[68]. It is the same case in the town of Gravina (Terra di Bari), where water is collected "from the streets"[69], a practice even more common in the rural areas of the province, where "a long time ago the practice began of building cisterns outside towns, at a lesser or greater distance" which "receive water from the streets, always full of dust and earth, of excremental and vegetable waste in decomposition" and from which "people and animals drink"[70].

The technologies for water provisioning vary according to the circumstances, making the most of local topographical realities to capture precious rainwater. The editor for Terra d'Otranto refers to the presence of a typology of "cistern of characteristic structure" for rainwater capture in the countryside, found "in Martano, Castrignano and other places": "these are dug out of a concave layer of clay, more or less at depth, conical in shape and covered in undressed stone" and "into which water drips, filtered through the clay-stone layer" or else "into which rainwater is channeled from the ground above"[71]. As to quality, "the water keeps very well"[72].

---

65 *Ibid.*, II, pp. 172–173. F. Mineccia, *Soppressione degli enti religiosi e liquidazione del patrimonio ecclesiastico nel Regno di Napoli (1806–1815)*, in "Itinerari di ricerca storica", 26, 2012, pp. 71–92.

66 D. Demarco, *La "Statistica"*, II, p. 172.

67 *Ibid.*

68 *Ibid.*, I, p. 390. The *linea* was a unit of measurement used in the kingdom.

69 *Ibid.*, II, p. 10.

70 *Ibid.*, II, p. 40.

71 *Ibid.*, II, p. 171.

72 *Ibid.*, II, p. 155.

Although the editor does not name them, he is describing the *pozzelle* of the Greek-speaking part of Salento, small stone-built underground reservoirs built into Karst-like depressions, into which precious rainwater would filter and collect[73]. Similarly, in the Gargano plain (Capitanata), at Cagnano, the water "drips down into a small oblong basin; but it is of good quality"[74]. Nearby in Manfredonia, the lack of "spring water forced the ancient inhabitants to construct pools there, that is public rainwater reservoirs", the rain coming in "great storms from the northeast in torrents from the heights of the Gargano", then flowing "through a tortuous channel from the foot of the mountain towards these basins", the channel itself being three miles in length and "dug into layers of earth and rock of calcium carbonate"[75]. Finally, near the town of Rossano (Calabria Citeriore), near the sea, located "on a boulder surrounded by other crags", "because of the lack of spring water, rainwater is normally used, drawn basins commonly known as *wells*, kept clean and with care"[76].

Nothing is wasted in any case. Even brackish water gets used, whether to "water the vegetables" or for various "domestic uses", and "when the animals are accustomed to it they will drink it, if the salt content is not too high" (Terra d'Otranto)[77].

4 Water improvement techniques

To remedy limitations in water quality there exist various methods for improving it, according to our provincial editors. In the province of Molise, newly created in 1806[78], rainwater destined for cisterns "is captured in the eves troughs and filtered by passing either through silica sand or small round calcareous stones collected from rivers"[79]. Likewise in Oriolo (Calabria Citeriore), "the waters are filtered through sand and the reservoirs are cleaned often"[80]. The same technique is employed in Lecce (Terra d'Otranto); in addition to which, "the comfortable and better

73 A. Chiga / P. Durante / S. Giammaruco (eds.), *Conservare l'acqua. Le Pozzelle di Zollino tra memoria storica e indagini scientifiche*, Lecce 2015.
74 D. Demarco, *La "Statistica"*, I, p. 390.
75 Unfortunately, "the water when it comes is quite cloudy, of unpleasing taste, unable to wash soap away, not easy to boil, very heavy on the stomach and slowing digestion", *ibid.*, I, pp. 391–392.
76 *Ibid.*, II, pp. 330–331.
77 *Ibid.*, II, p. 173.
78 A. Spagnoletti, *Territorio e amministrazione nel Regno di Napoli (1806–1816)*, in "Meridiana", 9, 1990, pp. 86–87.
79 D. Demarco, *La "Statistica"*, I, p. 292.
80 *Ibid.*, II, p. 330.

off [. . .] do not allow the rainwater from summer and early autumn storms into their cisterns, but let it flow away by other conduits into the streets"[81]. In the Gargano (Capitanata) "a very few houses" have basins known as *purgatoi* "which rid the rainwater of foreign substances before it passes into the cisterns"[82].

In the Arienzo valley (Terra di Lavoro) the "cisterns are spherical in shape, in the middle of which is a small well, where all the extraneous substances and dissolved earths are deposited"[83]. In Abruzzo Ultra the cisterns "are cleaned with sponges and pebbles" (although the editor bemoans the small number of cisterns in the province, "found only in monastic cloisters and in the occasional private house"[84]). Another method, reported for Abruzzo Citra, is "to put live fish of the goatfish species in the cisterns, which purify the water, both because they eat the insects and other substances analogous to their normal diet and because their continuous motion keeps the water uncorrupted, helping to mix air particles into the water"[85]. In Miglionico (Basilicata) the inhabitants believe that the cistern water "is kept entirely pure by the movement made in drawing it"[86]. Evidently, this is not always enough. In the provinces of Terra di Bari and Terra d'Otranto "when [cistern water] assumes a bad smell, mastic branches are immersed into them"; unfortunately, "only seldom is this successful"[87] since the practice can only "hide the natural fetor of these waters"[88]. Another practice in such situations is to toss quicklime into the cistern[89].

When it comes to the quality of well water, in the province of Molise the waters "are purified by rest alone, which sometimes lasts a long time"[90]. When the well water is low, in Abruzzo Ultra, the wells "abound with small eels or other tiny red worms", the solution to which is to toss quicklime into them, believing that this will kill them. "And this is usually the effect", according to the editor[91].

In addition to this, it was common practice in the Kingdom of Naples, as throughout Europe, to store water in large earthenware vessels for household use. Not only was the water easily accessible, but "resting" it in this way allowed

81 *Ibid.*, II, pp. 154–155.
82 *Ibid.*, I, pp. 389–390.
83 *Ibid.*, IV, p. 146.
84 *Ibid.*, I, p. 13.
85 *Ibid.*, I, p. 210.
86 *Ibid.*, III, p. 129.
87 *Ibid.*, II, p. 10.
88 *Ibid.*, II, p. 172.
89 *Ibid.*
90 *Ibid.*, I, p. 292.
91 *Ibid.*, II, p. 10.

"foreign elements" to settle to the bottom as "sediment"[92]. In Calabria Citeriore – but probably everywhere – "the jars (*giarre*) used for water" are made locally out of clay "which is the only earth used in their manufacture"[93]. The editor for Calabria Ulteriore goes further, suggesting that those dwelling along the costs use actual "filtering vases", "to purify their waters full of clay particles and stink of silt, as used by those living along the banks of the Thames"[94].

Even where local water quality is perceived as good by the editors, the fact of not treating it in any way is seen as a negative social indicator. Thus, in the words of the editor for Abruzzo Ultra II: "Nowhere in the province is there the practice of filtering the water before drinking it, whether out of laziness or ignorance of how to do it"[95]. The editor, with reference to the sulfurous water of the town fountain in Antrodoco, notes how "it is amazing that the town continues to use this water, when with not much expense it could supply itself with better potable water"[96].

But as the editor for Abruzzo Citra states, "if nature does not fatefully provide water good for digestion and suitable for other economic uses, generally the water is used as it springs forth, whether out of ignorance or to avoid the bother of filtering it artificially"[97]. The inhabitants of Villalago (Abruzzo Ultra II) are likewise criticized for their habit of drawing their water from a spring of Lake Pio, "and since dirty clothes are washed in the lake and all the town's rubbish ends up there, so the said spring also remains infected". And yet, as the same editor tells us, "Villalago has another fountain of good water which is called *della frescura*"[98]. Rather than a question of poor judgement, it is just as likely that the inhabitants are simply employing the two waters for different purposes.

The editors make a similar social criticism of the perceived laziness of the locals when it comes to sourcing their water, preferring poor-quality water that is close by to better water further away (I wonder how often the editors had to draw and carry their own water). Thus the editor for Terra d'Otranto, commenting on

---

92 *Ibid.*, I, pp. 51–52.

93 *Ibid.*, II, p. 504.

94 *Ibid.*, II, p. 534.

95 Mind you, the editor contradicts himself just a few sentences later, commenting on how, with regard to the water of Lake Fucino, "there is no practice other than filtering it if it is cloudy or allowing it to rest and settle in wooden vessels". And the solution to water quality he proposes merely consists in "immersing a red-hot poker into it before drinking, in winter, and in summer dosing it with a small amount of mineral acid or larger amounts of vegetable acid". *Ibid.*, I, p. 50.

96 *Ibid.*, I, p. 51.

97 *Ibid.*, I, p. 211.

98 *Ibid.*, I, p. 51.

Galatina and Massafra, notes how "in town, the spring water is either bad or not very good, and in the surrounding country there is excellent water but at a distance of a half or full mile, and naturally the inhabitants drink the bad water and ignore the good"[99]. Similarly, the editor for Abruzzo Citra reports:

> If it happens that in some towns use is made of water that is less healthy and more than often sludgy [*molle*] because full of clay, this is due to the laziness of the inhabitants who, to avoid having to draw it in faraway places, content themselves with threatening their health by using water which is full of harmful substances, only because it is close by[100].

5 Hydraulic hierarchies: multiple uses and privileged access

In the province of Naples more generally "all the perennial waters gushing out of the valleys in the branch of the Apennines are channeled from their point of origin and through stone conduits, mostly uncovered, arrive in the towns, where they serve for domestic uses and to power mills, and then the residual waters flow out at the sea"[101]. Communities practice a distinction between different water quality and uses. For instance, in Bolognano (Abruzzo Citra), "the townsfolk judiciously water the animals and other less important uses, reserving the good potable water, although distant, for drinking and the cooking of food"[102]. In the town of S. Marco in Lamis (Capitanata), where "they drink rainwater", "the cisterns are uncovered in the countryside and covered in town", and "the waters of the former are destined for the watering of animals, those of the latter for human uses"[103]. Different waters are used for different purposes, as in Potenza (Basilicata), where the inhabitants distinguish between "drinking water", "which is fountain water [. . .] and [which] is believed to possess all potable qualities", and water reserved "for cooking and other household uses", "for which they use the water that gushes into wells dug at a certain depth in town"[104]. Elsewhere, such distinctions are made more out of necessity, as in the towns of Schiavone di S. Felice, Ripalda and Montemitro (Molise), where "the waters are so bad, so little

99 *Ibid.*, II, p. 173.
100 *Ibid.*, I, p. 210.
101 *Ibid.*, IV, p. 28.
102 *Ibid.*, I, p. 226.
103 *Ibid.*, I, p. 391.
104 *Ibid.*, III, pp. 68–69.

potable [. . .] that the [inhabitants] are forced to limit and reserve the only well providing mediocre water they have for the use of the sick"[105].

In contrast to this, at the other end of the spectrum, the editors elsewhere criticize a promiscuous use of water. In places where the only sources of water are "open fountains built like watering troughs", "people dip their hands in along with water pitchers of either wood or copper to draw water" and "animals also drink from them and sometimes water is also drawn there for the washing of dirty clothes"[106]. In Calabria Citeriore river water is reserved for animals and, "given their abundance, the owners of animals have not seen the need to build troughs and basins specifically for their use"[107]. The same is true in Principato Citeriore, where "waters are normally springs or flowing streams"[108].

But not everything is always as it seems. In Molise, the provincial editor Pepe – reformer, essayist and agronomist – tells us, "the people are not very careful in their choice of drinking water: they take it where they find it". And yet elsewhere in his report the editor notes that "to cook his legumes the peasant goes in search of cooking water, which easily soften them, waters which the people in local dialect call *cocevoli*"[109]. The fact that the local inhabitants not only went in search of such waters but had a specific word to indicate them, suggests they made evident distinctions regarding water use and were perhaps more "careful" than the editor was aware.

As this suggests, everywhere water is an essential resource, subject to a multiplicity of uses – sometimes complementary, sometimes in competition with one another. By way of example, the mineral spring "called the water of Crassano" (Terra di Lavoro), gushes out "in such quantity [. . .] that as soon as it appears from a chasm it powers a mill", after which, "in the summertime many people come here to use its waters, internally and externally" (that is, drinking and bathing in it), and then last, "linen and hemp are retted in its waters, acquiring an extraordinary whiteness"[110].

Water was not only necessary for life, for drinking and other domestic uses; in the form of flowing water it was also the most reliable source of power available to communities, as well as having other uses in industry and agriculture. But the supply was limited and so had to be portioned out. As a result, there was a hierarchy of water use, more or less regulated by local authorities. Each use had different, often competing, needs in terms of water power, volume/reliability, and

105 *Ibid.*, I, p. 299.
106 *Ibid.*, I, pp. 53–54.
107 *Ibid.*, II, p. 359.
108 *Ibid.*, IV, p. 607.
109 *Ibid.*, I, p. 300.
110 *Ibid.*, IV, p. 106.

quality. Thus, water for drinking and other domestic uses, such as cooking and laundry, needed purity; irrigation of agricultural land and retting of linen required reliability of supply above all. Reliability was also crucial for milling uses – grain, silk, fulling, paper, wood – although even more important was the force of water[111].

These competing needs for limited resources lead to a hydro-politics of a sort at the local level, only implied in the comments of the provincial editors. For example, even where significant infrastructure works have been undertaken, these can have a negative impact at the local level. A community may lose its waters when these are conducted elsewhere, given that the kingdom's hydro-politics privileges the city over the countryside. Acerra (Terra di Lavoro), whose nearby lake is the source of the Carmignano aqueduct which supplies the kingdom's capital, and which "passes by near the town", finds itself not benefitting "in any way" from it[112]. One part of a city may deprive another of water, especially when the former is the site of an important royal palace. Thus "old Caserta is entirely without water", according to the editor of Terra di Lavoro, because "the waters of the Fontanelle and Giove springs, although they gush forth in the valley where old Caserta lies [. . .] do not provide any water to the inhabitants, because [. . .] they were channeled into a covered aqueduct which leads to new Caserta"[113]. Thus a significant engineering achievement – the Caroline aqueduct designed by Luigi Vanvitelli and completed in 1762 (and today a UNESCO world heritage site) – warrants barely a mention in the *Statistica*, and this in a negative context.

Within towns, the arrangements for meeting different water needs can appear quite efficient. A hydraulic hierarchy is most evident where the infrastructure is at its most complex, the two Abruzzi provinces. Thus, in the town of Leonessa (Abruzzo Ultra), supplied with water by an aqueduct (as noted above), a branch of which "leads [. . .] to the beautiful fountain in the square", which in addition to its aesthetic qualities supplies water for domestic uses, and "then going down exits outside Porta di Regno to irrigate various vegetable gardens". Just as important, for the town's economic life, is "the other branch, greater in volume", which "serves to power seven mills", after which the water, "agitated and shaken by the action of the mill wheels, is collected in a large reservoir, from which it exits wending its way through various conduits inside the town, for the

111 A. Guenzi / C. Poni, *Un "network" plurisecolare: acqua e industria a Bologna*, in "Studi storici", 30, 1989, 2, pp. 359–377; S. Ciriacono, *L'eau comme enjeu économique: l'irrigation entre époques anciennes et l'époque modern*, in S. Ciriacono (ed.), *Eau et développement dans l'Europe moderne*, Paris 2004, pp. 1–34.

112 D. Demarco, *La "Statistica"*, IV, p. 159.

113 *Ibid.*, IV, p. 141.

convenience of the private uses of the townsfolk". In the final two levels of Leonessa's hydraulic hierarchy, "what is left ends up in a trough at Porta de lo Stato used for watering animals and as washbasin for clothing", and finally, "it is channeled outside town to irrigate the farmland located below"[114].

Despite constituting a crucial part of the hydraulic infrastructure, washbasins (and indeed clothes-washing in general) are rarely mentioned by the provincial editors. In any case, we find a similar hierarchy in the town of Aquila, beginning at the Fonte della Novantanove Cannelle, where

> there are everywhere convenient basins or containers, where the water exiting from the second level of taps, is collected for the washing of clothes and other similar ordinary uses such as the watering of animals, and subsequently filtered goes further downwards to water vegetable gardens[115].

Similarly, in the capital, the hydraulic infrastructure allows for a differentiation in water use. The waters "of the Carmignano, so called", after the aqueduct of the same name, "arrive [in Naples] divided into two branches", one of which "provides water to dwellings of the upper part of the city, the other powers many mills and various craft machinery, and after having served for the bleaching of cloths, flows into the Marinella in the area known as Fiumicello". The city's second aqueduct, the Bolla (or Volla) also divides into two branches upon its arrival in Naples. One "provides water to the lower part of the city and also serves to power manufacturing devices", the other "makes up the famous [river] Sebeto, which after having powered many mills, flows into the sea under the Maddalena bridge"[116].

In the Kingdom of Naples at the start of the nineteenth century, the machinery of manufacturing relied on the power of water, the most reliable source of energy, as it had done for centuries[117]. According to the editor of Calabria Ulteriore, "the flour mills, sawmills, fulling mills for the rough cloth of the common people are the mills powered by the waters of our rivers"[118]. Not without a note of pride he adds that "this province would seem to be born to unite all the means necessary to give the best of the wealth coming out of the earth"[119]. In Basilicata

---

114 D. Demarco, *La "Statistica"*, I, p. 53. It is not as idyllic as it seems, since a few pages later the editor notes how outside the town "a good portion" of the aqueduct is "broken and exposed". Meanwhile, in the town, the conduits located under the streets leak because not well connected and there are piles of waste put there by the millers to regulate the flow of water (*ibid.*, I, p. 55).

115 *Ibid.*, I, p. 53.

116 *Ibid.*, IV, p. 23.

117 J. Sawday, *Engines of the Imagination. Renaissance Culture and the Rise of the Machine*, London 2007, p. 32.

118 D. Demarco, *La "Statistica"*, II, p. 520.

119 *Ibid.*

the Mount Vulture region is rich in streams which "spring forth in such abundance, especially the famous Fonte della Francesca, to power fulling mills and flour mills", while also serving to "irrigate vegetable fields" and for "the retting of linen"[120]. In the province of Naples the river Sarno has multiple uses, industrial and agricultural, serving "the royal armories, gunpowder mills and flour mills of Torre dell'Annunziata, after which along its whole course of some seven miles it irrigates many adjacent fields, including those belonging to the Crown"[121].

In Calabria Citeriore, although there are fulling mills "everywhere", their "imperfections prevent the best sort of production"[122]. This consists of the preparation of "heavy and coarse cloth, known as *arbascio*, and rough and poorly woven woolen flannels, known locally as *fiandine*"[123]. Indeed, when it comes to fulling mills in particular, an ideal functionality seems evident only in the town of Palena (Abruzzo Citra). Here "the machines are built as they should be, without having superfluous elements or lacking necessary ones; the water is well collected and conducted, so that it creates the most power possible, accomplishing the task with a notable time saving"[124]. But Palena seems to be the exception. Even if every district in the province, according to the same editor, "boasts one or more fulling mills [. . .] not all of them are well suited to the preparation of wool manufactures, either because they are not well maintained or poorly built"[125]. This is exacerbated by the fact that reliance on water power in a Mediterranean climate comes with its own natural limitations, such as seasonality. In Abruzzo Ultra II, "with winter cold [the waters] acquire a certain degree of substance and heaviness", such that in the district of Amatrice "the mills rotate much less in winter than in other seasons"[126]. Not surprisingly, the opposite is more common: a diminution of water power during the summer months because of the lack of water, as in the case of the river Alento (Abruzzo Citra), which "can only power a few mills, that oftentimes in summer cannot function at all"[127].

The *Statistica* also provides examples of manufacturing decline. Along the river Verde (Abruzzo Citra), for example, activity "has declined to just a few mills, with the closure of the Fara S. Martino woolen mills"[128]. In Terra d'Otranto, the

120 *Ibid.*, III, p. 22.
121 *Ibid.*, IV, pp. 29–30.
122 *Ibid.*, II, p. 496.
123 *Ibid.*, II, p. 493.
124 *Ibid.*, I, pp. 273–274.
125 *Ibid.*
126 *Ibid.*, I, p. 51.
127 *Ibid.*, I, p. 216.
128 *Ibid.*, I, p. 219.

lack of rivers of any size means an absence of fulling mills, with the exception of those at Taranto "known as *battinteri*" which "made cloths for monks' habits"[129], now presumably no longer in use because of the Napoleonic "reform" of the religious orders. There are also missed opportunities when it comes to maximizing water use. The so-called Ceraso spring serves the town of S. Mango (Principato Citeriore) "to power many flour mills", and yet, according to the editor, "the inhabitants do not take the advantage of it that one might hope, since they could construct fulling mills, paper mills and tanneries, as well as set up regular irrigation"[130].

When it came to local manufactures, water was also an essential resource in the production of linen and hemp, in particular during the phases of retting and washing, where large quantities of stagnant water were needed. In Abruzzo Ultra "almost all the places if the province have lands given over to flax and hemp retting, especially where they can be easily irrigated"[131]. The statement could probably be extended to the entire kingdom, given that most communities produced their own linen and hemp, the main textiles, along with wool, before cotton became more widely available. As the editor of Principato Citeriore explains, "there is no town in which both sexes of the lower class are not engaged in [linen production], each according to their role". In fact – and this is one of the rare occasions in which gender is specifically addressed in the *Statistica* – the gendering of linen and hemp production meant that while "the men are normally tasked with the planting and cultivation, as well as the pulling, retting and breaking; the women are engaged in the manufacture, undertaking all of the tasks required"[132]. This would have included spinning, dying, weaving and sewing. The textiles produced could be marketed or consumed locally. Thus, in Avigliano (Basilicata) the linen "is of good quality and is sought after for purchase in Basilicata and in the provinces of Bari and Otranto"[133], whereas in Molise "every peasant, every poor woman cultivates it [flax], to patch her own rags and not to sell", in the words of the provincial editor Raffaele Pepe[134]. And yet, even in Basilicata there was room for improvement, as the editor notes with regard to the town of Castelgrande:

> the obstacles against the increase in these manufactures are that everything is done according poorly established practices, and in particular the retting of flax and hemp in waters

129 *Ibid.*, II, p. 281.
130 *Ibid.*, IV, p. 672.
131 *Ibid.*, I, p. 181.
132 *Ibid.*, IV, pp. 657–658.
133 *Ibid.*, III, p. 484.
134 *Ibid.*, I, p. 332. Among Pepe's numerous activities, as a means of combating peasant poverty, was the encouragement of potato cultivation in his native Molise. D. Gentilcore, *Italy and The Potato: A History, 1550–2000*, London 2012, pp. 58, 67.

> that are full of clay, and piling up large stones on top of them, so that the retting is neither even nor is it evident when it is complete[135].

When it came to textile production, water was also important in the dying process. This was especially so when the water possessed special qualities, as at the Olmitella springs on the island of Ischia (province of Naples), which were used in "the manufacture of blue cloth, containing naturally occurring phlogisticated alkalis"[136].

The final use of water in the local economy concerned irrigation. In the province of Calabria Citeriore, according to the editor, "we have many irrigable lands and we generally practice irrigation in the cultivation of maize, cotton (*bambagia*) and legumes"[137]. At S. Giorgio (Basilicata) "irrigation is practiced in the vegetable gardens and in some places planted with maize"[138]. These two simple statements represent the exception; almost everywhere else irrigation represented something of a bone of contention for the provincial editors, which the local peasants never seem to get right. Indeed, Piero Bevilacqua has pointed out that contemporaries frequently failed to appreciate the specific uses of water in southern Italian agriculture[139].

In some areas there is too little: irrigation is presented as a missed opportunity. The editors recognize the natural limitations. To work well, according to the editor for Capitanata, "the need for irrigation" must be wedded to "a sufficient supply of flowing water", but all too often "it happens that just when adjacent cultivated lands need the water, the nearby stream has little or none"[140]. Available water supply and agriculture rarely seem to coincide, as the editor of Terra di Lavoro notes with regard to the rich Campania plain. If "it is without doubt the best and most fertile part of the province and one of the most beautiful areas of the kingdom", unfortunately "it can be said quite honestly that in very few sites the goodness of the land, the water and the climate are found all together [. . .]. If the land is fertile, the waters are mediocre and the airs tend towards insalubrity and damp"[141].

And this with regard to one of the few areas of the kingdom where irrigation was extensively practiced, even seeing an expansion during the course of the "French decade"! Not far away, in the Salerno plain (Principato Citeriore) irrigation was also widely practiced, extensively and more or less efficiently, according

135 D. Demarco, *La "Statistica"*, III, p. 463.
136 *Ibid.*, IV, p. 28.
137 *Ibid.*, II, p. 420.
138 *Ibid.*, III, p. 442.
139 P. Bevilacqua, *Acque e bonifiche nel Mezzogiorno nella prima metà dell'Ottocento*, in "Studi Storici", 27, 1986, 2, p. 339.
140 *Ibid.*, I, p. 383.
141 *Ibid.*, IV, p. 173.

to Bevilacqua[142]. But for the cathedral canon and Salerno native Gennaro Guida, provincial editor for Principato Citeriore, there was far too much of it. "Wherever there are irrigable lands, wherever water can be brought in, even from far away, irrigation is practiced". He even complained that the fruit and vegetables "would taste better if the fields were not irrigated with water"[143]. Guida also objected to the fact that "continuous irrigation", accompanied by "much manure", was used to grow vegetables in the fields located all around Salerno, "causing the development of poisonous gases which render the air unhealthy and pestiferous"[144].

Elsewhere, it is not the "right" kind of irrigation. Thus the editor for Abruzzo Ultra, the patrician and agronomist Alferi Osorio, points out that there are towns "which have abundant water and could take full advantage of it, but by the abuse they make of it they render the land infertile rather than nourish it". This is due to poor irrigation practices, which cause "these beautiful farmlands" to be "exhausted and removed of their humus or loam, reduced to a mass of stones and pebbles as a result of the frequent flooding". Alas, Osorio concludes, "there is no way of disabusing or persuading those peasants otherwise"[145].

Finally, there were missed opportunities when it came to irrigation, according to the provincial editors. In the province of Molise, where "all the good lowlands on the banks [of the river Biferno], as of those on the [river] Trigno could be irrigable; they are veritable thirsty Tantaluses surrounded by water", as the editor Pepe comments in a flight of lyricism[146]. And in Abruzzo Citra the editor – the teacher and former Piarist priest Paolo d'Aquila – proposes the canalization of river water as the solution. As it stands, the benefits of the river Pescara are limited to the powering of "a few mills", whereas if its waters were channeled they could serve "to irrigate the fields which make up this province's wealth"[147]. He makes the same point with regard to the river Sangro, the waters of which could provide the province with "many benefits", in particular "the irrigation of the farmland on both of its banks"[148].

---

142 P. Bevilacqua, *Acque e bonifiche*, pp. 338–340.

143 D. Demarco, *La "Statistica"*, IV, p. 550.

144 *Ibid.*, p. 556. The latter point was certainly a legitimate one, given the contemporary association between miasmatic air and disease. I explore this link more fully in my companion piece, *"La qualità delle acque"*.

145 *Ibid.*, I, p. 137. Osorio refers here to the case of a certain Bonanni, "worthy member of Aquila's Istituto agrario-economico", who "in vain sought to introduce and promote the use of canals horizontal and parallel to rivers, as practiced in China".

146 *Ibid.*, I, p. 293. The reference here is to the mythological figure Tantalus, punished by being made to stand in a pool of water beneath a fruit tree with low branches, but unable to access either.

147 *Ibid.*, I, pp. 213–214.

148 *Ibid.*, I, p. 218.

Hitherto in this section we have discussed distinctions in water use; what about access to that water? On a European level, water was often characterized as a "universal good" in legislation; but in reality water access was not the same for everyone in society[149]. The basic fact of the social elites not only having many more possibilities when it comes to water access, but also jealously guarding their own privileges often at the expense of the wider community, is seen by Monticelli as part and parcel of the kingdom's economic decline. It is also amply borne out by the *Statistica*. In Diano (Principato Citeriore), "the persons of means normally make use of rainwater captured from the rooftops of their houses and stored in cisterns" while "the common people make use of the little water that flows from springs, and when this is lacking they are forced to use water from a river one mile distant from the town". The editor concludes that "Diano is rather infelicitous is this regard"[150] – although one is not sure whether this refers to the class distinction in water access or the shortage of water more generally. If the townsfolk of the low-lying towns of Oriolo and Bollita (Calabria Citeriore) are forced to utilize cisterns for rainwater storage – a great shame as far as the provincial editor is concerned – he also notes how "the well-off have the waters they need drawn from the nearby mountain, leaving to the multitudes without this possibility the use of town waters"[151]. In Principato Citeriore, "in addition to spring water, there are dug wells [*pozzi artificiali*] [. . .] and these belong to private landowning families"[152]. The same is true in Castellamare (province of Naples), where "many private landowners prefer to have the benefit of spring water wells in their houses, which are commonly found in most places"[153]. In the old part of Caserta (Terra di Lavoro), "entirely without water", as we have seen, an aqueduct passes "through the hilltop on which it is built [. . .] used only by the wealthiest people, who alone can afford the expense of having their water drawn from it"[154]. The better-off can afford to have their water brought from greater distances, which allows them to access better quality water, also the case for the wealthy of the hamlets of S. Felice (Terra di Lavoro), who have their water drawn and brought

149 U. Sowina, *Water, Towns and People. Polish Lands Against a European Background until the Mid-16th Century*, trans. by J. Woldanska, Frankfurt 2016.

150 D. Demarco, *La "Statistica"*, IV, p. 585. The marshy valley (Vallo di Diano) was drained in an ongoing public works project during the first half of the nineteenth century, not without local opposition. P. Bevilacqua, *Acque e bonifiche*; C. D'Elia, *Supplicanti e vandali. Testi scritti, testi non scritti, testi scritti dagli storici*, in "Quaderni Storici", 31, 1996, 2, pp. 459–485.

151 *Ibid.*, III, p. 330.

152 *Ibid.*, IV, p. 540.

153 *Ibid.*, IV, p. 25.

154 *Ibid.*, IV, p. 141.

to them from "a small spring popularly known as the Fontana di Capo di Conca"[155]. Even the use of water jars, referred to above, has its social limitations (and one wonders how widespread throughout the kingdom these were). Thus, among the inhabitants of Castelvolturno (Terra di Lavoro), forced to use poor quality river water, "some of the better off put it in large earthenware vases, in which it rests, slowing depositing the impurities with which it abounds, and then decanted as needed it would seem to acquire a degree of clarity making it potable and less harmful"[156].

Despite this social distinction in terms of water access, it is very occasionally members of the same local elites who have necessary hydraulic infrastructure works undertaken. For instance the "Fiumarello, or canal of the count of Sarno, which the former baron S. Pietro had done for the population of his feudal estate with its mediocre potable waters" (Principato Citeriore)[157]. More commonly, however, the elites take full advantage of their powers. Monticelli writes of how the large landowners and the well-off are wanting in this regard, with their generalized aversion to "rural cares", due to a mixture of ignorance and private business interests[158].

This is also evident in the *Statistica*. In S. Bartolomeo (Capitanata) "there is a beautifully built fountain, which would supply abundant water to the whole population if the egoism and bad faith of an arrogant family of the town had not fraudulently conducted all the water to itself"[159], an event which, for greed and betrayal, recalls the plot of Marcel Pagnol's 1952 film (and later two-part novel) *Manon des sources*, set in the parched hills of Provence. In other cases, spring water is jealously guarded by its owners, as those of the Fontana di S. Angelo, on the outskirts of Capua (Terra di Lavoro), which is "used by its owners to water their extensive vegetable gardens". As the editor comments, the family could cede a portion of the spring's water to the town, which could certainly use it, "but the owner's obstinacy is invincible, and only the authority of the government could bring about this cession"[160]. A similar story on the outskirts of Orsogna (Abruzzo Citra), where there is a spring of brackish water, possibly due to the salt mines nearby, the water of which is highly prized to water vegetable gardens. But, the editor notes, "the owners of the land have maliciously dug the spring over, to exempt their estates from

155 *Ibid.*, IV, p. 146.
156 *Ibid.*, IV, p. 165.
157 *Ibid.*, IV, p. 573.
158 T. Monticelli, *Sulla economia delle acque*, p. 43, note 26.
159 D. Demarco, *La "Statistica"*, I, p. 393.
160 *Ibid.*, IV, p. 142.

any subjugation"[161]. A final dispute is recounted by the editor of Terra di Lavoro. "Around 1750", he writes, "the feudal lord Buoncompagno" attempted to revive the use of the Catane springs, only to meet with "the opposition of the town authorities, whose land it was"[162].

The issue of mineral bathing springs brings up a final characterization of decay and decline, as the provincial editors highlight the lack of suitable establishments and structures for what is still a widespread medical (and indeed social) practice. The springs at Catane (Terra di Lavoro) "are today abandoned due to a reprehensible negligence", but "from the ruins of buildings and mosaic floors near the springs, it is evident that in ancient times they must have been very busy"[163]. In Calabria Ulteriore the thermal springs are still much used despite "the total lack of buildings to protect the sick from the impact of the airs above", with the result that "the sick, if they want to use them, are forced to build temporary protection from plant materials themselves or else run the risk of possible chills from being exposed to the open air". The provincial editor, the doctor Giuseppe Grio, wonders how it is possible "for the sick to cure themselves of one illness without coming down with others"[164]. In Terra di Lavoro the waters of Montetto could be "of greater usefulness" if "the doctors of the surrounding areas took greater care in prescribing the sick in their use and if, in the vicinity, there was some covered building and properly built baths to protect the sick from the inclemency of the air"[165].

The decay is most evident at the thermal springs of Bagno della Rogna (Terra di Lavoro), which translates as the not very attractive sounding "Scabies Springs", but is an indication of its importance as a site for treating afflictions of the skin. Located near the "small ruined convent of S. Antonio", one can "see evidence of bath-houses, including among the many some double ones, the water passing from one to another". However, "these have been buried under fallen buildings, so that one cannot stay for long". The same provincial editor concludes his discussion asking "by what fatal destiny these health-giving waters were abandoned, which are perhaps among the best in the kingdom". The answer may lie, he suggests, "in the insalubrity of the climate due to the proximity of the Minturna

161 *Ibid.*, I, p. 212.
162 *Ibid.*, IV, p. 74.
163 *Ibid.*
164 *Ibid.*, II, p. 517. Grio was a native of Polistena and a mathematician, planner and philosopher, in addition to being a doctor. Secretary of the provincial agricultural society, he introduced treatment for typhus in the province and was charged with the division of the waters of the rivers Sciarapotamo e Jerapotamo.
165 *Ibid.*, IV, p. 159.

marshes, the pestiferous exhalations of which extend all around and which are deadly at precisely the same time of year when the mineral waters should be most visited"[166].

6 Conclusion

What the views of the provincial editors of the *Statistica* reveal is a kingdom divided by its hydraulic infrastructure, from areas of sophistication in the Abruzzi provinces and Terra di Lavoro to areas of quite basic standards in the Calabrian provinces, to areas of scarcity in Molise. There is a tendency to concentrate on what is lacking rather than what works: decay, abandonment and poor maintenance are frequent themes. Despite this, what is also striking is the ability of local communities throughout the kingdom to achieve a level of self-sufficiency, making a virtue of necessity by growing and milling their own food (with or without the aid of irrigation), producing their own cloth (linen, wool), and treating their own illnesses (mineral springs).

If both Monticelli and the contributors to the *Statistica* had a tendency to look back to the past in their evaluation of the present, what about the future? And what impact did they have on hydraulic infrastructure in the kingdom of Naples during the nineteenth century?

In terms of looking forwards, we might consider what proposals they make to rectify the present ills, as they saw them. As a general solution to difficulties linked to the "economy of the waters", Monticelli proposed undertaking three "great things": i) restoring the "ancient healthiness" of the coasts and plains by draining stagnant water, ii) reforesting the mountains, and iii) furnishing arid zones with water reservoirs[167]. In a similar vein, some of the provincial editors also propose specific solutions to local problems linked to water resources.

However, the only one to provide broad solutions is the editor of the Terra di Lavoro submission, Perrini, "because it is now well known that the diminution of disease, good digestion, personal vigor, fresh skin color, whiteness of teeth largely depend on the use of good and limpid waters"[168].

His solutions pertain to four water sources: aqueducts, fountains, wells and river water. In terms of aqueducts, Perrini argues that it would be important that "the appreciation of aqueducts was reborn among the people, which signal the

166 *Ibid.*, IV, p. 184.
167 T. Monticelli, *Sulla economia delle acque*, p. 42.
168 D. Demarco, *La "Statistica"*, IV, p. 211.

progresses of civilizations and announce the affluence and wealth of a people". For fountains, one would need "to oversee the cleanness of fountains, to use conduits to remove water (*purgatoi*) from cisterns and other rainwater receptacles". When it came to wells, one should "prohibit the digging of wells in waterlogged land and always at a set distance from sewers, burial grounds, sites which attract rain water and places where hides are cured, and all wells to be equipped with corresponding ventilation". And, finally, in terms of river resources, it would be necessary "to construct at public expense machines for filtering river waters and to teach in a gentle way those populations forced to drink unhealthy and stagnant water the methods already proposed by Messers Ami, de Iusti and Porzio". Here Perrini goes so far as to refer to "the basin with vertical divider proposed by Mister Foderé, following details derived from Porzio's military medicine (*Igiene pub. ca*, tom. VII, pag. 56, Ediz. Napol.na)"[169]. This water filter would be especially useful to "all harvesters and farmers who work in the fields during the dog days of summer and the heat of the afternoons", a long way from town, such that "the weary peasant, drinking in search of refreshment, does not instead find a poisonous potion which attacks the very source of life"[170].

It is a long list, and an ambitious one. That said, the words of the provincial editors of the *Statistica*, as well as of Monticelli himself, did not fall on deaf ears. If Monticelli has an heir, it is the figure of Carlo Afan de Rivera, although they were virtual contemporaries (and may not have seen eye to eye)[171]. Afan de Rivera combined both intellectual studies of the kingdom's infrastructure and its requirements, hydraulic and otherwise[172], with a significant technical role as state official. From 1825, under the restored Bourbon dynasty, which followed the decade of French rule that produced the *Statistica*, Afan de Rivera was director general of the office of "Ponti e Strade, Acque, Foreste e Caccia", a corps of engineers in charge of

169 Perrini names the originators of various water filtration devices, such as the Neapolitan military physician Luca Antonio Porzio (1639–1723) and the Savoyard forensic and public health doctor François-Emmanuel Fodéré (1764–1835). *Ibid.*

170 *Ibid.*

171 G. Foscari, *Teodoro Monticelli*, pp. 114–117.

172 Taking his lead from Monticelli, Afan de Rivera identifies the barbarian invasions, followed by Saracen incursions along the coast, as the beginning of the kingdom's decline. C. Afan de Rivera, *Memoria intorno alle devastazioni prodotte dalle acque a cagion de' diboscamenti*, Napoli 1825, p. 7. His ideas concerning the previous natural wealth of the kingdom, the subsequent decline as a result of poor water management and deforestation, as well as solutions to remedy them were more fully developed in his major work, published eight years later: C. Afan de Rivera, *Considerazioni su i mezzi da restituire il valore proprio a' doni che ha la natura largamente conceduto al regno delle Due Sicilie*, 2 vols., Napoli 1833.

public works concerning bridges, roads, waters, forests and hunting. The "Acque" (waters) in the title extended to waterways, canals, ports and land reclamation. In this guise he was able to implement some of the infrastructure projects proposed in earlier decades, in addition to undertaking new ones, even if the full promise of his role was not realized – but that, as they say, is another story[173].

173 G. Foscari, *Prassi amministrativa e attività pubblicistica a tutela del territorio: l'opera di Carlo Afan de Rivera nell'Ottocento borbonico*, in "Clio", 30, 1994, 2, pp. 223–255, and S. Conti, *Il problema delle bonifiche e del diboscamento nel pensiero di Carlo Afan de Rivera*, in *Carlo Afan de Rivera e la scuola napoletana di ponti e strade*, Napoli 2020, pp. 9–21. On the kingdom's hydraulic issues and solutions, in particularly regarding land reclamation and flooding, see: P. Bevilacqua, *Acque e bonifiche*, pp. 335–357; A. Di Biasio, *Politica e amministrazione del territorio nel mezzogiorno d'Italia tra settecento e ottocento*, Napoli 2004, pp. 213–270; and W. Palmieri, *Natura, uomini e dissesti. Le alluvioni di Nola agli inizi dell'Ottocento*, in "Società e Storia", 32, 2009, 126, pp. 615–633. On administrative reforms and public works, see: N. Ostuni, *Riforme amministrative e viabilità nel Regno di Napoli durante il periodo francese*, in *Villes et territoire pendant la période napoléonienne: France et Italie*, Roma 1987, pp. 161–181, and A. Spagnoletti, *Territorio e amministrazione nel Regno di Napoli (1806–1816)*, pp. 79–101. Finally, on the wider context, see F. D'Angelo, *Scienze e viaggio: ingegneri e architetti nel Regno delle due Sicilie*, Villasanta 2014.

V. Conclusion

John R. McNeill

Afterword: Reflections on Environmental Infrastructure

One characteristic is common to the chapters in this volume: their high quality. They give a taste of the depth of research and the varied perspectives that inform European environmental history at the moment. Taken together, they raise a handful of questions and themes that I will reflect upon briefly in the next few pages.

First of all is the difficulty surrounding the term "infrastructure" as used in environmental history. Almost every chapter in this book relies on this concept. Some attempt to define it, while others do not. And the definitions employed vary. They must vary because in each setting the infrastructure that communities used to exploit their local environments, or to protect themselves from its occasional extremes (such as flood), differed. Technological capabilities grew over time, and the range of potential infrastructure expanded accordingly. The *stue* used to ease the flotation of timber in the Friuli region centuries ago have no counterparts in an abandoned Honduran banana port re-purposed late in the twentieth century to receive toxic waste. A definition of environmental infrastructure for a book as capacious as this one might not be attainable, at least not unless it was very vague and general.

That problem does not detract from the utility of the concept. A decade ago, Emmanuel Kreike devoted a book to environmental infrastructure in southern Africa. He hoped the concept might bridge the dubious divide between nature and culture[1]. Without using the term, others before him had deployed the same concept, arguing that some things are neither wholly natural nor wholly cultural, but both at once[2]. Indeed, every society since the invention of wooden tools has devised some sort of environmental infrastructure. Nonetheless, the term and concept remain rarer than they should be in the work of environmental historians. It is helpful to see so many versions of it within one book, which might inspire more imitation.

Another issue raised in these chapters concerns the role of labor in environmental infrastructure. *Stue*, canals, aqueducts, wells, fountains, sea walls and all the rest required labor both in their creation and, what is sometimes forgotten, their maintenance. Some societies had plenty of labor to deploy, either because of

1 E. Kreike, *Environmental Infrastructure in African History: Examining the Myth of Natural Resource Management in Namibia*, New York 2013.
2 E.g. North America's Columbia River in the estimation of R. White, *The Organic Machine*, New York 2000.

https://doi.org/10.1515/9783111112756-012

dense populations (uncommon in the premodern Alpine region featured in several of these chapters) or because of a "dead season" when tasks were few and people (perhaps only men) had time to spare on what were often communal projects. The history of canals around the world points to the importance of abundant cheap labor, without which the irrigation and navigation canals that crisscross the North China plain, Gangetic plain, Mesopotamia, or the Nile Delta could neither have been built nor maintained. (Note, moreover, that a successful system of canals helped to raise agricultural yields and typically to increase population size, and sustain it, providing more labor power for system maintenance).

Sometimes the labor involved in building or maintaining environmental infrastructure had to be specialized skilled labor, rather than legions of peasants with spades or shovels. In some parts of the world, for example, well-digger was a skilled profession. Itinerant well-diggers traveled about offering their services. Larger projects, such as canals, might require a skilled engineer but not skilled labor. The chapters here touch on questions of labor, skill, specialization, but they leave opportunity for further exploration of that subject. Attention to environmental infrastructure invites fuller consideration of the place of labor in environmental histories.

Another issue that makes an occasional appearance in these chapters, but might deserve more consistent attention, is the role of military priorities in the construction and maintenance of environmental infrastructure. Decisions about what to build and where to put it could reflect many preferences and priorities, but among them, often enough, were military ones. In the early modern centuries explored by Stöger, Lorenzini, Graber, Di Tullio and Soens, for example, communities – villages, town, cities, states – had to take into account their capacity to resist sieges. They needed reliable access to food and water, without which they could not last long, and, over longer times scale, they needed access to wood and other materials. In later eras, access to coal or oil, and the complex infrastructure needed to process and transport modern fossil fuels, were added to the list of strategic requirements. The exploitation of uranium in Saxony and Thuringia is a further case in point: it made sense only during the Cold War, when the Soviet bloc needed uranium for nuclear weapons and to power its industry, a large share of which was military production. After 1985, with increased momentum in strategic arms limitation negotiations, and then German reunification, the military priority attached to uranium disappeared and the Wismut mines closed.

A loosely related issue is the role of public vs. private agency and capital in creating and maintaining environmental infrastructure. Several of the chapters discuss this theme. Most environmental infrastructure benefited a variety of people and institutions. Canals might serve the purpose of merchants and farmers in their private capacities, but also serve the state as it sought to move military equipment and manpower around its domains. Uranium mining, port facilities, and even seawalls might also serve both private and public interests at the same time. It might be interesting to search for patterns in the varying roles of public and private interests in promoting environmental infrastructure. Are there discernible changes over the past 500 years? Are there differences among regions of the world, or regions of Europe? Are mountainous regions any different from valleys and plains in this regard? Are seacoasts any different from continental interiors? Surely heavily militarized societies are different in their environmental infrastructure investments from those societies with minimal security concerns (e.g. modern Costa Rica, which has no military). Proper investigation would, no doubt, reveal less obvious patterns.

Umbrella terms such as public and private hide many distinctions. As Graber's chapter concerning *enquêtes publiques* in France shows, public authorities found it easy enough to manipulate the citizenry in order to muster adequate support for the approval of public works projects. In other settings, no doubt, the richest or most influential private citizens attempted much the same manipulation. Looking just a little below the surface, one is likely to find a welter of different institutions, ministries, agencies, offices involved in public initiatives to build or maintain environmental infrastructure. And by the same token, one is sure to find a range of private citizens, some acting as individuals, others in pressure groups, trying to influence what their community or government chooses to do with respect to environmental infrastructure. Thus, the patterns one is likely to find if pursuing this course of research might look fairly complicated – but we can't be sure until these questions are pursued in depth.

When it comes to private citizens and their roles, it would surely prove worthwhile to attempt a more gendered understanding of who gets involved in environmental infrastructure and why. The standard sources available to historians are often little help in this ambition, but as countless historians of women, family, and gender have shown, with enough ingenuity it is possible to overcome, at least in part, the obstacles inherent in the surviving sources. With respect to the villages and towns of the early modern Alpine region, so prominent in this book, the water and fuel infrastructure they created probably affected the lives of women and children at least as much as those of men. This might well be true of the water infrastructure in the early nineteenth-century Kingdom of Naples as detailed in the sources analyzed in Gentilcore's chapter. Indeed, it ought to be the rule everywhere that fetching water and gathering fuelwood for daily living was women and children's work. Their voices, no doubt, are muffled in the surviving archival documents, and even more so in the contemporaneous published sources (e.g. the study of Naples's water infrastructure published by Teodoro Monticelli). Environmental infrastructure probably was not built with their lives in mind. And yet, women and children were deeply bound up in the operation of the systems that supplied water and fuel. This too seems deserving of further investigation, even if extra ingenuity will be required in, so to speak, persuading the sources to talk.

Given the prominence today of climate change in almost every discourse concerning the environment and environmental management efforts, these chapters might serve as a springboard for further work in another way as well. Water infrastructure is of course highly vulnerable to short-term fluxes – floods and droughts – and, less evidently, to changes in long-term precipitation patterns (as Parrinello's chapter emphasizes). Systems of timber transport were vulnerable to fluctuations in snowfall, which could be either too heavy or too light for the smooth skidding of logs. Several of the chapters touch on the possible relevance of climate change to the continuing viability of environmental infrastructure. But they can also inspire deeper investigations in this direction.

Turning now to issues of historical craft, these chapters display a considerable range in the choices their authors have made about the appropriate scale – or scales – on which to pursue environmental history research. Some go to lengths to integrate local and international scales, as in Müller's chapter, zooming in and zooming out. Others prefer a tighter focus. Here I attempt to arrange the chapters by the scales that predominate within each chapter, starting with the largest, geographically speaking, and the longest, chronologically speaking. The table below should be understood not as a rating or evaluation of the chapters, but as a heuristic device created to illustrate a point. I readily admit there is room to dispute the specific characterizations of scale that I make here: the chapter by Trischler and Will on the Anthropocene, which I list below as dealing with the largest and longest of scales, might alternatively be judged as an intellectual history of a single idea over the past 20 years. And one could claim that Di Tullio's Lombardy is bigger than Soens's North Sea coastlands. The point here is not the positioning of this, that, or the other chapter, but the range of choices in evidence.

TIME	SPACE
Trischler & Will: all geological time	Trischler & Will: the Earth
Soens ~ 10 centuries	Graber: France
Di Tullio ~ 3 centuries	Gentilcore: Kingdom of Naples
Stöger ~ 3 centuries	Soens: North Sea
Parrinello ~ 2 centuries	Parrinello: Po watershed
Graber ~ 2 centuries	Müller: littoral of Greater Caribbean
Müller ~ 60 years	Di Tullio: Lombardy
Lorenzini ~ 50 years	Stöger: hinterlands of 3 cities
Kirchhof et al. ~ 30 years	Lorenzini: upper Tagliamento basin
Gentilcore ~ 20 years	Kirchhof et al.: archipelago of Wismut mining towns

To a large extent, questions of scale are questions of authors' pre-dispositions. Some scholars are "lumpers", who like to lump things together because of their resemblances or perhaps because of their differences. Others are "splitters" who prefer to cherish to differences among cases and treat one at a time. Each approach has its merits, and I often claim that for historians, including environmental historians, work at all scales is equally valid (some scholars disagree vigorously). Further, work at any particular scale complements, and is complemented by, work at larger or smaller scales – or so I claim. All that is admittedly rather abstract.

When one gets down to specific work, there often is an inherent logic to one or another choice of spatial scale. It might derive from the sources. Archives often reflect a particular political jurisdiction, a single empire, nation-state, province, town, or village. This often shapes decisions about scale, especially for scholars who need to take practical considerations (travel, expense, time) into account – which means almost all scholars. Alternatively, choice of one or another scale might derive more directly from the subject: Gentilcore's study of the work of Monticelli deals with the Kingdom of Naples at the very beginning of the nineteenth century because that is what Monticelli took as his subject. Graber's chapter on *enquêtes publiques* deals with France because *enquêtes publiques* were a nation-wide French phenomenon. The Wismut conglomerate mined uranium only in a handful of settings in East Germany, and those who remember life in, or close to, the mines, and can be interviewed today, are clustered around those locations. But often enough there is still room for judgment and an author's predisposition: should one take on all of the Po watershed or just one tributary's valley? The chapters display a range of possible choices about spatial scale, and are complementary in that way.

With respect to chronological scale, much the same is true. But in this collection it is striking how many of the authors have opted for two or more centuries (6 out of 10 by my count). This may be a fluke, a reflection of the particular collection of authors assembled for this book. But it might be, to some extent at least, a result of the opportunities presented by the deep documentary record available in the circum-alpine region and around the shores of the North Sea. In western North America, which has been a favorite field of research for environmental historians in the US, the written record scarcely extends back before 1850 (there are exceptions especially in the former Spanish territories). In most of Africa, the same is true. Longer chronological scales in these latter places require supplementing the written record with archeology and various paleosciences such as dendrochronology or paleogenomics. The documentary record in many European settings, like the Chinese, Ottoman, and a few other settings, invites consideration of longer time spans. The fact that such work is so difficult in some other places makes it all the more valuable in Europe.

Continuing with the theme of historical craft, I offer one final reflection on the variety of work within this volume – on sources and methods. The bulk of this collection relies on traditional sources for historians, the written record. In some chapters, those sources are published works from the period under examination (e.g. Gentilcore, Parrinello); in others, such published sources are blended together with archival findings (e.g. Stöger, Lorenzini, Graber, Müller, Di Tullio). In two chapters, perhaps unsurprisingly those that take on the longest chronologies, the research is based on published modern scholarship (Soens, Trischler & Will). The most conspicuous outlier in terms of sources and method is the lone chapter that relies on oral history (Kirchhof, Koshelev, Manthey, Pelkner, Schein and Uhlig). While the historical profession as a whole long ago accepted, and even embraced, oral history, within the confines of environmental history it remains exceptional. The example here might serve as inspiration for more scholars to conduct the interviews on which such work is always based, although sadly it won't help much for deep histories of the distant past.

In one respect, the chapters in this book, despite their variety and quality, do not represent one methodological trend that is increasingly evident in the work of European environmental historians, and indeed environmental historians everywhere. That is reliance on bio- and geo-archives via the work of paleoscientists, practitioners of palynology, geo-archeology, paleoclimatology and so forth. While the richness of the documentary record is a luxury that historians elsewhere often do not have, it does not mean that the wealth of information that survives on paper is all one can get. Nor does it mean that the deeper history that was not recorded in any written records, is beside the point when thinking about early modern, or modern centuries[3]. No book, however, can contain everything, and readers, I trust, will recognize the merits of this one.

3 One paper I recently stumbled across offers an example pertinent to the alpine region: B. Dietre et al., *Steady Transformation of Primeval Forest into Subalpine Pasture during the Late Neolithic to Early Bronze Age (2300–1700 BC) in the Silvretta Alps, Switzerland*, in "Holocene", 30, 2020, 3, pp. 355–368. This paper uses palynology, charcoal analysis and other techniques to show that deforestation and erosion accelerated after 2300 BCE as the practice of deliberately burning forests to create mountain pasture for cattle developed and intensified. This pattern of land use, which substantially reduced the forest cover of the Alps, made sense only after a genetic adaptation had swept through circum-alpine populations, one that allowed them to digest milk and other dairy products as adults. This adaptation, the European version of which probably resulted from a mutation among some northern European populations that originated as long as 9,000 years ago, but spread most rapidly among Europeans between ~2000 BCE and 500 CE, influenced land use practices in the Alps to this day by ensuring a robust market for milk, cheese, cream, and yogurt. The genetic trait that allows digestion of milk in adulthood is the "most strongly selected single gene trait over the last 10,000 years in multiple human populations". See J. Burger et al., *Low Prevalence of Lactase Persistence in Bronze Age Europe Indicates Ongoing Strong Selection over the Last 3,000 Years*, in "Current Biology", 30, 2020, 21, https://doi.org/10.1016/j.cub.2020.08.033.

Contributors

Giacomo Bonan, Assistant Professor in Modern History, University of Turin

Matteo Di Tullio, Assistant Professor in Early Modern History, University of Pavia

David Gentilcore, Professor of Early Modern History, Ca' Foscari University of Venice

Frédéric Graber, CNRS Researcher, Center Marc Bloch, Berlin

John R. McNeill, Professor of Environmental History, Georgetown University

Astrid Mignon Kirchhof, Senior Researcher, Institute for Technology Assessment and Systems Analysis, Karlsruhe

Yaroslav Koshelev, Researcher, Institute for Technology Assessment and Systems Analysis, Karlsruhe

Claudio Lorenzini, Associate Researcher, Laboratory of the History of the Alps, Mendrisio, Switzerland

Florian Manthey, Editor, Exhibition Office Beier+Wellach Projekte, Berlin

Simone M. Müller, Project Director of the DFG Emmy Noether Research Group "Hazardous Travels", Rachel Carson Center for Environment and Society, University of Munich (LMU)

Katia Occhi, Researcher, Istituto Storico Italo-Germanico, Fondazione Bruno Kessler, Trento

Giacomo Parrinello, Assistant Professor in Environmental History, Center for History, Sciences Po (CHSP), Paris

Anna-Katharina Pelkner, Sociologist, Pedagogist and Activist, Berlin

Judith Schein, Visual Anthropologist, The Leibniz Institute for Jewish History and Culture – Simon Dubnow, Leipzig

Tim Soens, Professor of Medieval and Environmental History, University of Antwerp

Georg Stöger, Associate Professor of Economic, Social and Environmental History, University of Salzburg

https://doi.org/10.1515/9783111112756-013

Helmuth Trischler, Head of Research, Deutsches Museum / Professor of Modern History and History of Technology, LMU Munich and Co-Director of the Rachel Carson Center for Environment and Society

Christiane Uhlig, Human Geographer, Sociologist and Systemic Consultant with a Focus on Biographical Research Methods, Berlin

Fabienne Will, Research Assistant, Munich Science Communication Lab on Planetary Health / Deutsches Museum, Munich

Bei Fragen zur Produktsicherheit wenden Sie sich bitte an:
If you have any questions regarding product safety,
please contact:

Walter de Gruyter GmbH
Genthiner Straße 13
10785 Berlin
productsafety@degruyterbrill.com